the
BOOK
book

the BOOK book

STEVEN GILBAR

ST. MARTIN'S PRESS
NEW YORK

To
DEBORAH
and
SKY
whose love
gave me energy
when I was
listless

10 9 8 7 6 5 4 3 2 1

First Edition

Library of Congress Cataloging in Publication Data

Gilbar, Steven.
    The book book.
    1. Books—Miscellanea.   2. Literature—Miscellanea.
I. Title.
Z1034.G54   01'.3   80-27703
ISBN 0-312-08803-5

■ FOREWORD

What shall I read next? There is no easy answer to that question. There is at once so much to read and so much difficulty in choosing. We are inundated by the tens of thousands of books published each year, to say nothing of the countless volumes already published that repose quietly on the shelves of libraries and bookshops. At the same time, unless you are a regular book review reader, there is no way to discover which among this Niagara of books you might enjoy reading. You must rely on word of mouth, dust-jacket blurbs, and bestseller lists. For different reasons, none of these methods is totally satisfactory.

This book attempts to remedy the problem by providing the pleasure reader with lists of worthwhile books arranged by subject matter. The books are generally of the kind referred to as *belles lettres*—that is, books that can be read and enjoyed for their own sake, that aspire toward literature. Thus cookbooks, self-help books, reference works, and the like are not included

The book list is probably almost as ancient as writing itself. No doubt some literary citizen of Babylon listed the ten best clay tablets of 1981 B.C. Many famous modern lists are included in this book, but most have been compiled by the author. Rather than list, for example, the "best" books of a particular category—a difficult and arbitrary task—ten "of the best" have been selected. The titles on each list do not just reflect the caprices of the author but have been thought worth reading by at least one book reviewer. There are many more books that deserve to be read, but because of space limitations they are not included. So if one of your favorite books is not on a list where you think it belongs, that does not mean that you have rotten taste or even that there are ten "better" books, but only that it is in the nature of lists to be imperfect and, inevitably, somewhat personal.

If, as you browse through this book, you are led to discover new reading adventures, then its purpose will have been accomplished. Good reading!

■ ACKNOWLEDGMENTS

I wish to thank the patient and helpful staff of the Santa Barbara Public Library for their assistance, Fred Failla and Ralph B. Sipper for the use of their books and comments, E. R. Zirpoli for her incisive critique, P. S. Kallenberg, K. J. Levy, and D. F. Zickerman for their wit, and all the other bibliophiles, trivia nuts, and list lovers who contributed to the making of this book.

the
BOOK
book

■ IN THE FIRST PLACE

The First Book Printed in Europe
The first book printed in Europe, the first Bible to be printed, and the first large book to be printed from movable metal type was the Gutenberg Bible, named after the inventor of movable metal type. It was printed in 1456.

The First Book Printed in English
The Recuyell of the Historyes of Troye, a French romance of the Trojan War, was translated and then printed by William Caxton at Bruges in 1475.

The First Book Printed in England
William Caxton returned to England and set up his press in Westminster. The first book to come off the press was his own *The Dictes and Sayinges of the Philosophers,* in 1477.

The First Book Printed in America
The Bay Psalm Book (1640), a metrical translation of the Psalms by the ministers of the Massachusetts Bay Colony, was the first bound book printed in the English colonies.

The First Book Printed at Sea
This dubious distinction belongs to *The Bloddy Journal Kept by William Davidson on Board a Russian Pirate in the Year 1789.* It was printed on board H.M.S. *Caledonia* in 1812 while she was cruising the Mediterranean Sea.

The First Volume of Poems Written in America
Anne Bradstreet, the daughter of one governor of the

Massachusetts Bay Colony and the wife of another, wrote *The Tenth Muse Lately Sprung up in America* in 1650.

The First Book Entered for Copyright
The Philadelphia Spelling Book was registered by its author, John Barry, on June 9, 1790.

The First Bookseller in America
The first bookseller of importance seems to have been Hezekiah Usher, who established himself at Cambridge, Massachusetts, in 1639.

The First Antiquarian Bookstore
Samuel Gardner Drake appears to have opened up the first such store in 1830. Located in Boston, it specialized in writings about American Indians.

The First Book Club in America
The Book-of-the-Month Club was established in New York City in 1926. The original book judges were Heywood Broun, Henry Seidel Canby, Dorothy Canfield, Christopher Morley, and William Allen White. The first selection to be distributed to the club's 4,750 members was Sylvia Townsend Warner's novel *Lolly Willowes*.

The First Dime Novel
The early precursor of the popularly priced paperback novel was the Beadle dime novel printed in New York. The first of that series was Mrs. Ann S. Stephens' *Malaeska*, printed in 1860.

The First Paperback Bookshop
The first bookshop to sell paperbacks exclusively was the City Lights Book Shop, established by the poet Lawrence Ferlinghetti in San Francisco's North Beach in 1953.

■ FOR OPENERS

In the first column are some memorable opening lines drawn from fifteen distinguished novels. Match them with the proper title and author in the opposite column.

1. A screaming comes across the sky. It has happened before, but there is nothing to compare it to now.

2. Someone must have traduced Joseph K., for without having done anything wrong he was arrested one fine morning.

3. Whether I shall turn out to be the hero of my own life, or whether that station will be held by anybody else, these pages must show.

4. If you really want to hear about it, the first thing you'll probably want to know is where I was born, and what my lousy childhood was like, and how my parents were occupied before they had me, and all that David Copperfield kind of crap . . .

5. The first time I saw Brenda she asked me to hold her glasses.

6. Call me Ishmael.

7. Call me Jonah.

A. *David Copperfield* Charles Dickens

B. *The Trial* Franz Kafka

C. *The Adventures of Augie March* Saul Bellow

D. *Cat's Cradle* Kurt Vonnegut

E. *Fear of Flying* Erica Jong

F. *Goodbye, Columbus* Philip Roth

G. *Catch-22* Joseph Heller

H. *Moby Dick* Herman Melville

I. *A Tale of Two Cities* Charles Dickens

8. It was the best of times, it was the worst of times.

9. It was love at first sight.

10. I wish either my father or my mother, or indeed both of them . . . had minded what they were about when they begot me. . . .

11. There were 117 psycho-analysts on the Pan Am flight to Vienna and I'd been treated by at least six of them.

12. I am an American, Chicago born. . . .

13. Happy families are all alike; every unhappy family is unhappy in its own way.

14. Many years later, as he faced the firing squad, Colonel Aureliano Buendía was to remember that distant afternoon when his father took him to discover ice.

15. It was a bright cold day in April, and the clocks were striking thirteen.

J. *The Catcher in the Rye* J. D. Salinger

K. *Tristram Shandy* Laurence Sterne

L. *1984* George Orwell

M. *One Hundred Years of Solitude* Gabriel García Márquez

N. *Anna Karenina* Leo Tolstoy

O. *Gravity's Rainbow* Thomas Pynchon

Answers:

1–O; 2–B; 3–A; 4–J; 5–F; 6–H; 7–D; 8–I; 9–G; 10–K; 11–E; 12–C; 13–N; 14–M; 15–L

A book you haven't read is a new book.

—ANONYMOUS

■ THE ORIGINAL MODERN LIBRARY

The Modern Library of the World's Best Books first appeared in 1912 under the Boni & Liveright imprint. It was subsequently purchased by Bennett Cerf and published by Random House. Here are the twelve original titles.

1. Fëdor Dostoevski, *Poor People*
2. Anatole France, *The Red Lily*
3. Henrik Ibsen, *Plays*
4. Rudyard Kipling, *Soldiers Three*
5. Maurice Maeterlinck, *Plays*
6. Friedrich Nietzsche, *Thus Spake Zarathustra*
7. Arthur Schopenhauer, *Studies in Pessimism*
8. Robert Louis Stevenson, *Treasure Island*
9. August Strindberg, *Married*
10. H.G. Wells, *The War in the Air*
11. Oscar Wilde, *The Picture of Dorian Gray*
12. Oscar Wilde, *Plays*

Where the Term "Classic" Came From
Servius divided the Romans into five classes. A citizen of the highest class was called *classicus*. The rest were said to be *infra classem*, that is, beneath the class. Accordingly, authors of the best or first class were termed *classici auctores* ("classic authors"). The term has come to describe any work of the first or highest order.

■ FIRST-NAME BASIS: A QUIZ

Each woman in the first column is both the principal character in, and the title of, a novel. Match each with her author in the second column.

1. Candy	A. Emile Zola
2. Carmen	B. André Breton
3. Chéri	C. Samuel Richardson
4. Clea	D. Prosper Mérimée
5. Emma	E. Terry Southern and

6. Fanny   Mason Hoffenberg
7. Gertrude   F. Daphne DuMaurier
8. Ida   G. Daniel Defoe
9. Isabel   H. Herman Hesse
10. Justine   I. Jane Austen
11. Lolita   J. Stephen Crane
12. Maggie   K. Vladimir Nabokov
13. Nadja   L. Gérard de Nerval
14. Nana   M. Marquis de Sade
15. Pamela   N. Erica Jong
16. Roxana   O. Gertrude Stein
17. Rebecca   P. Colette
18. Shirley   Q. Charlotte Brontë
19. Sylvie   R. Lawrence Durrell
20. Thérèse   S. François Mauriac
     T. André Gide

Answers:

1–E, 2–D, 3–P, 4–R, 5–I, 6–N, 7–H, 8–O, 9–T, 10–M, 11–K, 12–J, 13–B, 14–A, 15–C, 16–G, 17–F, 18–Q, 19–L, 20–S

■ 100 MOST SIGNIFICANT BOOKS

Reprinted from *Good Reading* with permission of R. R. Bowker Company. Copyright © 1978 by the Committee on College Reading.

Compiled by The Committee on College Reading in consultation with many distinguished teachers, writers, and critics, this list offers a representative selection of 100 books that many people have found "rewarding to know."

Ancient Times
Aeschylus, *The Oresteia*
Aesop, *Fables*
Aristophanes, *Comedies*
Aristotle, *Nicomachean Ethics*
The Bible
Confucius, *The Analects*
Euripides, *Dramas*
Homer, *Iliad, Odyssey*
Lao-Tzu, *The Way of Life*
Lucretius, *The Nature of Things*
Plato, *Republic, Symposium*
Plutarch, *Lives*
Sophocles, *The Theban Plays*

Thucydides, *The Peloponnesian Wars*

Vergil, *Aeneid*

Middle Ages and Renaissance

The Arabian Nights
Bacon, *Essays*
Boccaccio, *Decameron*
Cervantes, *Don Quixote*
Chaucer, *Canterbury Tales*
Dante, *Divine Comedy*
Omar Khayyám, *The Rubáiyát*

Machiavelli, *The Prince*
Malory, *Le Morte D'Arthur*
Mohammad, *Koran*
Montaigne, *Essays*
More, *Utopia*
Rabelais, *Gargantua and Pantagruel*
Shakespeare, *Complete Tragedies, Comedies, and Histories*

Seventeenth and Eighteenth Centuries

Boswell, *Life of Samuel Johnson*
Bunyan, *The Pilgrim's Progress*
Burns, *Poems*
Defoe, *Robinson Crusoe*
Descartes, *Discourse on Method*
Donne, *Poems*
Fielding, *Tom Jones*
Gibbon, *The Decline and Fall of the Roman Empire*
Hamilton et al., *Federalist Papers*
Kant, *Critique of Pure Reason*

Locke, *Essay Concerning Human Understanding*
Malthus, *Principles of Population*
Milton, *Paradise Lost*
Molière, *Comedies*
Paine, *The Rights of Man*
Rousseau, *The Social Contract*
Smith, *The Wealth of Nations*
Spinoza, *Ethics*
Sterne, *Tristram Shandy*
Swift, *Gulliver's Travels*
Voltaire, *Candide*

Nineteenth Century

Austen, *Pride and Prejudice*
Balzac, *Eugénie Grandet*
Browning (Robert), *Poems*
Byron, *Poems*
Chekhov, *Plays*
Darwin, *On the Origin of the Species*

Dickens, *Great Expectations*
Dickinson, *Poems*
Dostoevski, *The Brothers Karamazov*
Eliot, *Middlemarch*
Emerson, *Essays*
Flaubert, *Madame Bovary*

Goethe, *Faust*
Hardy, *Tess of the D'Urbervilles*
Hawthorne, *The Scarlet Letter*
Hugo, *Les Misérables*
Ibsen, *Dramas*
Keats, *Poems*
Marx, *Das Capital*
Melville, *Moby Dick*
Nietzsche, *Thus Spake Zarathustra*

Poe, *Short Stories*
Shelley, *Poems*
Stendhal, *The Red and the Black*
Thackeray, *Vanity Fair*
Thoreau, *Walden*
Tolstoy, *War and Peace*
Twain, *Huckleberry Finn*
Whitman, *Leaves of Grass*
Wordsworth, *Poems*

Twentieth Century

Einstein, *The Meaning of Relativity*
Eliot, *Poems and Plays*
Ellison, *Invisible Man*
Faulkner, *The Sound and the Fury*
Frazer, *The Golden Bough*
Freud, *Introduction to Psychoanalysis*
Frost, *Poems*
Hemingway, *The Sun Also Rises*

Joyce, *Ulysses*
Lawrence, *Sons and Lovers*
Mann, *The Magic Mountain*
O'Neill, *Plays*
Proust, *Remembrance of Things Past*
Shaw, *Plays*
Steinbeck, *The Grapes of Wrath*
Veblen, *The Theory of the Leisure Class*
Yeats, *Poems*

◼ BIBLIORRHEA: A BOOKISH LEXICON

BIBLIOCLASM: The destruction of books
BIBLIOGONY: The production of books
BIBLIOKLEPT: A book thief
BIBLIOMANCY: Divination by books
BIBLIOMANIA: A rage for collecting books
BIBLIOPEGY: Bookbinding as a fine art
BIBLIOPHAGIST: A devourer of books
BIBLIOPHILE: A book lover
BIBLIOPHOBIA: A dread of books
BIBLIOPOESY: The making of books

BIBLIOPOLE: Bookseller

BIBLIOTAPH: One who buries books by keeping them under lock and key

BIBLIOTHECA: Library

Biblia Pauperum (Lat., "the poor man's Bible")
Picture books widely used by the illiterate in the Middle Ages in place of the Bible. They probably were among the earliest books to be printed, first from blocks, later from moveable type.

There are some people who read too much, the bibliobibuli. I know some who are constantly drunk on books, as other men are drunk on whiskey or religion. They wander through this most diverting and stimulating of worlds in a haze, seeing nothing and hearing nothing.

—H. L. MENCKEN

■ NOBEL PRIZE LAUREATES

The literary awards are selected by the Swedish Academy of Literature and consist of a substantial cash prize paid out of a fund established by the will of Alfred Nobel. After the name of each recipient set forth below is the year in which the award was bestowed and a letter indicating the recipient's principal literary field (F—fiction, P—poetry, D—drama, Ph—philosophy, H—history). Authors are listed under the country of their citizenship.

France

Réné F. A. Sully Prudhomme—1901 (P)

Frédéric Mistral—1904 (P)

Romain Rolland—1915 (F)

Anatole France—1921 (F)

Henri Bergson—1927 (Ph)

Roger M. Du Gard—1937 (F)

André Gide—1947 (F)

François Mauriac—1952 (F)

Albert Camus—1957 (F)

Alexis Léger (St. John Perse)—1960 (P)

Jean-Paul Sartre—1964 (F, D, Ph)

Samuel Beckett—1969 (F, D)

England
Rudyard Kipling—1907 (F, P)
George Bernard Shaw
—1925 (D)
John Galsworthy—1932 (F)
T. S. Eliot—1948 (P, D)
Sir Winston Churchill
—1953 (H)

Scandinavia
Björnstjerne Björnson
—1903 (D)
Selma Lagerlöf—1909 (F)
Verner von Heidenstam
—1916 (P)
Karl A. Gjellerup—1917 (F)
Hendrik Pontoppidan
—1917 (F)
Knut Hamsun—1920 (F)
Sigrid Undset—1928 (F)
Erik Axel Karlfeldt—1931 (P)
Johannes V. Jensen
—1944 (F, P)
Pär Lagerkvist—1951 (F)
Halldor Laxness—1955 (F)
Nelly Sachs—1966 (P)
Eyvind Johnson—1974 (F)
Edmund Martinson
—1974 (F)

Germany
Theodor Mommsen
—1902 (H)
Rudolf Eucken—1908 (Ph)
Paul von Heyse—1910 (F)
Gerhart Hauptmann
—1912 (D)
Thomas Mann—1929 (F)
Herman Hesse—1946 (F)
Heinrich Böll—1972 (F)

Spain
José Echegaray y Eizaguirre
—1904 (D
Jacinto Benavente y
Martinez—1922 (D)
Vicente Aleixandre—1977 (P)

Italy
Giosuè Carducci—1906 (P)
Grazia Deledda—1926 (F)
Luigi Pirandello—1934 (D)
Salvatore Quasimodo
—1959 (P)
Eugenio Montale—1975 (P)

Russia
Ivan Bunin—1933 (F)
Boris Pasternak—1958 (F, P)
Mikhail Sholokov—1965 (F)
Aleksandr I. Solzhenitsyn
—1970 (F)

Greece
Giorgos Sefeiades (Seferis)
—1963 (P)
Odysseus Elytis—1979 (P)

United States
Sinclair Lewis—1930 (F)
Eugene O'Neill—1936 (D)
Pearl S. Buck—1938 (F)
William Faulkner—1949 (F)
Ernest Hemingway—1954 (F)
John Steinbeck—1962 (F)
Saul Bellow—1976 (F)
Isaac Bashevis Singer
—1978 (F)
Czeslaw Milosc—1980 (P)

Poland
Henryk Sienkiewicz
—1905 (F)

Wladislaw S. Reymont
—1924 (F)

Chile
Gabriela Mistral—1945 (P)
Pablo Neruda—1971 (P)

Belgium
Maurice Maeterlinck
—1911 (D)

India
Rabindranath Tagore
—1913 (P)

Ireland
William Butler Yeats
—1923 (P)

Guatemala
Miguel Angel Asturias
—1967 (F)

Finland
Frans Eemil Sillanpää
—1939 (F)

Australia
Patrick White—1973 (F)

Switzerland
Carl Spitteler—1919 (P)

Puerto Rico
Juán Ramón Jiméniz
—1956 (P)

Yugoslavia
Ivo Andric—1961 (F)

Japan
Yasunari Kawabata—1968 (F)

Israel
S. Y. Agnon—1966 (F)

■ WRITING ON THE WALL

Here is a choice assortment of literary graffiti from the littlest rooms of some of the biggest libraries and institutions of the nation.
George Orwell is an optimist.
Henry Miller is a virgin.
I was here. Wait for me.—*Godot*
Hester Prynne was a nymphomaniac.
Herman Melville eats blubber.
Renata Adler is smarter than Susan Sontag.
Franz Kafka is a *kvetch*.
Leo Tolstoy drinks tea from a glass.
Marcel Proust is a *yenta*.
Othello was a bigot.
Norman Mailer is the master of the single *entendre*.

'Twas brillig and the slithy toads got screwed.
Moby Dick was a honkie.
Thoreau was a hippie.
Electra loves daddy.
Who's afraid of Virginia Woolf.
Emily Dickinson doesn't have a date for the senior prom.
Frodo lives.

■ COSI TAN FRUTTI

Even though some of these works may not have met with critical or economic success, they need not have been fruitless efforts—as their titles attest. Match each title with its author.

1. *A Clockwork Orange*
2. *The Lime Twig*
3. *The Grapes of Wrath*
4. *A Raisin in the Sun*
5. *The Cherry Orchard*
6. *Bitter Lemons*
7. *The Golden Apples*
8. *Blackberry Winter*
9. *Big Sur and the Oranges of Hieronymous Bosch*
10. *Rubyfruit Jungle*
11. *The Kandy-Kolored Tangerine Flake Streamline Baby*
12. *Grapefruit*
13. *The Strawberry Statement*
14. *Strange Fruit*
15. *If Life Is a Bowl of Cherries—What Am I Doing in the Pits?*

A. Tom Wolfe
B. Lawrence Durrell
C. Margaret Mead
D. James Simon Kunen
E. Anton Chekhov
F. Anthony Burgess
G. Yoko Ono
H. Eudora Welty
I. Erma Bombeck
J. John Hawkes
K. Lillian Smith
L. Lorraine Hansberry
M. John Steinbeck
N. Rita Mae Brown
O. Henry Miller

■ LIBRARIANS' CHOICE: NOTABLE FICTION OF THE SEVENTIES

Each year the Notable Books Council of the American Library Association compiles a list of notable titles for use by librarians who work with adult readers. Both wide general appeal and literary merit are criteria.

1970
Donald Barthelme, *City Life*
Saul Bellow, *Mr. Sammler's Planet*
James Dickey, *Deliverance*
Joan Didion, *Play It as It Lays*
Gabriel García Márquez, *One Hundred Years of Solitude*
Louise Meriwether, *Daddy Was a Numbers Runner*
Johana Ostrow, . . . *In the Highlands Since Time Immemorial*
Eudora Welty, *Losing Battles*
Elie Wiesel, *A Beggar in Jerusalem*

1971
Jorge Amado, *Tent of Miracles*
Ann Cornelisen, *Vendetta of Silence*
E. L. Doctorow, *The Book of Daniel: A Novel*
Ernest J. Gaines, *The Autobiography of Miss Jane Pittman*
John Gardner, *Grendel*
George Garrett, *Death of the Fox*
James Houston, *The White Dawn*
Tommaso Landolfi, *Cancerqueen and Other Stories*
Tom McHale, *Farragan's Retreat*
Wright Morris, *Fire Sermon*

Yambo Ouologuem, *Bound to Violence*
Walker Percy, *Love in the Ruins*
Manuel Puig, *Betrayed by Rita Hayworth*

1972
Donald Barthelme, *Sadness*
Brock Bower, *The Late Great Creature*
Charles Gaines, *Stay Hungry*
John Gardner, *The Sunlight Dialogues*
Siegfried Lenz, *The German Lesson*
Thomas Rogers, *The Confessions of a Child of the Century by Samuel Heather: A Novel*
Isaac Bashevis Singer, *Enemies, A Love Story*
Alexandr I. Solzhenitsyn, *August 1914*
Hyemeyohsts Storm, *Seven Arrows*
Eudora Welty, *The Optimist's Daughter*

1973
Heinrich Böll, *Group Portrait With Lady*
Ruth Prawer Jhabvala, *Travelers*
Thomas McGuane, *Ninety-two in the Shade*
Brian Moore, *Catholics*
Iris Murdoch, *The Black Prince*
Manuel Puig, *Heartbreak Tango: A Serial*
Thomas Pynchon, *Gravity's Rainbow*
Hans Ruesch, *Back to the Top of the World*
André Schwarz-Bart, *A Woman Named Solitude*
Gore Vidal, *Burr*

1974
Richard Adams, *Watership Down*
Wendell Berry, *The Memory of Old Jack*
Italo Calvino, *Invisible Cities*
Gail Godwin, *The Odd Woman*
Joseph Heller, *Something Happened*
George Konrad, *The Case Worker*
Robert Stone, *Dog Soldiers*

1975
Saul Bellow, *Humboldt's Gift*
André P. Brink, *Looking on Darkness*
Alan Brody, *Coming To*
E. L. Doctorow, *Ragtime*
Margaret Drabble, *The Realms of Gold*
Ben Greer, *Slammer*
Peter Matthiessen, *Far Tortuga*
Judith Rossner, *Looking for Mr. Goodbar*
Paul Scott, *A Division of the Spoils*
Larry Woiwode, *Beyond the Bedroom Wall*

1976
Lisa Alther, *Kinflicks: A Novel*
Rosellen Brown, *The Autobiography of My Mother*
Robertson Davies, *World of Wonders*
Carlos Fuentes, *Terra Nostra*
Gabriel García Márquez, *The Autumn of the Patriarch*
John Gardner, *October Light*
Judith Guest, *Ordinary People*
Ruth Prawer Jhabvala, *Heat and Dust*
Richard Price, *Bloodbrothers*
Muriel Spark, *The Takeover*
William Trevor, *Angels at the Ritz*
Anne Tyler, *Searching for Caleb*
John Updike, *Marry Me: A Romance*
Gore Vidal, *1876: A Novel*
Richard Yates, *The Easter Parade: A Novel*
Helen Yglesias, *Family Feeling*

1977
Robert Brain, *Kolonialagent*
Marilyn French, *The Women's Room*
Thomas Gavin, *King-Kill*
James Hanley, *A Dream Journey*
Elsa Morante, *History: A Novel*
Toni Morrison, *Song of Solomon*
Walker Percy, *Lancelot*

Thomas Savage, *I Heard My Sister Speak My Name*
Paul Scott, *Staying On*
Susan Richards Shreve, *A Woman Like That*
Peter Taylor, *In The Miro District and Other Stories*
Paul Theroux, *The Consul's File*

1978
Rosellen Brown, *Tender Mercies*
John Cheever, *The Stories of John Cheever*
Carolly Erickson, *Bloody Mary*
Ernest J. Gaines, *In My Father's House*
Gabriel García Márquez, *Innocent Erendira and Other Stories*
Mary Gordon, *Final Payments*
Graham Greene, *The Human Factor*
John Irving, *The World According to Garp*
Josephine Jacobsen, *A Walk With Rachid and Other Stories*
Diane Johnson, *Lying Low*
James Jones, *Whistle*
Iris Murdoch, *The Sea, the Sea*
Tim O'Brien, *Going after Cacciato*
May Sarton, *A Reckoning*
Irwin Shaw, *Short Stories: Five Decades*
Paul Theroux, *Picture Palace*
Kate Wilhelm, *Somerset Dreams and Other Fictions*

1979
Alice Adams, *Beautiful Girl*
Leslie Epstein, *King of the Jews*
Stratis Haviaris, *When the Tree Sings*
Alice Hoffman, *The Drowning Season*
Thomas Keneally, *Passenger*
Norman Mailer, *Executioner's Song*
Bernard Malamud, *Dubin's Lives*
Alice Munro, *The Beggar Maid: Stories of Flo and Rose*
Joyce Carol Oates, *Unholy Love*
Manuel Puig, *Kiss of the Spider Woman*
Philip Roth, *Ghost Writer*
Scott Spencer, *Endless Love*
John Updike, *The Coup*

————, *Problem and Other Stories*
Kurt Vonnegut, *Jailbird*

■ PULITZER PRIZE WINNERS: FICTION

Awarded by the trustees of Columbia University, the prize is usually given annually to an American author for fiction in book form, preferably dealing with American Life.

In the years not listed below, no prize was awarded.

1918: Ernest Poole, *His Family*
1919: Booth Tarkington, *The Magnificent Ambersons*
1921: Edith Wharton, *The Age of Innocence*
1922: Booth Tarkington, *Alice Adams*
1923: Willa Cather, *One of Ours*
1924: Margaret Wilson, *The Able McLaughlins*
1925: Edna Ferber, *So Big*
1926: Sinclair Lewis, *Arrowsmith*
1927: Louis Bromfield, *Early Autumn*
1928: Thornton Wilder, *The Bridge of San Luis Rey*
1929: Julia M. Peterkin, *Scarlet Sister Mary*
1930: Oliver LaFarge, *Laughing Boy*
1931: Margaret Ayer Barnes, *Years of Grace*
1932: Pearl S. Buck, *The Good Earth*
1933: T. S. Stribling, *The Store*
1934: Caroline Miller, *Lamb in His Bosom*
1935: Josephine W. Johnson, *Now in November*
1936: Harold L. Davis, *Honey in the Horn*
1937: Margaret Mitchell, *Gone with the Wind*
1938: John P. Marquand, *The Late George Apley*
1939: Marjorie Kinnan Rawlings, *The Yearling*
1940: John Steinbeck, *The Grapes of Wrath*
1942: Ellen Glasgow, *In This Our Life*
1943: Upton Sinclair, *Dragon's Teeth*
1944: Martin Flavin, *Journey in the Dark*
1945: John Hersey, *A Bell for Adano*
1947: Robert Penn Warren, *All the King's Men*
1948: James A. Michener, *Tales of the South Pacific*

1949: James Gould Cozzens, *Guard of Honor*
1950: A. B. Guthrie, Jr., *The Way West*
1951: Conrad Richter, *The Town*
1952: Herman Wouk, *The Caine Mutiny*
1953: Ernest Hemingway, *The Old Man and the Sea*
1955: William Faulkner, *A Fable*
1956: MacKinlay Kantor, *Andersonville*
1958: James Agee, *A Death in the Family*
1959: Robert Lewis Taylor, *The Travels of Jaimie McPheeters*
1960: Allen Drury, *Advise and Consent*
1961: Harper Lee, *To Kill a Mockingbird*
1962: Edwin O'Connor, *The Edge of Sadness*
1963: William Faulkner, *The Reivers*
1965: Shirley Ann Grau, *The Keepers of the House*
1966: Katherine Anne Porter, *Collected Stories*
1967: Bernard Malamud, *The Fixer*
1968: William Styron, *The Confessions of Nat Turner*
1969: N. Scott Momaday, *House Made of Dawn*
1970: Jean Stafford, *Collected Stories*
1972: Wallace Stegner, *Angle of Repose*
1973: Eudora Welty, *The Optimist's Daughter*
1975: Michael Shaara, *The Killer Angels*
1976: Saul Bellow, *Humboldt's Gift*
1978: James Alan McPherson, *Elbow Room*
1979: John Cheever, *The Stories of John Cheever*
1980: Norman Mailer, *The Executioner's Song*

---

*The novelist in America today benefits . . . from the versatility
and power of his language, from the breadth of his landscapes, from
the company of many brilliant, gifted and adventurous colleagues,
from a group of readers who, beset with an unprecedented variety of
diversions, continue to read with great taste and intelligence.*

—JOHN CHEEVER

■ NATIONAL BOOK AWARDS: WINNERS AND NOMINEES FOR BEST FICTION

For almost thirty years this was considered by writers the
most prestigious, even if not the most remunerative, literary

award. The principal reason was that the panel of judges was comprised of other authors. The awards were discontinued after 1979. The first book listed after each date is the winner for that year, and the rest are the other nominees.

1950
Nelson Algren, *The Man with the Golden Arm*

1951
William Faulkner, *The Collected Stories*

1952
James Jones, *From Here to Eternity*

James Agee, *The Morning Watch*
Truman Capote, *The Grass Harp*
William Faulkner, *Requiem for a Nun*
Caroline Gordon, *The Strange Children*
Thomas Mann, *The Holy Sinner*
John P. Marquand, *Melville Goodwin USA*
Peter Martin, *The Landsman*
J. D. Salinger, *The Catcher in the Rye*
William Styron, *Lie Down in Darkness*
Jessamyn West, *The Witch Diggers*
Herman Wouk, *The Caine Mutiny*

1953
Ralph Ellison, *Invisible Man*

Isabel Bolton, *Many Mansions*
H. L. Davis, *Winds of Morning*
Thomas Gallagher, *The Gathering Darkness*
Ernest Hemingway, *The Old Man and the Sea*
Carl Jones, *Jefferson Selleck*
May Sarton, *A Shower of Summer Days*
Jean Stafford, *The Catherine Wheel*
John Steinbeck, *East of Eden*
William Carlos Williams, *The Build-up*

1954
Saul Bellow, *The Adventures of Augie March*

1955
William Faulkner, *A Fable*

Harriet Arnow, *The Dollmaker*
Hamilton Basso, *The View from Pompey's Head*
Davis Grubb, *The Night of the Hunter*
Randall Jarrell, *Pictures from an Institution*
Milton Lott, *The Last Hunt*
William March, *The Bad Seed*
Frederick Manfred, *Lord Grizzly*
Wright Morris, *The Huge Season*
Frank Rooney, *The Courts of Memory*
John Steinbeck, *Sweet Thursday*

1956
John O'Hara, *Ten North Frederick*

Shirley Ann Grau, *The Black Prince*
MacKinlay Kantor, *Andersonville*
Flannery O'Connor, *A Good Man is Hard to Find*
May Sarton, *Faithful are the Wounds*
Robert Penn Warren, *Band of Angels*
Eudora Welty, *Bride of the Innisfallen*
Herman Wouk, *Marjorie Morningstar*

1957
Wright Morris, *The Field of Vision*

James Baldwin, *Giovanni's Room*
Saul Bellow, *Seize the Day*
B. J. Chute, *Greenwillow*
A. B. Guthrie, *These Thousand Years*
John Hersey, *A Single Pebble*
John Hunt, *Generation of Men*
Edwin O'Connor, *The Last Hurrah*
J. F. Powers, *The Presence of Grace*
Elizabeth Spencer, *Voice at the Back Door*
James Thurber, *Further Fables for Our Time*

1958
John Cheever, *The Wapshot Chronicle*

James Agee, *A Death in the Family*
James Gould Couzzens, *By Love Possessed*
Mark Harris, *Something About a Soldier*
Andrew Lytle, *The Velvet Horn*
Bernard Malamud, *The Assistant*
Wright Morris, *Love Among the Cannibals*
Vladimir Nabokov, *Pnin*
Ayn Rand, *Atlas Shrugged*
Nancy Wilson Ross, *The Return of Lady Brace*
May Sarton, *The Birth of a Grandfather*

1959
Bernard Malamud, *The Magic Barrel*

J. P. Donleavy, *The Ginger Man*
William Humphrey, *Home from the Hill*
Vladimir Nabokov, *Lolita*
John O'Hara, *From the Terrace*
J. R. Salamanca, *The Lost Country*
Anya Seton, *The Winthrop Woman*
Robert Travers, *Anatomy of a Murder*

1960
Philip Roth, *Goodbye, Columbus*

Louis Auchincloss, *Pursuit of the Prodigal*
Hamilton Basso, *The Light Infantry Ball*
Saul Bellow, *Henderson the Rain King*
Evan S. Connell, *Mrs. Bridge*
William Faulkner, *The Mansion*
Mark Harris, *Wake Up, Stupid*
John Hersey, *The War Lover*
H. L. Humes, *Men Die*
Shirley Jackson, *The Haunting of Hill House*
Elizabeth Janeway, *The Third Choice*
James Jones, *The Pistol*
Warren Miller, *The Cool World*
James Purdy, *Malcolm*
Leo Rosten, *The Return of H.Y.M.A.N. K.A.P.L.A.N.*
John Updike, *The Poorhouse Fair*

Robert Penn Warren, *The Cave*
Morris West, *The Devil's Advocate*

1961
Conrad Richter, *The Waters of Kronos*

Louis Auchincloss, *The House of Five Talents*
John Hersey, *The Child Buyer*
John Knowles, *A Separate Peace*
Harper Lee, *To Kill a Mockingbird*
Wright Morris, *Ceremony in a Lone Tree*
Flannery O'Connor, *The Violent Bear It Away*
Elizabeth Spencer, *The Light in the Piazza*
Francis Steegmuller, *The Christening Party*
John Updike, *Rabbit, Run*
Mildred Walker, *The Body of a Young Man*

1962
Walker Percy, *The Moviegoer*

Hortense Calisher, *False Entry*
George P. Elliot, *Among the Dangs*
Joseph Heller, *Catch-22*
Bernard Malamud, *A New Life*
William Maxwell, *The Chateau*
J. D. Salinger, *Franny and Zooey*
Isaac Bashevis Singer, *The Spinoza of Market Street*
Edward Lewis Wallant, *The Pawnbroker*
Joan Williams, *The Morning and the Evening*
Richard Yates, *Revolutionary Road*

1963
J. F. Powers, *Morte D'Urban*

Katherine Anne Porter, *Ship of Fools*
Dawn Powell, *The Golden Spur*
Clancy Sigal, *Going Away*
John Updike, *Pigeon Feathers*

1964
John Updike, *The Centaur*

Mary McCarthy, *The Group*
Thomas Pynchon, *V*
Harvey Swados, *The Will*

1965
Saul Bellow, *Herzog*

Louis Auchincloss, *The Rector of Justin*
John Hawkes, *Second Skin*
Richard E. Kim, *The Martyred*
Wallace Markfield, *To an Early Grave*
Vladimir Nabokov, *Pale Fire*
Isaac Bashevis Singer, *Short Friday*

1966
Katherine Anne Porter, *The Collected Stories*

Jesse Hill Ford, *The Liberation of Lord Byron Jones*
Peter Matthiessen, *At Play in the Fields of the Lord*
James Merrill, *The (Diblos) Notebook*
Harry Petrakis, *Pericles on 31st Street*

1967
Bernard Malamud, *The Fixer*

Edwin O'Connor, *All in the Family*
Walker Percy, *The Last Gentleman*
Harry Petrakis, *A Dream of Kings*
Wilfrid Sheed, *Office Politics*

1968
Thornton Wilder, *The Eighth Day*

Norman Mailer, *Why Are We in Vietnam?*
Joyce Carol Oates, *A Garden of Earthly Delights*
Chaim Potok, *The Chosen*
William Styron, *Confessions of Nat Turner*

1969
Jerzy Kosinski, *Steps*

John Barth, *Lost in the Funhouse*

Frederick Exley, *A Fan's Notes*
Joyce Carol Oates, *Expensive People*
Thomas Rogers, *The Pursuit of Happiness*

1970
Joyce Carol Oates, *Them*

Leonard Gardner, *Fat City*
Leonard Michaels, *Going Places*
Jean Stafford, *The Collected Stories*

1971
Saul Bellow, *Mr. Sammler's Planet*

James Dickey, *Deliverance*
Shirley Hazzard, *The Bay of Noon*
John Updike, *Bech: A Book*
Eudora Welty, *Losing Battles*

1972
Flannery O'Connor, *The Complete Stories*

E. L. Doctorow, *The Book of Daniel*
Stanley Elkin, *The Dick Gibson Show*
Joyce Carol Oates, *Wonderland*
Cynthia Ozick, *The Pagan Rabbi and Other Stories*
Walker Percy, *Love in the Ruins*
Earl Thompson, *A Garden of Sand*
John Updike, *Rabbit Redux*

1973
John Barth, *Chimera*
John Williams, *Augustus*

Alan Friedman, *Hermaphrodeity*
Barry Hannah, *Geronimo Rex*
George V. Higgins, *The Friends of Eddie Coyle*
R. M. Koster, *The Prince*
Vladimir Nabokov, *Transparent Things*
Ishmael Reed, *Mumbo Jumbo*
Thomas Rogers, *The Confessions of a Child of the Century*

Isaac Bashevis Singer, *Enemies, A Love Story*
Eudora Welty, *The Optimist's Daughter*

1974
Thomas Pynchon, *Gravity's Rainbow*
Isaac Bashevis Singer, *A Crown of Feathers and Other Stories*

Doris Betts, *Beasts of the Southern Wild and Other Stories*
John Cheever, *The World of Apples*
Ellen Douglas, *Apostles of Light*
Stanley Elkin, *Searches & Seizures*
John Gardner, *Nickel Mountain*
John Leonard, *Black Conceit*
Thomas McGuane, *Ninety-Two in the Shade*
Wilfrid Sheed, *People Will Always Be Kind*
Gore Vidal, *Burr*
Joy Williams, *State of Grace*

1975
Robert Stone, *Dog Soldiers*
Thomas Williams, *The Hair of Harold Roux*

Donald Barthelme, *Guilty Pleasures*
Gail Godwin, *The Odd Woman*
Joseph Heller, *Something Happened*
Toni Morrison, *Sula*
Vladimir Nabokov, *Look at the Harlequins!*
Grace Paley, *Enormous Changes at the Last Minute*
Philip Roth, *My Life as a Man*
Mark Smith, *The Death of the Detective*

1976
William Gaddis, *JR*

Saul Bellow, *Humboldt's Gift*
Hortense Calisher, *The Collected Stories*
Johanna Kaplan, *Other People's Lives*
Vladimir Nabokov, *Tyrants, Destroyed and Other Stories*
Larry Woiwode, *Beyond the Bedroom Wall*

1977

Wallace Stegner, *The Spectator Bird*

Raymond Carver, *Will You Please Be Quiet, Please?*
McDonald Harris, *The Balloonist*
Ursula LeGuin, *Orsinian Tales*
Cynthia Proper Seton, *A Fine Romance*

1978

Mary Lee Settle, *Blood Tie*

Robert Coover, *The Public Burning*
Peter DeVries, *Madder Music*
James Alan McPherson, *Elbow Room*
John Sayles, *Union Dues*

1979

Tim O'Brien, *Going After Cacciato*

John Cheever, *The Stories of John Cheever*
John Irving, *The World According to Garp*
Diane Johnson, *Lying Low*
David Plante, *The Family*

The writer, using fragments of disorder, seeks to impose order on the world around him, that otherwise immense panorama of futility and anarchy. In that panorama the National Book Awards are both a beacon and a milestone . . . a shelter where writer and his public can meet for a moment, in the clearing, take heart from each other, before returning to the wilderness.

—WRIGHT MORRIS, ACCEPTANCE REMARKS

■ 10 FACTS TO CONTEMPLATE UPON REACHING 30 YEARS OF AGE

It's bad enough to cross over to the other side of the generation gap and make steely resolutions really to get serious now without having to think about what some writers were achieving while you frittered away your twenties. But for the guilt-ridden and envious, here are some precocious starters. You have some catching up to do.

By the time these authors were thirty:

The six-volume first edition of Yukio Mishima's collected works was published.

John Updike had seen published two novels, two short-story collections, and a book of verse.

François Sagan had five novels published and two plays produced.

F. Scott Fitzgerald had three novels in print, including *The Great Gatsby*.

Stephen Crane had ensured himself a permanent place in American literature and had been dead a year.

The bulk of Wordsworth's best-known poetry had been published.

Shelley and Keats were dead.

But they were late starters compared to:

Norman Mailer and Truman Capote, whose highly acclaimed first novels appeared before the authors were twenty-five.

Rimbaud, who had written all his known poetry before he was twenty.

Edgar Allan Poe, whose first volume of poetry was published when he was eighteen.

Thomas Mann, who had already completed *Buddenbrooks* and two brilliant long short stories, "Tonio Kröger" and "Tristan," while still in his mid-twenties.

■ HARD TO SAY: A PRONUNCIATION GUIDE

Sholom Aleichem: SHO-lem Ah-LAY-kem
Louis Auchincloss: AW-kin-claws
Karel Capek: KAH-rel CHAH-pek
William Cowper: KOO-per
Michael Crichton: CRY-tuhn
Isak Dinesen: EE-sahk DEE-nuh-suhn
Alain Robbe-Grillet: AH-LAN Rohb-gree-YAY

Nathalie Sarraute: Nah-ta-LEE Sah-ROTE
Lawrence Durrell: DUR-ul (as in "girl")
Vladimir Nabokov: VLAH-duh-meer Nah-BO-kof
Thomas Mann: TOE-mass MAHN
Bertolt Brecht: BER-tawlt BREKT
Anaïs Nin: AH-nah-EES NEEN
Johann Wolfgang von Goethe: GER-tuh
Samuel Taylor Coleridge: KOHL-er-idj
Peter Handke: PAY-ter HAHNT-keh
Evelyn Waugh: EEV-lin WAH
William Makepeace Thackeray: THACK-ree
Jorge Luis Borges: HOR-hay Lew-EES BOR-hays
Arthur Rimbaud: Artur Ram-BO
Rainer Maria Rilke: RYE-nahr Ma-REE-ah RIHL-kuh
Lytton Strachey: LIT-ahn STRAY-chih
Larry Woiwode: WHY-WOOD-ee
Herman Hesse: HARE-mahn HESS-eh
Elie Wiesel: AY-lee VEE-zl
Jerzy Kosinski: JER-sey Koh-SIN-ski
John LeCarré: Luh-car-RAY

■ 7 COME 11 QUIZ

The number seven has always had a mystical import.
There are seven days in Creation, seven graces, seven ages
in the life of man, and, of course, the seventh son of a
seventh son (a diminishing creature in this age of planned
parenthood). Literature, too, has had its sevens, ranging
from the ancient *The Seven Wise Masters* to Irving Wallace's
magnum opus, *The Seven Minutes*. Here are eleven "sevens"
to match with their authors.

1. *Seven Deadly Sins*	A. Leonid Andreyev
2. *Seven Against Thebes*	B. Fletcher Knebel and
3. *Seven Pillars of Wisdom*	Thomas Bailey
4. *The Seven That Were Hanged*	C. Leon Uris
5. *Seven Gothic Tales*	D. Nathaniel Hawthorne
6. *Seven Types of Ambiguity*	E. Thomas Merton
7. *77 Dream Songs*	F. Christopher Marlowe

8. *Seven Days in May*	G. Isak Dinesen
9. *The Seven Storey Mountain*	H. Aeschylus
10. *QB-VII*	I. T. E. Lawrence
11. *The House of the Seven Gables*	J. John Berryman
	K. William Empson

Answers
1–F, 2–H, 3–I, 4–A, 5–G, 6–K, 7–J, 8–B, 9.-E, 10–C, 11–D

■ THE BEST BOOKS: *THE NEW YORK TIMES BOOK REVIEW* EDITORS' CHOICE

Since 1968 the editors of *The New York Times Book Review* have selected what they take to be the best books of the year, books of "particular excellence."

1968
John Berryman, *His Toy, His Dream, His Rest*
Eldridge Cleaver, *Soul on Ice*
Michael Holroyd, *Lytton Strachey: A Critical Biography*
Norman Mailer, *The Armies of the Night*
Jan Myrdal, *Confessions of a Disloyal European*
George Orwell, *The Collected Essays, Journalism and Letters of George Orwell*
André Malraux, *Anti-Memoirs*
V. S. Pritchett, *A Cab at the Door*
Alexsandr I. Solzhenitsyn, *The First Circle*
James D. Watson, *The Double Helix*

1969
Dean Acheson, *Present at the Creation*
Sherwood Anderson, *Sherwood Anderson's Memoirs*
Ronald Blythe, *Akenfield: A Portrait of an English Village*
Louis-Ferdinand Céline, *Castle to Castle*
Erik H. Erikson, *Gandhi's Truth: The Origins of Militant Non-Violence*
Peter Gay, *The Enlightenment*
Joyce Carol Oates, *Them*

Philip Roth, *Portnoy's Complaint*
Jean Stafford, *The Collected Stories of Jean Stafford*
Peter Taylor, *The Collected Stories of Peter Taylor*
Kurt Vonnegut, Jr., *Slaughterhouse-Five*
T. Harry Williams, *Huey Long*

1970

Donald Bartheleme, *City Life*
James MacGregor Burns, *Roosevelt: The Soldier of Freedom*
Alvin Gouldner, *The Coming Crisis of Western Sociology*
Dumas Malone, *Jefferson the President: First Term, 1801–1805*
Gabriel García Márquez, *One Hundred Years of Solitude*
Nancy Mitford, *Zelda, A Biography*
Kate Millett, *Sexual Politics*
Charles E. Silberman, *Crisis in the Classroom: The Remaking of American Education*
Albert Speer, *Inside the Third Reich*
Francis Steegmuller, *Cocteau: A Biography*
John Updike, *Bech: A Book*
Eudora Welty, *Losing Battles*

1971

T. S. Eliot, *The Waste Land—A Facsimile and Transcript of the Original Drafts*
Joseph P. Lash, *Eleanor and Franklin*
Samuel Eliot Morison, *The European Discovery of America*
Yambo Ouologuem, *Bound to Violence*
Richard M. Titmuss, *The Gift Relationship: From Human Blood to Social Policy*
John Updike, *Rabbit Redux*
Edmund Wilson, *Upstate—Records and Recollections of Northern New York*

1972

Simone de Beauvoir, *The Coming of Age*
Frances Fitzgerald, *Fire in the Lake*
Leon Edel, *Henry James: The Master, 1901–16*
John Rawls, *A Theory of Justice*
Robert Manson Meyers (ed.), *The Children of Pride—A True Story of Georgia and the Civil War*

1973

Doris Lessing, *The Summer before the Dark*
John Clive, *Macauley: The Making of a Historian*
Thomas Pynchon, *Gravity's Rainbow*

1974

Richard Adams, *Watership Down*
Eugene D. Genovese, *Roll, Jordan, Roll: The World the Slaves Made*
Howard E. Gruber and Paul H. Barrett, *Darwin on Man*
Joseph Heller, *Something Happened*
Theodore Rosengarten, *All God's Dangers: The Life of Nate Shaw*
Aleksandr I. Solzhenitsyn, *The Gulag Archipelago*
Robert Stone, *Dog Soldiers*

1975

Saul Bellow, *Humboldt's Gift*
Peter Handke, *A Sorrow Beyond Dreams*
Peter Matthiessen, *Far Tortuga*
Susan Brownmiller, *Against Our Will*
David Brion Davis, *The Problem of Slavery in the Age of Revolution: 1770–1823*
Lucy S. Davidowicz, *The War Against the Jews, 1933–1945*
E. L. Doctorow, *Ragtime*
R. W. B. Lewis, *Edith Wharton*
Paul Theroux, *The Great Railway Bazaar*
Leonard Michaels, *I Would Have Saved Them If I Could*
V. S. Naipaul, *Guerrillas*
Aleksandr I. Solzhenitsyn, *The Gulag Archipelago: 1918–1956*

1976

Renata Adler, *Speedboat*
Saul Bellow, *To Jerusalem and Back*
Bruno Bettleheim, *The Uses of Enchantment*
Ann Cornelisen, *Women of the Shadows*
George Dangerfield, *The Damnable Question: A Study of Anglo-Irish Relations*
Gabriel García Márquez, *The Autumn of the Patriarch*
John Gardner, *October Light*

Alex Haley, Jr., *Roots*
Irving Howe, *The World of Our Fathers*
Maxine Hong Kingston, *The Woman Warrior: Memories of a Girlhood among Ghosts*
Ron Kovic, *Born on the Fourth of July*
Jean Lacoutoure, *André Malraux*
Vladimir Nabokov, *Details of the Sunset, and Other Stories*
Anthony Powell, *Hearing Secret Harmonies*
Abram Tertz, *A Voice from the Chorus*
Richard Yates, *The Easter Parade*

1977

James Atlas, *Delmore Schwartz: The Life of an American Poet*
W. Jackson Bate, *Samuel Johnson*
John Cheever, *Falconer*
Arlene Croce, *Afterimages*
Morris Dickstein, *Gates of Eden: American Culture in the Sixties*
Joan Didion, *A Book of Common Prayer*
Selma Fraiberg, *Every Child's Birthright: In Defense of Mothering*
Michael Herr, *Dispatches*
Simon Leys, *Chinese Shadows*
Robert Lowell, *Day by Day*
Toni Morrison, *Song of Solomon*
David McCullough, *The Path Between the Seas: The Creation of the Panama Canal, 1870–1914*
John McPhee, *Coming into the Country*
V. S. Naipaul, *India: A Wounded Civilization*
Robert Frost, *The World of Knowing*
V. S. Pritchett, *The Gentle Barbarian: The Life and Work of Turgenev*
Paul Scott, *Staying On*
Susan Sontag, *On Photography*
Edmund Wilson, *Letters on Literature and Politics, 1912–1972*

1978

Bruce Chatwin, *In Patagonia*
John Cheever, *The Stories of John Cheever*
Michel Foucault, *Discipline and Punish: The Birth of the Prison*
P. N. Furbank, *E. M. Forster: A Life*
Mary Gordon, *Final Payments*

Günter Grass, *The Flounder*
Alistair Horne, *A Savage War of Peace: Algeria, 1954–1962*
Maureen Howard, *Facts of Life*
Irving Howe, *Leon Trotsky*
John Irving, *The World According to Garp*
Diane Johnson, *Lying Low*
Doris Lessing, *Stories*
Charles Simmons, *Wrinkles*
John Updike, *The Coup*
Eudora Welty, *The Eye of the Storm: Selected Essays and Reviews*
Gary Wills, *Inventing America: Jefferson's Declaration of Independence*

1979
Joan Didion, *The White Album*
Leslie Epstein, *King of the Jews*
Elizabeth Hardwick, *Sleepless Nights*
Douglas R. Hofstadter, *Gödel, Escher, Bach: An Eternal Golden Braid*
Horace Freeland Judson, *Eighth Day of Creation: Makers of the Revolution in Biology*
The Nabokov-Wilson Letters: Correspondence Between Vladimir Nabokov and Edmund Wilson, 1940–1971
Henry Kissinger, *White House Years*
Christopher Lasch, *The Culture of Narcissism: American Life in an Age of Diminishing Expectations*
Norman Mailer, *The Executioner's Song*
Edmund Morris, *The Rise of Theodore Roosevelt*
V. S. Naipaul, *A Bend in the River*
Flannery O'Connor, *The Habit of Being*
Thomas Pakenham, *The Boer War*
Thomas Powers, *The Man Who Kept the Secrets: Richard Helms and the CIA*
Philip Roth, *The Ghost Writer*
William Shawcross, *Sideshow: Kissinger, Nixon and the Destruction of Cambodia*
John Updike, *Too Far to Go: The Maples Stories*

1980

Ann Beattie, *Falling in Place*
John Boswell, *Christianity, Social Tolerance, and Homosexuality*
Italo Calvino, *Italian Folktales*
E. L. Doctorow, *Loon Lake*
Max Frisch, *Man in the Holocene*
Justin Kaplan, *Walt Whitman*
Maxine Hong Kingston, *China Men*
Charles R. Morris, *The Cost of Good Intentions*
Barbara Novak, *Nature and Culture*
Ian Watt, *Conrad in the Nineteenth Century*
Eudora Welty, *The Collected Stories of Eudora Welty*

■ PROSE BY ANY OTHER NAME: 30 PEN NAMES

SHOLEM ALEICHEM: Solomon J. Rabinowitz
ANDREI BELY: Boris Nikolovich Bugaev
ANTHONY BURGESS: John Burgess Wilson
LEWIS CARROLL: Charles Dodgson
LOUIS-FERDINAND CÉLINE: Louis-Ferdinand Destouches
ISAK DINESEN: Karen Blixen
GEORGE ELIOT: Mary Ann Evans
ANATOLE FRANCE: Jacques Anatole Thibault
MAXIM GORKY: Alexei Peshkov
HENRY GREEN: Henry Yorke
KNUT HAMSUN: Knut Pederson
JOHN LeCARRÉ: David Cornwall
KATHERINE MANSFIELD: Katherine Beauchamp
ANDRÉ MAUROIS: Emile Herzog
YUKIO MISHIMA: Hiraoka Kimitake
ALBERTO MORAVIA: Alberto Pincherle
FLANN O'BRIEN: Brian Nolan
FRANK O'CONNOR: Michael O'Donovan
GEORGE ORWELL: Eric Blair
MARY RENAULT: Mary Challans
JULES ROMAINS: Louis Farigoule
FRANCOISE SAGAN: Francoise Quoirez
GEORGE SAND: Amantine Aurore Dupin

IGNAZIO SILONE: Secondo Tranquilli
STENDHAL: Marie Henri Beyle
ITALO SVEVO: Ettore Schmitz
MARK TWAIN: Samuel Clemens
VOLTAIRE: Francois Marie Arouet
NATHANAEL WEST: Nathan Weinstein
REBECCA WEST: Cecily Andrews

■ LIFE AND DEATH IN THE MODERN NOVEL

Can you match the titles of the novels in the first column with their respective authors in the second column? Give it your best effort; it's a matter of life and death.

1. *A Death in the Family*	A. Susan Sontag
2. *A Short and Happy Life*	B. Irving Stone
3. *Death in Venice*	C. Leo Tolstoy
4. *The Death of a Nobody*	D. Elizabeth Bowen
5. *The Death of Ivan Ilyich*	E. Willa Cather
6. *A Charmed Life*	F. Thomas Mann
7. *Death Ship*	G. Nathanael West
8. *Death of the Fox*	H. Jules Romains
9. *The Death of the Heart*	I. James Agee
10. *Lust for Life*	K. Reynolds Price
11. *Death on the Installment Plan*	L. Mary McCarthy
12. *Death Comes for the Arch-bishop*	M. Louis-Ferdinand Céline
13. *The Dream Life of Balso Snell*	N. Carlos Fuentes
14. *Death Kit*	O. George Garrett
15. *The Death of Artemio Cruz*	P. B. Traven

Answers
1–I, 2–K, 3–F, 4–H, 5–C, 6–L, 7–P, 8–O, 9–D, 10–B, 11–M, 12–E, 13–G, 14–A, 15–N

I cannot live without books.

—THOMAS JEFFERSON

■ AND I QUOTE

All the following titles were derived from literary antecedents. Can you name the source of each title?

1. Noel Coward, *Blithe Spirit*
2. Norman Mailer, *The Armies of the Night*
3. John Steinbeck, *Of Mice and Men*
4. Mary Webb, *Precious Bane*
5. Ernest Hemingway, *The Sun Also Rises*
6. Lilli Palmer, *Change Lobsters and Dance*
7. Evelyn Waugh, *A Handful of Dust*
8. Thornton Wilder, *The Skin of our Teeth*
9. W. Somerset Maugham, *Cakes and Ale*
10. Aldous Huxley, *Brave New World*
11. Gary Wills, *Bare Ruin'd Choirs*
12. James Herriot, *All Creatures Great and Small*
13. Robert Penn Warren, *World Enough and Time*
14. Frederick Forsyth, *The Dogs of War*
15. Isaiah Berlin, *The Hedgehog and the Fox*

Answers

1. Hail to thee, blithe Spirit!/Bird thou never wert,/That from Heaven, or near it,/Pourest thy full heart/In profuse strains of unpremeditated art./—PERCY BYSSHE SHELLEY, "To a Skylark"
2. And we are here as on a darkling plain/Swept with confused alarms of struggle and flight,/Where ignorant armies clash by night./—MATTHEW ARNOLD, "Dover Beach"
3. The best laid schemes o' mice and men/Gang aft a-gley. —ROBERT BURNS, "To a Mouse"
4. Let none admire/That riches grow in Hell; that soil may best/Deserve the precious bane./—JOHN MILTON, "Paradise Lost"
5. One generation passeth away, and another cometh, but the earth abideth forever. . . . The sun also riseth, and the sun goeth down, and hasteth to the place where he arose. . . . —ECCLESIASTES 1:2-6
6. LEWIS CARROLL, *Alice's Adventures in Wonderland*, Chapter 10, "The Lobster-Quadrille."
7. I will show you fear in a handful of dust. —T. S. ELIOT, "The Waste Land"
8. I am escaped with the skin of my teeth. —JOB 19:20

9. Dost thou think, because thou art virtuous, there shall be no more cakes and ale? —SHAKESPEARE, Twelfth Night, *II, iii, 124*
10. O Brave new world,/That has such people in't! —SHAKESPEARE, The Tempest, *V, i, 183*
11. That time of year thou mayst in me behold/When yellow leaves, or none, or few, do hang/Upon those boughs which shake against the cold,/Bare ruin'd choirs, where late sweet the birds sang. —SHAKESPEARE, *Sonnet 73*
12. All things bright and beautiful,/All creatures great and small,/All things wise and wonderful,/The Lord God made them all. —CECIL FRANCES ALEXANDER, *"All Things Bright and Beautiful"*
13. Had we but world enough, and time,/This coyness, lady, were no crime. —ANDREW MARVELL, *"To His Coy Mistress"*
14. Cry "Havoc!" and let slip the dogs of war. —SHAKESPEARE, Julius Caesar, *III, i, 273*
15. The fox knows many things, but the hedgehog knows one big thing. ARCHILOCHUS, *fragment from ancient Greek poem*

■ THE FAME OF THE NAME GAME

Clarissa Harlowe and Moll Flanders, to name just two, were the protagonists of eponymous works in the early years of the novel. Here are twenty that followed. Match each woman of title with her creator.

1. *Jane Eyre*	A. Sinclair Lewis
2. *Zuleika Dobson*	B. Theodore Dreiser
3. *Lorna Doone*	C. George Moore
4. *Violet Clay*	D. John O'Hara
5. *Jennie Gerhardt*	E. Charlotte Brontë
6. *Kristin Lavransdatter*	F. Christopher Morley
7. *Alice Adams*	G. Herman Wouk
8. *Kitty Foyle*	H. Arnold Bennett
9. *Elsie Venner*	I. Henry James
10. *Lucy Crown*	J. Oliver Wendell Holmes
11. *Elizabeth Appleton*	K. Max Beerbohm
12. *Ann Vickers*	L. Booth Tarkington
13. *Janice Meredith*	M. Gail Godwin
14. *Esther Waters*	N. Irwin Shaw
15. *Marjorie Morningstar*	O. Paul Leicester Ford

16. *Myra Breckenridge*	P. Leo Tolstoy
17. *Anna Karenina*	Q. Sigrid Undset
18. *Daisy Miller*	R. Gore Vidal
19. *Hilda Lessways*	S. John Cleland
20. *Fanny Hill*	T. R. D. Blackmore

Answers

1–E, 2–K, 3–T, 4–M, 5–B, 6–Q, 7–L, 8–F, 9–J, 10–N, 11–D, 12–A, 13–O, 14–C, 15–G, 16–R, 17–P, 18–I, 19–H, 20–S

■ NOTABLE NOTABLES, 1944–74: LIBRARIANS' CHOICE

This list was chosen by subcommittee of the American Library Association from the annual Notable Book lists.

Richard Adams, *Watership Down*
James Agee, *A Death in the Family*
A. R. Ammons, *Collected Poems*
Robert Ardrey, *The Territorial Imperative*
Harriet S. Arnow, *The Dollmaker*
W. H. Auden, *Collected Poetry*
John Barth, *The Sot-Weed Factor*
Wendell Berry, *The Memory of Old Jack*
Charles E. Bohlen, *Witness to History*
Heinrich Böll, *The Clown*
Robert Bolt, *A Man for All Seasons*
Catherine Drinker Bowen, *Yankee from Olympus*
Jacob Bronowski, *The Ascent of Man*
Gwendolyn Brooks, *In the Mecca*
Claude Brown, *Manchild in the Promised Land*
Dee Brown, *Bury My Heart at Wounded Knee*
James M. Burns, *Roosevelt: The Lion and the Fox*
John H. Burns, *The Gallery*
Albert Camus, *The Plague*
Rachel L. Carson, *The Sea Around Us*
Bruce Catton, *A Stillness at Appomattox*
Harry M. Caudill, *Night Comes to the Cumberlands*
C. W. Ceram, *Gods, Graves, and Scholars*

Winston Churchill, *The Second World War*
Eldridge Cleaver, *Soul on Ice*
Samuel L. Clemens, *Letters from the Earth*
Robert Coles, *Children of Crisis*
Sharon R. Curtin, *Nobody Ever Died of Old Age*
Annie Dillard, *Pilgrim at Tinker Creek*
T. S. Eliot, *Complete Poems and Plays*
Ralph Ellison, *Invisible Man*
Frances Fitzgerald, *Fire in the Lake*
Joseph Francis Fletcher, *Situation Ethics*
John Fowles, *The French Lieutenant's Woman*
Anne Frank, *The Diary of a Young Girl*
Antonia Fraser, *Mary, Queen of Scots*
Robert Frost, *Complete Poems*
Christopher Fry, *The Lady's Not for Burning*
Günter Grass, *The Tin Drum*
Germaine Greer, *The Female Eunuch*
John Gunther, *Death Be Not Proud*
Moss Hart, *Act One*
Joseph Heller, *Catch-22*
Ernest Hemingway, *The Old Man and the Sea*
John Hersey, *Hiroshima*
Jane Jacobs, *The Death and Life of Great American Cities*
John XXIII, *Journal of a Soul*
Russell Kirk, *The Conservative Mind*
Jonathan Kozol, *Death at an Early Age*
Harper Lee, *To Kill a Mockingbird*
Oscar Lewis, *The Children of Sanchez*
Norman Mailer, *The Naked and the Dead*
Malcolm X, *Autobiography of Malcolm X*
Robert K. Massie, *Nicholas and Alexandra*
Bill Mauldin, *Up Front*
Margaret Mead, *Male and Female*
Thomas Merton, *The Seven Storey Mountain*
Arthur Miller, *Death of a Salesman*
Jason Miller, *That Championship Season*
Merle Miller, *Plain Speaking*
Jessica Mitford, *The American Way of Death*
Marianne Moore, *Complete Poems*

Alan Moorehead, *The White Nile*
Samuel Eliot Morison, *The European Discovery of America*
Gunnar Myrdal, *An American Dilemma*
Eugene O'Neill, *Long Day's Journey into Night*
George Orwell, *1984*
Boris Pasternak, *Doctor Zhivago*
Raphael Patai, *The Arab Mind*
Alan Paton, *Cry, The Beloved Country*
Robert M. Pirsig, *Zen and the Art of Motorcycle Maintenance*
Theodore Roethke, *Collected Poems*
Philip Roth, *Portnoy's Complaint*
Cornelius Ryan, *The Longest Day*
J. D. Salinger, *The Catcher in the Rye*
Carl Sandburg, *Complete Poetry*
Arthur M. Schlesinger, *The Imperial Presidency*
Rachel Scott, *Muscle and Blood*
William Shirer, *The Rise and Fall of the Third Reich*
B. F. Skinner, *Beyond Freedom and Dignity*
Edgar Snow, *Red Star Over China*
Albert Speer, *Inside the Third Reich*
William Styron, *The Confessions of Nat Turner*
Pierre Teilhard de Chardin, *The Future of Man*
Dylan Thomas, *Collected Poems*
Piri Thomas, *Down These Mean Streets*
J. R. R. Tolkien, *The Lord of the Rings*
Arnold J. Toynbee, *A Study of History*
Barbara Tuchman, *The Guns of August*
Carl Van Doren, *The Great Rehearsal*
Gore Vidal, *Burr*
Theodore H. White, *The Making of the President, 1960*
Tennessee Williams, *A Streetcar Named Desire*
Richard Wright, *Black Boy*

The First Novel

The first full-fledged novel is generally held to be Lady Murasaki's *The Tale of Genji*, a large-scale chronicle of tenth-century Japanese court life. It is one of the monuments of literature and can be enjoyed today in excellent translations.

■ WHOSE WHAT?

Fill in the blank of each title of the fictional works in the first column with the correct word in the opposite column.

1. *The Rise of* ——	A. *Theron Ware*
2. *The Crime of* ——	B. *Albion Moonlight*
3. *The Ordeal of* ——	C. *Lord Byron Jones*
4. *The Confessions Of* ——	D. *Ivan Ilyich*
5. *The Education of* ——	E. *Silas Lapham*
6. *The Picture of* ——	F. *Duddy Kravitz*
7. *The Liberation of* ——	G. *Sylvestre Bonnard*
8. *The Death of* ——	F. *Eddie Coyle*
9. *The Mystery of* ——	G. *Jamie McPheeters*
10. *The Adventures of* ——	H. *Richard Feverel*
11. *The Apprenticeship of* ——	I. *Augie March*
12. *The Journal of* ——	J. *Dorian Gray*
13. *The Travels of* ——	K. *Edwin Drood*
14. *The Damnation of* ——	L. *H.Y.M.A.N. K.A.P.L.A.N.*
15. *The Friends of* ——	M. *Nat Turner*
16. *The Luck of* ——	N. *A. Gordon Pym*
17. *The Story of* ——	O. *Ginger Coffey*
18. *The Expedition of* ——	P. *Francis Macomber*
19. *The Short Happy Life of* ——	Q. *Humphry Clinker*
20. *The Narrative of* ——	R. *Gösta Berling*

Answers
1–E, 2–G, 3–H, 4–M, 5–L, 6–J, 7–C, 8–D, 9–K, 10–I, 11–F, 12–B, 13–G, 14–A, 15–F, 16–O, 17–R, 18–Q, 19–P, 20–N

■ THE VERSE TITLES: 10 NOVELS' TITLES DERIVED FROM ENGLISH VERSE

Anthony Burgess, *Nothing Like the Sun* (Shakespeare, Sonnet 90)

William Faulkner, *The Sound and the Fury* (Shakespeare, Macbeth)

F. Scott Fitzgerald, *Tender is the Night* (Keats, "Ode to a Nightingale")

E. M. Forster, *Where Angels Fear to Tread* (Pope, "An Essay on Criticism")

Thomas Hardy, *Far From the Madding Crowd* (Gray, "Elegy Written in a Country Churchyard")

Aldous Huxley, *Eyeless in Gaza* (Milton, "Samson Agonistes")

James Jones, *From Here to Eternity* (Kipling, "Gentlemen Rankers")

Vladimir Nabokov, *Pale Fire* (Shakespeare, *Timon of Athens*)

Wallace Stegner, *On a Darkling Plain* (Arnold, "Dover Beach")

John Steinbeck, *In Dubious Battle* (Milton, *Paradise Lost*)

■ THE FIRST TITLES: ORIGINAL TITLES OF 10 FAMOUS NOVELS

William Faulkner, *The Sound and the Fury: Twilight*

F. Scott Fitzgerald, *This Side of Paradise: The Romantic Egoists*

Ernest Hemingway, *The Sun Also Rises: Fiesta*

James Joyce, *A Portrait of the Artist as a Young Man: Stephen Hero*

D. H. Lawrence, *Lady Chatterley's Lover: Tenderness*

Sinclair Lewis, *Main Street: The Village Virus*

John Steinbeck, *East of Eden: Salinas Valley*

Leo Tolstoy, *War and Peace: All's Well that Ends Well*

Robert Penn Warren, *All the King's Men: Proud Flesh*

Thomas Wolfe, *Look Homeward, Angel: O Lost*

■ PUBLISHED AND PERISHED: 25 NOVELS OF THE SIXTIES TO BE REDISCOVERED

From polls of writers and critics in *American Scholar* (Spring 1970) and *Rediscoveries* (ed. David Madden, 1971)

Chester Aaron, *About Us* (1967)

Yves Berger, *The Garden,* (1963)

Wendell Berry, *A Place on Earth* (1967)

Italo Calvino, *Cosmicomics* (1968)

John Stewart Carter, *Full Fathom Five* (1965)

Lester Goren, *The Candy Butcher's Farewell* (1964)
Hiram Haydn, *The Hands of Esau* (1962)
Cecil Hemley, *Young Cranshaw* (1963)
Romulus Linney, *Heathen Valley* (1962)
Alison Lurie, *The Nowhere City* (1965)
James McConkey, *Crossroads* (1968)
Olivia Manning, *The Great Fortune Trilogy* (1966)
P. H. Newby, *The Barbary Light* (1962)
Gil Orlovitz, *Milkbottle H* (1968)
Jane Phillips, *Mojo Hand* (1966)
Piotr Rawicz, *Blood from the Sky* (1964)
Louis D. Ruben, Jr., *The Golden Weather* (1961)
James Salter, *A Sport and a Pastime* (1967)
André Schwartz-Bart, *The Last of the Just* (1960)
Jorge Semprun, *The Last Voyage* (1964)
David Stacton, *A Dancer in Darkness* (1962)
Walter Tevis, *The Man Who Fell to Earth* (1963)
Edward Lewis Wallant, *The Tenants of Moonbloom* (1963)
Henry Williamson, *It Was the Nightingale* (1962)
Marguerite Young, *Miss Macintosh, My Darling* (1965)

And Five More from Joseph the Provider
Bookman and critic Ralph B. Sipper, proprietor of Joseph the Provider, the eminent California rare-book dealers, adds:

Alice Adams, *Careless Love* (1961)
John Gardner, *The Resurrection* (1966)
Diane Johnson, *Fair Game*, (1965)
Joseph McElroy, *Smuggler's Bible* (1966)
Cynthia Ozick, *Trust* (1966)

Every man who knows how to read has it in his power to magnify himself, to multiply the ways in which he exists, to make his life full, significant, and interesting.

—ALDOUS HUXLEY

■ THE BEST TWENTIETH-CENTURY AMERICAN NOVELS

Reprinted from *Good Reading* with permission of R. R. Bowker Company. Copyright © 1978 by The Committee on College Reading.

Selected by the Committee on College Reading.

1900–45

Sherwood Anderson, *Winesburg, Ohio* (1919)
————, *Poor White* (1920)
Erskine Caldwell, *God's Little Acre* (1933)
Willa Cather, *My Antonia* (1918)
————, *The Professor's House* (1925)
John Dos Passos, *U.S.A.* (1937)
Theodore Dreiser, *Sister Carrie* (1900)
————, *The Financier* (1912)
————, *An American Tragedy* (1925)
James T. Farrell, *Studs Lonigan* (1935)
William Faulkner, *The Sound and the Fury* (1929)
————, *As I Lay Dying* (1930)
————, *Light In August* (1932)
————, *Absalom, Absalom* (1936)
F. Scott Fitzgerald, *The Great Gatsby* (1925)
————, *Tender Is the Night* (1934)
————, *The Last Tycoon* (1941)
Ellen Glasgow, *Barren Ground* (1925)
————, *Vein of Iron* (1935)
Ernest Hemingway, *The Sun Also Rises* (1926)
————, *A Farewell to Arms* (1929)
————, *For Whom the Bell Tolls* (1940)
Sinclair Lewis, *Main Street* (1920)
————, *Babbitt* (1922)
————, *Arrowsmith* (1925)
Jack London, *The Call of the Wild* (1903)
J. P. Marquand, *The Late George Apley* (1937)
Henry Miller, *Tropic of Cancer* (1931)
John O'Hara, *Appointment in Samarra* (1934)
Upton Sinclair, *The Jungle* (1906)

Gertrude Stein, *Three Lives* (1909)
John Steinbeck, *In Dubious Battle* (1936)
———, *The Grapes of Wrath* (1939)
Glenway Wescott, *The Grandmothers* (1927)
Nathanael West, *Miss Lonelyhearts* (1933)
———, *The Day of the Locust* (1939)
Edith Wharton, *The House of Mirth* (1905)
———, *Ethan Frome* (1911)
Thornton Wilder, *The Bridge of San Luis Rey* (1927)
———, *Heaven's My Destination* (1934)
Thomas Wolfe, *Look Homeward, Angel* (1929)
Richard Wright, *Native Son* (1940)

1945–78
Louis Auchincloss, *The Rector of Justin* (1964)
James Baldwin, *Go Tell It on the Mountain* (1953)
John Barth, *End of the Road* (1958)
———, *The Sot-Weed Factor* (1960)
Donald Barthelme, *Snow White* (1967)
———, *The Dead Father* (1975)
Saul Bellow, *The Adventures of Augie March* (1953)
———, *Seize the Day* (1956)
———, *Herzog* (1964)
———, *Mr. Sammler's Planet* (1969)
Thomas Berger, *Little Big Man* (1964)
William Burroughs, *Naked Lunch* (1969)
Truman Capote, *Other Voices, Other Rooms* (1948)
John Cheever, *The Wapshot Chronicle* (1958)
———, *The Wapshot Scandal* (1964)
Robert C. Coover, *The Universal Baseball Association, Inc., J. Henry Waugh, Prop.* (1968)
Joan Didion, *Play It As It Lays* (1970)
J. P. Donleavy, *The Ginger Man* (1955)
Ralph Ellison, *the Invisible Man* (1952)
William Gaddis, *Recognitions* (1955)
John Gardner, *The Sunlight Dialogues* (1972)
William Gass, *Omensetter's Luck* (1966)
Herbert Gold, *Fathers* (1967)
John Hawkes, *The Lime Twig* (1961)

————, *Second Skin* (1964)
Joseph Heller, *Catch-22* (1961)
James Jones, *From Here to Eternity* (1951)
————, *The Thin Red Line* (1962)
Ken Kesey, *One Flew Over the Cuckoo's Nest* (1962)
Jerzy Kosinski, *The Painted Bird* (1965)
Carson McCullers, *The Heart Is a Lonely Hunter* (1940)
Norman Mailer, *The Naked and the Dead* (1948)
————, *An American Dream* (1964)
————, *Why Are We in Vietnam?* (1967)
Bernard Malamud, *The Assistant* (1957)
Wright Morris, *The Works of Love* (1952)
————, *The Fields of Vision* (1956)
Vladimir Nabokov, *Lolita* (1955)
————, *Pale Fire* (1962)
Joyce Carol Oates, *Them* (1969)
Flannery O'Connor, *The Violent Bear It Away* (1960)
Walker Percy, *The Moviegoer* (1961)
James Purdy, *Malcolm* (1959)
Thomas Pynchon, *V* (1963)
————, *Gravity's Rainbow* (1973)
Philip Roth, *Portnoy's Complaint* (1969)
————, *My Life as a Man* (1974)
J. D. Salinger, *The Catcher in the Rye* (1951)
William Styron, *Lie Down in Darkness* (1951)
John Updike, *Rabbit, Run* (1960)
————, *Rabbit Redux* (1971)
Kurt Vonnegut, *Slaughterhouse-Five* (1969)
Robert Penn Warren, *All the King's Men* (1946)
Elie Wiesel, *Night* (1960)
————, *A Beggar in Jerusalem* (1970)
Larry Woiwode, *Beyond the Bedroom Wall* (1975)

■ MEN OF LETTERS

The tradition of using only initials before one's last name is a relatively recent one. In the nineteenth century, literary lions proudly used their full names, sometimes three or four if they had them. Although use of initials is customarily associated with English writers, not a few Americans, generally incorrigible Anglophiles, have adopted it. Here are the full names of some prominent "men of letters."

W(ystan) H(ugh) Auden
G(ilbert) K(eith) Chesterton
A(rchibald) J(oseph) Cronin
E(dward) E(stlin) Cummings
J(ames) P(atrick) Donleavy
W(illiam) E(dward)
  B(urghardt) Du Bois
T(homas) S(tearns) Eliot
E(dward) M(organ) Forster
A(lfred) E(dward) Housman
W(illiam) H(enry) Hudson
D(avid) H(erbert) Lawrence
T(homas) E(dward) Lawrence
C(live) S(taples) Lewis
H(enry) L(ouis) Mencken
W(illiam) S(tanley) Merwin

A(lan) A(lexander) Milne
V(idiadhar) S(urajprasad)
  Naipaul
S(idney) J(oseph) Perelman
J(ohn) B(oynton) Priestly
V(ictor) S(awdon) Pritchett
J(erome) D(avid) Salinger
C(harles) P(ercy) Snow
D(aisetz) T(eitaro) Suzuki
J(ohn) M(illington) Synge
J(ohn) R(onald) R(euel)
  Tolkein
H(erbert) G(eorge) Wells
E(lwyn) B(rooks) White
P(elham) G(renville)
  Wodehouse

The intensely, stiflingly human quality of the novel is not to be avoided; the novel is sogged with humanity; there is no escaping the uplift and the downpour, nor can they be kept out of criticism. We may hate humanity, but if it is exorcised or even purified, the novel wilts, little is left but a bunch of words.

—E. M. FORSTER

■ A LOVE MATCH

Madame Bovary and Rodolphe, Anna Karenina and Vronsky, Scarlet O'Hara and Rhett Butler are but a few of literature's memorable pairs of lovers. Here are some more; see if you can match the pairs and their novels.

1. Dick Diver	A. Jenny Cavillere	i. *Green Mansions*, W. H. Hudson
2. Darcy	B. Dolores Haze	ii. *Lady Chatterley's Lover*, D. H. Lawrence
3. Heathcliff	C. Mrs. Esther Jack	iii. *Tender is the Night*, F. Scott Fitzgerald
4. Mr. Abel	D. Connie	iv. *War and Peace*, Leo Tolstoy
5. Neal Klugman	E. Nicole Warren	v. *The Web and the Rock*, Thomas Wolfe
6. Gabriel Oak	F. Sarah Woodruff	vi. *Far From the Madding Crowd*, Thomas Hardy
7. Frederic Henry	G. Elizabeth Bennet	vii. *Lolita*, Vladimir Nabokov
8. Prince Andrei	H. Brenda Patimkin	viii. *Pride and Prejudice*, Jane Austen
9. Sgt. Milt Warden	I. Karen Holmes	ix. *Fear of Flying*, Erica Jong
10. Mellors	J. Catherine Earnshaw	x. *A Farewell to Arms*, Ernest Hemingway
11. Charles Smithson	K. Rima	xi. *Goodbye, Columbus*, Philip Roth
12. Oliver Barrett IV	L. Bathsheba Everdene	xii. *From Here to Eternity*, James Jones
13. Humbert Humbert	M. Catherine Barkley	xiii. *Love Story*, Erich Segal
14. Adrian Goodlove	N. Natasha Rostova	xiv. *The French Lieutenant's Woman*, John Fowles
15. George Webber	O. Isadora Wing	xv. *Wuthering Heights*, Emily Brontë

Answers
1–E–iii, 2–G–viii, 3–J–xv, 4–K–i, 5–H–xi, 6–L–vi, 7–M–x, 8–N–iv, 9–I–xii, 10–D–ii, 11–F–xiv, 12–A–xiii, 13–B–vii, 14–O–ix, 15–C–v

■ A TITLE MATCH

Match the first name in the first column with the last name in the second column to come up with the title of a novel; then match that title with its author in the third column.

1. *Adam*	A. *Random*	i. Laurence Sterne
2. *Daniel*	B. *Esmond*	ii. Charles Dickens
3. *Tristram*	C. *Grandet*	iii. Sinclair Lewis
4. *Anthony*	D. *Durward*	iv. Henry James
5. *Humphry*	E. *Bede*	v. Walter Scott
6. *Martin*	F. *Wolfe*	vi. Tobias Smollett
7. *Tom*	G. *Timberlane*	vii. Wilfrid Sheed
8. *Eugénie*	H. *Adverse*	viii. George Eliot
9. *Henry*	I. *Clinker*	ix. Honoré de Balzac
10. *Cass*	J. *Martin*	x. Hervey Allen
11. *Quentin*	K. *Shandy*	xi. John Fowles
12. *Turbott*	L. *Leuwen*	xii. William Plomer
13. *Lucien*	M. *Chuzzlewit*	xiii. William Thackeray
14. *Max*	N. *Jones*	xiv. Henry Fielding
15. *Roderick*	O. *Jamison*	xv. Stendhal

Answers
1–E–viii, 2–J–xi, 3–K–i, 4–H–x, 5–I–vi, 6–M–ii, 7–N–xiv, 8–C–ix, 9–B–xiii, 10–G–iii, 11–D–v, 12–F–xii, 13–L–xv, 14–O–vii, 15–A–iv.

■ ONLY *TIME* WILL TELL: BEST NONFICTION

The weekly newsmagazine has annually selected the "best books" since 1973. In 1979, in lieu of picking the best for that year, it chose the best of the decade; they are marked by asterisks. In addition, one pre-1973 work was included, Gary Wills's *Nixon Agonistes*, and one 1979 work, Tom Wolfe's *The Right Stuff*.

1973
John Clive, *Macauley: The Making of an Historian*
Myra Freedman, *Buried Alive*
John Kenneth Galbraith, *Economics and the Public Purpose*

Edward Hoagland, *Walking the Dead Diamond River*
Emmet John Hughes, *The Living Presidency*
Steven Rose, *The Conscious Brain*
Anthony Sampson, *The Soveriegn State of ITT*
Arthur Schlesinger, *The Imperial Presidency*
Louis Shaeffer, *O'Neill: Son and Artist*
Kevin Starr, *American and the California Dream (1850–1915)*

1974
Robert Caro, *The Power Broker*
Noel Mostert, *Supership*
*Robert M. Pirsig, *Zen and the Art of Motorcycle Maintenance*
*Aleksandr I. Solzhenitsyn, *The Gulag Archipelago*
Lewis Thomas, *Lives of a Cell*

1975
Michael J. Arlen, *Passage to Ararat*
Jimmy Breslin, *How the Good Guys Finally Won*
Shelby Foote, *The Civil War, A Narrative*
*Paul Fussell, *The Great War and Modern Memory*
R. W. B. Lewis, *Edith Wharton: A Biography*

1976
C. D. B. Bryan, *Friendly Fire*
Lillian Hellman, *Scoundrel Time*
Irving Howe, *World of our Fathers*
*Maxine Hong Kingston, *The Woman Warrior*
Richard Kluger, *Simple Justice*

1977
Ann Douglas, *The Feminization of American Culture*
*Michael Herr, *Dispatches*
Simon Leys, *Chinese Shadows*
John McPhee, *Coming into the Country*
Evelyn Waugh, *The Diaries of Evelyn Waugh*

1978
Harry Crews, *A Childhood*

Josh Greenfield, *A Place for Noah*
William Manchester, *American Caesar: Douglas Macarthur 1880–1964*
Barbara Tuchman, *A Distant Mirror: The Calamitous Fourteenth Century*
Theodore H. White, *In Search of History: A Personal Adventure*

1980
Justin Kaplan, *Walt Whitman*
Maxine Hong Kingston, *Chinamen*
Carl E. Schorske, *Fin-de-siecle Vienna: Politics and Culture*
Ronald Steel, *Walter Lippmann and the American Dream*
Studs Terkel, *The American Dream*

■ BEST FICTION: *TIME*'s ANNUAL PICKS

Since 1973 *Time* magazine has made an annual "best books" selection. In 1979, rather than picking the best for that year, it selected the best of the decade. Those selections are marked by asterisks. Also picked was Gabriel García Márquez, *One Hundred Years of Solitude* (1970).

1973
John Cheever, *The World of Apples*
Graham Greene, *The Honorary Consul*
Doris Lessing, *The Summer Before the Dark*
Thomas McGuane, *Ninety-Two in the Shade*
Iris Murdoch, *The Black Prince*
*Thomas Pynchon, *Gravity's Rainbow*
Susan Fromberg Schaeffer, *Falling*
Wilfrid Sheed, *People Will Always be Kind*
Richard G. Stern, *Other Men's Daughters*
Gore Vidal, *Burr*

1974
Evan S. Connell, *The Connoisseur*
John Fowles, *The Ebony Tower*
*Vladimir Nabokov, *Look at the Harlequins*
Jonathan Rubin, *The Barking Deer*
Robert Stone, *Dog Soldiers*

1975
*Saul Bellow, *Humboldt's Gift*
*E. L. Doctorow, *Ragtime*
William Gaddis, *JR*
Doris Lessing, *The Memoirs of a Survivor*
Peter Matthiessen, *Far Tortuga*

1976
Renata Adler, *Speedboat*
John Gardner, *October Light*
Gabriel García Márquez, *The Autumn of the Patriarch*
Paul Theroux, *The Family Arsenal*
Gore Vidal, *1876*

1977
John Cheever, *Falconer*
John Fowles, *Daniel Martin*
John LeCarré, *The Honourable Schoolboy*
Toni Morrison, *Song of Solomon*
Philip Roth, *The Professor of Desire*

1978
*John Cheever, *The Stories of John Cheever*
Gunter Grass, *The Flounder*
*John Irving, *The World According to Garp*
*Isaac Bashevis Singer, *Shosha*
John Updike, *The Coup*

1980
Thomas Berger, *Neighbors*
Italo Calvino, *Italian Folktales*

E.L. Doctorow, *Loon Lake*
Mordecai Richler, *Joshua, Then and Now*
Eudorea Welty, *The Collected Stories of Eudora Welty*

■ WHAT'S BLACK AND WHITE AND RED ALL OVER?

No, not a blushing zebra, but the titles of the novels in the first column. Match each with its author in the opposite column.

1. *Black Mischief*	A.	Wilkie Collins
2. *Poor White*	B.	Iris Murdoch
3. *The Red Badge of Courage*	C.	John Fowles
4. *The Black Book*	D.	Henry Miller
5. *White Jacket*	E.	Stendhal
6. *The Red Pony*	F.	Lawrence Durrell
7. *Black Spring*	G.	Evelyn Waugh
8. *White Fang*	H.	Stephen Crane
9. *Red Cavalry*	I.	Ross McDonald
10. *The Black Prince*	J.	D. H. Lawrence
11. *The Woman in White*	K.	Pierre La Mure
12. *The Scarlet Letter*	L.	John Steinbeck
13. *The Red and the Black*	M.	Sherwood Anderson
14. *White Nights*	N.	Sir Arthur Conan Doyle
15. *Snow White*	O.	Isaac Babel
16. *A Study in Scarlet*	P.	Herman Melville
17. *The Ebony Tower*	Q.	Nathaniel Hawthorne
18. *The White Peacock*	R.	Donald Barthelme
19. *Moulin Rouge*	S.	Jack London
20. *The Zebra-Striped Hearse*	T.	Fedor Dostoevski

Answers
1–G, 2–M, 3–H, 4–F, 5–P, 6–L, 7–D, 8–S, 9–O, 10–B, 11–A, 12–Q, 13–E, 14–T, 15–R, 16–N, 17–C, 18–J, 19–K, 20–I

Reading is to the mind what exercise is to the body.
—SIR RICHARD STEELE

■ THE CRITICS' CHOICE: NATIONAL BOOK CRITICS CIRCLE AWARD—FICTION

Established in 1976 because of differences of opinion over choices made by other award panels on which critics were not represented, the National Book Critics Circle annually presents an award for the best work of American fiction of the previous year. The first book in each group below is the winner, and the rest are the other nominees for that year.

1976
E. L. Doctorow, *Ragtime*

Alice Adams, *Families and Survivors*
Saul Bellow, *Humboldt's Gift*
William Kotzwinkle, *Swimmers in the Secret Sea*
Larry Woiwode, *Beyond the Bedroom Wall*

1977
John Gardner, *October Light*

Renata Adler, *Speedboat*
Vladimir Nabokov, *Details of a Sunset and Other Stories*
Cynthia Ozick, *Bloodshed and Three Novellas*
Richard Yates, *The Easter Parade*

1978
Toni Morrison, *Song of Solomon*

John Cheever, *Falconer*
Joan Didion, *A Book of Common Prayer*
Philip Roth, *The Professor of Desire*
John Sayles, *Union Dues*

1979
John Cheever, *The Stories of John Cheever*

Mary Gordon, *Final Payments*
John Irving, *The World According to Garp*
Charles Simmons, *Wrinkles*
John Updike, *The Coup*

1980
Thomas Flanagan, *The Year of the French*

Leslie Epstein, *The King of the Jews*
William Styron, *Sophie's Choice*
Elizabeth Hardwick, *Sleepless Nights*
Norman Mailer, *The Executioner's Song*
Philip Roth, *The Ghost Writer*

1981
Shirley Hazzard, *The Transit of Venus*

E. L. Doctorow, *Loon Lake*
William Maxwell, *So Long, See You Tomorrow*
Walker Percy, *The Second Coming*
Anne Tyler, *Morgan's Passing*

■ THE ACADEMY AWARDS: FICTION

The American Academy and Institute of Arts and Letters, in an effort to encourage writers in their work, administers, among others, these two important literary awards.

Howells Medal
This prestigious award, named after William Dean Howells, is conferred every five years in recognition of the most distinguished work of American fiction during that period. Prior to 1955 it was made for the recipient's body of work.

1925: Mary E. Wilkins Freeman
1930: Willa Cather
1935: Pearl S. Buck
1940: Ellen Glasgow
1045: Booth Tarkington
1950: William Faulkner,
1955: Eudora Welty, *The Ponder Heart*
1960: James Gould Cozzens, *By Love Possessed*

1965: John Cheever, *The Wapshot Scandal*
1970: William Styron, *The Confessions of Nat Turner*
1975: Thomas Pynchon, *Gravity's Rainbow*
1980: William Maxwell, *So Long, See You Tomorrow*

Richard and Hinda Rosenthal Foundation Award
Presented annually to the author of an American work of fiction that, though not a commercial success, is a "considerable literary achievement," this award consists of a $3,000 cash prize.

1957: Elizabeth Spencer, *The Voice at the Back Door*
1958: Bernard Malamud, *The Assistant*
1959: Frederick Buechner, *The Return of Ansel Gibbs*
1960: John Updike, *The Poorhouse Fair*
1961: John Knowles, *A Separate Peace*
1962: Paule Marshall, *Soul Clap Hands and Sing*
1963: William Melvin Kelley, *A Different Drummer*
1964: Ivan Gold, *Nickel Miseries*
1965: Thomas Berger, *Little Big Man*
1966: Tom Cole, *An End to Chivalry*
1967: Thomas Pynchon, *The Crying of Lot 49*
1968: Joyce Carol Oates, *A Garden of Earthly Delights*
1969: Frederick Exley, *A Fan's Notes*
1970: Jonathan Strong, *Tike and Five Stories*
1971: Christopher Brookhouse, *Running Out*
1972: Thomas McGuane, *The Bushwhacked Piano*
1973: Thomas Rogers, *The Confessions of a Child of the Century*
1974: Alice Walker, *In Love and Trouble*
1975: Ishmael Reed, *The Last Days of Louisiana Red*
1976: Richard Yates, *Disturbing the Peace*
1977: Spencer Holst, *Spencer Holst Stories*
1978: Douglas Day, *Journey of the Wolf*
1979: Diane Johnson, *Lying Low*
1980: Stanley Elkin, *The Living End*

The book is man's best invention so far.

—CAROLINA MARIA DE JESUS

■ THE NUMBERS GAME

There are numberless works of fiction with numbers in their titles. Here are 10 for you to fill in the blanks.

1. Ray Bradbury, *Fahrenheit——*
2. J. D. Salinger, *——— Stories*
3. Joseph Heller, *Catch———*
4. W. Somerset Maugham, *The Moon and ———pence*
5. Robert Gover, *The———Hundred Dollar Misunderstanding*
6. John O'Hara, *Butterfield———*
7. Gertrude Stein, *———Lives*
8. Agatha Christie, *———Little Indians*
9. Dorothy L. Sayers, *———Red Herrings*
10. Fletcher Knebel and Charles W. Bailey II, *———Days in May*

Answers
1–451; 2–Nine; 3–22; 4–Six; 5–One; 6–8; 7–Three; 8–Ten; 9–Five; 10–Seven.

■ MIXED PAIRS

The great Russian classics *War and Peace* and *Crime and Punishment* first spring to mind when one thinks of novels with paired titles. Here are some others, many more obscure, that have been scrambled. Try to combine them correctly and then match them with their authors.

1. *Saturday Night* and *Wine*	A. D. H. Lawrence
2. *Bread* and *Soda-Water*	B. W. Somerset Maugham
3. *Fathers* and *Brothers*	C. Francine DuPlessix Gray
4. *Lovers* and *The Fury*	D. F. Scott Fitzgerald
5. *Sense* and *Sunday Morning*	E. Norman Mailer
6. *The Red* and *The Mighty*	F. John O'Hara
7. *Sermons* and *Sons*	G. Ignazio Silone
8. *The Beautiful* and *The Dead*	H. Ivan Turgenev
9. *The Sound* and *The Sea*	I. Ernest K. Gann

10. *The High* and *The Black*	J. C. P. Snow
11. *Strangers* and *Tyrants*	K. William Faulkner
12. *The Old Man* and *Sixpence*	L. Ernest Hemingway
13. *Sons* and *Sensibility*	M. Alan Sillitoe
14. *The Moon* and *Lovers*	N. Stendhal
15. *The Naked* and *Damned*	O. Jane Austen

Answers
1. *Saturday Night and Sunday Morning*–M, 2, *Bread and Wine*–G, 3. *Fathers and Sons*–H, 4. *Lovers and Tyrants*–C, 5. *Sense and Sensibility* –O, 6. *The Red and The Black*–N, 7. *Sermons and Soda Water*–F, 8. *The Beautiful and Damned*–D, 9. *The Sound and The Fury*–K, 10. *The High and The Mighty*–I, 11. *Strangers and Brothers*–J, 12. *The Old Man and The Sea*–L, 13. *Sons and Lovers*–A, 14. *The Moon and Sixpence*–B, 15. *The Naked and The Dead*–E

■ JEWISH LITERATURE

National Jewish Book Awards: Fiction

The William and Janice Epstein Fiction Award was established by the Jewish Book Council of America to honor a book of fiction on a Jewish theme published during the preceding year.

1950: John Hersey, *The Wall*
1951: Sonia Morgenstern, *The Testament of the Lost Son*
1952: Zelda Popkin, *Quiet Street*
1953: Michael Blankfort, *The Juggler*
1954: Charles Angoff, *In the Morning Light*
1955: Louis Zara, *Blessed Is the Land*
1956: Jo Sinclair, *The Changelings*
1957: Lion Feuchtwanger, *Raquel: The Jewess of Toledo*
1958: Bernard Malamud, *The Assistant*
1959: Leon Uris, *Exodus*
1960: Philip Roth, *Goodbye, Columbus*
1961: Edward L. Wallant, *The Human Season*
1962: Samuel Yellen, *The Wedding Band*
1963: Isaac Bashevis Singer, *The Slave*
1964: Joanne Greenberg, *The King's Persons*

1965: Elie Wiesel, *The Town Beyond the Wall*
1966: Meyer Levin, *The Stronghold*
1967: No Award
1968: Chaim Grade, *The Well*
1969: Charles Angoff, *Memory of Autumn*
1970: Leo Litwak, *Waiting for the News*
1971: No award
1972: Cynthia Ozick, *The Pagan Rabbi and Other Stories*
1973: Robert Kotlowitz, *Somewhere Else*
1974: Francine Prose, *Judah the Pious*
1975: Jean Karsavina, *White Eagle, Dark Skin*
1976: Johanna Kaplan, *Other People's Lives*
1977: Cynthia Ozick, *Bloodshed and Three Novellas*
1978: Chaim Grade, *The Yeshiva*, Vols. 1 and 2
1979: Gloria Goldreich, *Leah's Journey*
1980: Daniel Fuchs, *The Apathetic Bookie Joint*

Some Honorable *Mensch* in Books: Great Yiddish Stories
Sholem Aleichem, *The Best of Sholem Aleichem* (1979)
David Bergelson, *After All* (1919)
Chaim Grade, *The Yeshiva* (1977)
Joseph Opatoshu, *A Day in Regensburg* (1968)
I. L. Peretz, *Selected Stories* (1974)
Mendele Moicher Seforim, *Fishke the Lame* (1869)
Isaac Bashevis Singer, *The Magician of Lublin* (1960)
I. J. Singer, *The Brothers Ashkenazi* (1936)

10 Jewish-American Classics
Saul Bellow, *Herzog* (1964)
Abraham Cahan, *The Rise of David Levinsky* (1917)
Arthur A. Cohen, *In the Days of Simon Stern* (1963)
Daniel Fuchs, *The Williamsburg Trilogy* (1934–1937)
Herbert Gold, *Fathers* (1966)
Noah Gordon, *The Rabbi* (1965)
Bernard Malamud, *The Assistant* (1957)
Henry Roth, *Call It Sleep* (1934)
Philip Roth, *Goodbye, Columbus* (1959)
Chaim Potok, *The Chosen* (1967)

10 Jewish Novels

Charles Angoff, *Journey to the Dawn* (1951)
Joseph Heller, *Good As Gold* (1979)
Myron Kaufman, *Remember Me to God* (1961)
Meyer Levin, *The Old Bunch* (1937)
Wallace Markfield, *To an Early Grave* (1964)
Frederic Morton, *Asphalt and Desire* (1952)
Hugh Nissenson, *My Own Ground* (1976)
Edward Lewis Wallant, *The Pawnbroker* (1961)
Jerome Weidman, *I Can Get It for You Wholesale* (1937)
Herman Wouk, *Marjorie Morningstar* (1955)

■ THE GOOD BOOKS

True Confessions: 15 Modern Catholic Novels

Werner Bergengruen, *A Matter of Conscience* (1952)
Rumer Godden, *In This House of Brede* (1969)
Julian Green, *Each in His Own Darkness* (1960)
Graham Greene, *Brighton Rock* (1938)
Kathryn Hulme, *The Nun's Story* (1956)
Thomas Keneally, *Three Cheers for the Paraclete* (1968)
David Lodge, *The British Museum Is Falling Down* (1965)
Bruce Marshall, *The World, the Flesh, and Father Smith* (1945)
François Mauriac, *Woman of the Pharisees* (1946)
Brian Moore, *Catholics* (1972)
Pier Pauls Read, *A Married Man* (1979)
Henry Morton Robinson, *The Cardinal* (1950)
Sylvia Townsend Warner, *The Corner That Held Them* (1948)
Evelyn Waugh, *Brideshead Revisited* (1945)
Morris W. West, *The Devil's Advocate* (1959)

The First Catholic Novel
Allessandro Manzoni, *The Betrothed* (1826)

---

10 American Catholic Novels

Elizabeth Cullinan, *House of Gold* (1970)
John Gregory Dunne, *True Confessions* (1977)

Thomas Fleming, *The Good Shepherd* (1974)
Mary Gordon, *Final Payments* (1978)
N. Richard Nash, *The Last Magic* (1978)
Walker Percy, *Love in the Ruins* (1971)
Crawford Power, *The Encounter* (1950)
J. F. Powers, *Morte D'Urban* (1962)
John A. Powers, *The Last Catholic in America* (1973)
Wilfrid Sheed, *The Hack* (1963)

The Best Novel by an American Cardinal
Francis Cardinal Spellman, *The Foundling* (1951)

Pastoral Idylls: 10 Novels of the Protestant Clergy
Frederich Buechner, *The Bebb Trilogy* (1971–74)
Peter De Vries, *The Mackerel Plaza* (1958)
Harold Frederic, *The Damnation of Theron Ware* (1896)
Oliver Goldsmith, *The Vicar of Wakefield* (1776)
Richard E. Kim, *The Martyred* (1964)
D. Keith Mano, *Bishop's Progress* (1968)
Conrad Richter, *A Simple Honorable Man* (1962)
Anthony Trollope, *Barchester Towers* (1857)
Agnes Sligh Turnbull, *The Bishop's Mantle* (1947)
John Updike, *A Month of Sundays* (1975)

That Old-Time Religion: 5 Evangelist Novels
Harry Crews, *The Gospel Singer* (1968)
George Garrett, *Do, Lord, Remember Me* (1965)
Sinclair Lewis, *Elmer Gantry* (1927)
Joyce Carol Oates, *Son of the Morning* (1978)
Dotson Rader, *Miracle* (1978)

The Old Story: 5 Old Testament Novels
Stefan Heyim, *The King David Report* (1973)
Dan Jacobson, *The Rape of Tamar* (1970)
Gladys Malvern, *The Foreigner* (1954)
Thomas Mann, *Joseph and His Brothers Tetralogy* (1933–43)
Gladys Schmitt, *David the King* (1946)

Gospel Truths: 10 Novels of Christ
Sholem Asch, *The Nazarene* (1939)
Anthony Burgess, *Man of Nazareth* (1979)
Robert Graves, *King Jesus* (1946)
Marcus Harrison, *Memoirs of Jesus Christ* (1975)
Nikos Kazantzakis, *The Last Temptation of Christ* (1960)
David Kossoff, *The Book of Witnesses* (1971)
Pär Lagerkvist, *Barabbas* (1950)
Theo Long, *The Word and the Sword* (1974)
George Moore, *The Brook Kerith* (1916)
Leonard Wibberly, *The Centurion* (1967)

A Novel of the Second Coming
Upton Sinclair, *They Call Me Carpenter* (1922)

■ BLACK AMERICANS

15 Classics

William Attaway, *Blood on the Forge* (1941)
James Baldwin, *Go Tell It on the Mountain* (1953)
Arna Bontemps, *Black Thunder* (1936)
William Demby, *Beetlecreek* (1950)
Ralph Ellison, *Invisible Man* (1952)
Ernest J. Gaines, *The Autobiography of Miss Jane Pittman* (1971)
Chester Himes, *The Third Generation* (1954)
Zora Neale Hurston, *Their Eyes Were Watching God* (1937)
James Weldon Johnson, *The Autobiography of an Ex-Colored Man* (1912)
William Melvin Kelly, *A Different Drummer* (1959)
Toni Morrison, *Song of Solomon* (1977)
Ann Petry, *Country Place* (1947)
Jean Toomer, *Cane* (1923)
John A. Williams, *The Man Who Cried I Am* (1967)
Richard Wright, *Native Son* (1940)

15 Modern Works

Wesley Brown, *Tragic Magic* (1979)
Toni Cade Bambara, *The Sea Birds Still Alive* (1977)
George Cain, *Blueschild Baby* (1970)
Alice Childress, *A Short Walk* (1979)
Leon Forrest, *The Bloodworth Orphans* (1977)
Gayl Jones, *Corregidora* (1975)
John Oliver Killens, *The Cotillion* (1971)
Paule Marshall, *Soul Clap Hands and Sing* (1976)
James Alan McPherson, *Elbow Room* (1977)
Robert Deane Pharr, *Books of Numbers* (1969)
Ishmael Reed, *The Last Days of Louisiana Red* (1974)
William Gardner Smith, *Last of the Conquerors* (1948)
John Stewart, *Curving Roads* (1975)
Alice Walker, *In Love and Trouble* (1974)
Al Young, *Sitting Pretty* (1976)

■ ITALIAN-AMERICANS

Joseph Caruso, *The Priest* (1956)
Elizabeth Christman, *A Nice Italian Girl* (1976)
Guido D'Agostino, *Olives on an Apple Tree* (1940)
Raymond DiCapite, *The Coming of Fabrize* (1960)
Pietro DiDonato, *Christ in Concrete* (1939)
John Fante, *Dago Red* (1940)
Gerre Mangione, *Mount Allegro* (1972)
Jo Pagano, *The Paisanos* (1940)
Mario Puzo, *The Fortunate Pilgrim* (1965)
Mari Tomasi, *Like Lesser Gods* (1949)

You think your pains and your heartbreaks are unprecedented in the history of the world, but then you read. It was books that taught me that the things that tormented me most were the very things that connected me with all the people who were alive, or who have ever been alive.

—JAMES BALDWIN

■ CHICANOS

Oscar Zeta Acosta, *The Revolt of the Cockroach People* (1973)
Rudolfo A. Anaya, *Bless Me, Ultima* (1972)
Ron Arias, *The Road to Tamazuncha* (1975)
Raymond Barrio, *The Plum Plum Pickers* (1969)
Frank Bonham, *Viva Chicano* (1970)
Tomas Rivera, *". . . Yo no Se lo Trago la Tierra" (". . . and the Earth Did Not Part")* (1970)
Orlando Romero, *Nambe: Year One* (1976)
Richard Vasquez, *Chicano* (1971)
José Antonio Villareal, *Pocho* (1959)
Edmund Villasenor, *Macho!* (1973)

■ THE NATIVE-AMERICAN WAY

Ralph K. Andrist, *The Long Death* (1964)
Dee Brown, *Bury My Heart at Wounded Knee* (1971)
Vine Deloria, Jr., *Custer Died for Your Sins* (1970)
Peter Farb, *Man's Rise to Civilization: The Cultural Ascent of the Indian of North America* (rev. 1978)
Theodora Kroeber, *Ishi: Last of His Tribe* (1964)
Nancy O. Lurie, *Mountain Wolf Woman* (1961)
Mari Sandoz, *These Were the Sioux* (1961)
Dan C. Talayson, *Sun Chief* (1942)
Estelle Thomas, *Gift of Laughter* (1967)
Mary Warren, *Walk in My Moccasins* (1966)

5 Indian Profiles

Coye "Nino" Cochise as told to A. Kinney Griffith, *The First Hundred Years of Nino Cochise* (1971)
John Lame Deer and Richard Erdoes, *Lame Deer, Seeker of Visions* (1972)
Black Hawk, Sauk Chief, *Autobiography* (1833)
John Joseph Mathews, *Wah'kon-Tah: The Osage and the White Man's Road* (1932)
John C. Niehardt, *Black Elk Speaks* (1961)

Novels of Indian Life

Adolf Bandelier, *The Delight Makers* (1890)
Betty Baker, *Walk the World's Rim* (1965)
Thomas Berger, *Little Big Man* (1964)
Hal Borland, *When the Legends Die* (1963)
Dee Brown, *Creek Mary's Blood* (1980)
Edwin Corle, *Fig Tree John* (1935)
Dan Cushman, *Stay Away, Joe* (1953)
Christine Harris, *Raven's Cry* (1966)
Frederick Manfred, *Conquering Horse* (1959)
Florence Means, *Our Cup is Broken* (1969)
Thomas Sanchez, *Rabbit Boss* (1972)
Mari Sandoz, *The Story Catcher* (1963)
Virginia Sorensen, *The Proper Gods* (1951)
Frank Waters, *The Man Who Killed Deer* (1942)

The Most Painstakingly Written Indian Novel

Ruth Beebe Hill, *Hanta Yo* (1979). The author and Chunksa Yuha translated the 2,000 pages of original manuscript into the archaic Dakotah/Lakotah language and back into English to ensure that there would be no loss of Indian idiom.

Novels by Full-Blooded Indians

Denton R. Bradford, *Tsali* (1972)
Dallas Chief Eagle, *Winter Count* (1967)
Jamake Highwater, *The Sun, He Dies* (1980)
Darcy McNickle, *Wind from an Evening Sky* (1978)
N. Scott Momaday, *House Made of Dawn* (1968)
Leslie Marmon Silko, *Ceremony* (1977)
Hyemeyohsts Storm, *Seven Arrows* (1972)
James Welch, *The Death of Jim Loney* (1979)

What particularly excites me nowadays is the growing strength of literature written by American Indians themselves—Scott Momaday, Jr., Vine Deloria, Jr., James Welch, Jamake Highwater, Leslie Silko. When an Indian learns how to write, he's as good as they come.

—DEE BROWN

■ HOMOSEXUALITIES

Man to Man: 10 Novels
Daniel Curzon, *Something to Do in the Dark* (1971)
Andrew Holleran, *The Dancer From the Dance* (1979)
Christopher Isherwood, *A Single Man* (1964)
Joseph Pintauro, *Cold Hands* (1979)
John Rechy, *City of Night* (1963)
Gore Vidal, *The City and the Pillar* (1949)
Patricia Nell Warren, *The Front Runner* (1974)
David Watmough, *Mo More Into the Garden* (1978)
Denton Welch, *A Voice Through a Cloud* (1950)
Edmund White, *Nocturnes for the King of Naples* (1979)

As One Woman to Another: 10 Novels
Rita Mae Brown, *Rubyfruit Jungle* (1973)
Maureen Duffy, *The Microcosm* (1966)
Radclyffe Hall, *The Well of Loneliness* (1928)
Henry James, *The Bostonians* (1886)
Isobel Miller, *Patience and Sarah* (1970)
Claire Morgan, *The Price of Salt* (1958)
Marge Piercy, *The High Cost of Living* (1978)
May Sarton, *A Reckoning* (1978)
Gale Wilhelm, *We Too Are Drifting* (1935)
Monique Wittig, *The Lesbian Body* (1973)

Out of the Closet: Homosexual Emergence
J. R. Ackerly, *My Father and Myself* (1969)
Quentin Crisp, *The Naked Civil Servant* (1977)
Merle Miller, *On Being Different* (1972)
Elana Nachman, *Riverfinger Woman* (1974)
John Reid, *The Best Little Boy in the World* (1973)

The Gender Trap; Transsexual Experiences
Nancy Hunt, *Mirror Image* (1978)
Christine Jorgenson, *A Personal Autobiography* (1973)
Marco Martino with Harriet, *Emergence: A Transsexual Autobiography* (1977)
Jan Morris, *Conundrum* (1974)

■ WHAT'S MY LINE

We all know that Figaro is a barber *(of Seville)* and that Willy Loman is *(Death of)* a salesman, but how many of the following characters' occupations can you guess? Clue: They are all described in the novels' titles.

1. Dr. Charles Primrose
2. Felix Krull
3. Stephen Dedalus
4. Michael Henchard
5. Jean Latour
6. Yuri Zhivago
7. Natty Bumppo
8. Billy Budd
9. Frank Algernon Cowperwood
10. George Smiley
11. Captain Ashburnham
12. Athos, Porthos, and Aramis
13. Yasha Mazur
14. Yakov Bok
15. Gertie Nevels

Answers
1. *The VICAR of Wakefield* (Goldsmith), 2. *Confessions of Felix Krull: CONFIDENCE MAN* (Mann), 3. *A Portrait of the ARTIST as a Young Man* (Joyce), 4. *The MAYOR of Casterbridge,* (Hardy), 5. *Death Comes for the ARCHBISHOP* (Cather), 6. *DR. Zhivago* (Pasternak), 7. *The DEERSLAYER* or *The PATHFINDER* (Cooper), 8. *Billy Budd, FORETOPMAN* (Melville), 9. *The FINANCIER* or *The TITAN* (Dreiser), 10. *Tinker, Tailor, Soldier, SPY* (Le Carré), 11. *The Good SOLDIER* (Ford), 12. *The Three MUSKETEERS* (Dumas), 13. *The MAGICIAN of Lublin* (Singer), 14. *The FIXER* (Malamud), 15. *The DOLLMAKER* (Arnow)

■ PRESCRIBED READINGS

A Critical List: 10 Medical Novels
James Gould Cozzens, *The Last Adam* (1933)
Lloyd Douglas, *Magnificent Obsession* (1929)
Kenneth Fearing, *The Hospital* (1939)
Gerald Green, *The Last Angry Man* (1957)
Richard Clark Hirschhorn, *A Pride of Healers* (1977)
Sinclair Lewis, *Arrowsmith* (1925)
Morton Thompson, *Not As A Stranger* (1954)
Mildred Walker, *Medical Meeting* (1949)

Linda Wolfe, *Private Practices* (1979)
Agatha Young, *Dr. Moore's Legacy* (1973)

The Novelist-Practitioners: 15 Medical Novels by Doctors

Christian Barnaard, *In the Night Season* (1978)
Martin Bax, *The Hospital Ship* (1976)
Robin Cook, *Coma* (1977)
I. S. Cooper, *It's Hard to Leave While the Music's Playing* (1977)
Michael Crichton, *The Andromeda Strain* (1969)
A. J. Cronin, *The Citadel* (1937)
Colin Douglas, *The Greatest Breakthrough Since Lunchtime* (1979)
Marshall Goldberg, *The Anatomy Lesson* (1974)
John Hejinian, *Extreme Remedies* (1974)
James Kerr, *Emergency Room* (1975)
Samuel Shem, *The House of God* (1978)
Frank Slaughter, *Women in White* (1974)
David R. Slavitt, *King of Hearts* (1976)
Irwin Philip Sobel, *The Virus Killer* (1975)
André Souberan, *The Doctors* (1947)

Professional Reading: 10 True Cases

Peggy Anderson, *Nurse* (1978)
Ronald Glasser, *Ward 402* (1973)
Victor George Heiser, *An American Doctor's Odyssey* (1936)
Rachel MacKenzie, *Risk* (1971)
Theodore I. Malinin, *Surgery and Life: The Extraordinary Career of Alexis Carrel* (1979)
Wilder Penfield, *No Man Alone: A Surgeon's Story* (1977)
Berton Roueché, *The Orange Man and Other Narratives of Medical Detection* (1971)
Richard Selzer, *Mortal Lessons: Notes on the Art of Surgery* (1976)
Lawrence Shainberg, *Brain Surgeon: An Intimate View of His World* (1979)
Thomas Thompson, *Heart* (1971)

Let's Play Doctor

The authors of the books below were all physicians, which is about all they may have had in common. Do you know them by their works?

1. *Of Human Bondage*
2. *Gargantua and Pantagruel*
3. *The Cherry Orchard*
4. *The Expedition of Humphrey Clinker*
5. *The Autocrat of the Breakfast Table*
6. *Paterson*
7. *The Citadel*
8. *The Moviegoer*
9. *The Death of a Nobody*
10. *A Study in Scarlet*

Answers
1. W. Somerset Maugham, 2. François Rabelais, 3. Anton Chekhov, 4. Tobias Smollett, 5. Oliver Wendell Holmes, 6. William Carlos Williams, 7. A. J. Cronin, 8. Walker Percy, 9. Jules Romains, 10. Sir Arthur Conan Doyle

READING THE LAW

15 Legal Fictions

Louis Auchincloss, *The Partners* (1973)
Stephen Becker, *Covenant with Death* (1965)
Henry Cecil, *Brief Tales from the Bench* (1968)
Robert Cenedella, *A Little to the East* (1963)
James Gould Cozzens, *The Just and the Unjust* (1942)
Al Dewlin, *Twilight of Honor* (1961)
Bruce Ducker, *Rule by Proxy* (1977)
George V. Higgins, *Kennedy for the Defense* (1979)
Richard Kluger, *Star Witness* (1979)
Edward Linn, *The Adversaries* (1973)
Michael Meltsner, *Short Takes* (1979)
John Jay Osborne, Jr., *The Associates* (1979)
Arthur R. G. Solmssen, *The Comfort Letter* (1975)
Arthur Train, *Mr. Tutt at his Best* (1961)
Edmund Ward, *The Main Chance* (1977)

Letters of the Law: 10 Real Lawyers

Catherine Drinker Bowen, *Yankee from Olympus* (1944)
William O. Douglas, *Go East, Young Man* (1974)

Jacob Ehrlich, *Life in My Hands* (1965)

Milton S. Gould, *The Witness Who Spoke with God and Other Tales from the Courtroom* (1979)

William Harbaugh, *Lawyers' Lawyer: The Life of John W. Davis* (1973)

Paul O'Dwyer, *Counsel for the Defense* (1979)

Louis Nizer, *My Life in Court* (1961)

Helene Schwartz, *Lawyering* (1975)

Irving Stone, *Clarence Darrow for the Defense* (1949)

Scott Turow, *One-L: An Inside Account of Life in the First Year at Harvard Law School*, (1977)

Lawyers as Writers: A Literary Bar Exam

Can you identify each of these lawyers, some of whom never practiced law, others of whom practiced throughout their careers? Take out your legal pad and a pen and get down to cases.

1. This great Renaissance figure established the English form of the essay.
2. A pioneering American dramatist, his best-remembered play is *The Adding Machine*, 1923.
3. This poet's most enduring work is *Spoon River Anthology* (1915).
4. This nineteenth-century Scotsman is best known today for such historical romances as *Kidnapped*.
5. One of America's greatest modern poets, he was an officer of one of the Hartford insurance companies until retirement.
6. A marine lawyer during his career, he wrote one book—about his voyage to California as an ordinary seaman in 1834–36—that has remained a sea classic.
7. A former lawyer with the United States Attorney's office, he used his experience to give his crime novels—beginning with *The Friends of Eddie Coyle*—verisimilitude.
8. This nineteenth-century American poet is remembered by every high school English student for "To a Waterfowl" and "Thanatopsis."
9. The author of one of the greatest biographies ever written, he preserved the conversations of his subject—*the* man of eighteenth-century English literature.

10. He created the most famous lawyer-sleuth in all of detective fiction.
11. A Nobel Prize laureate, this British novelist and playwright is best remembered today for *The Forsyte Saga* (1906–22).
12. The prolific output of this most popular novelist of his day includes *Ivanhoe, Waverly, Rob Roy* and *Kenilworth.*
13. This Greek novelist and poet is best known in this country for *Zorba the Greek.*
14. Virtually the founder of American drama, he wrote *The Contrast* (1787) the first comedy by a native American.
15. A three-time Pulitzer Prize winner, this American poet and verse-dramatist was Librarian of Congress and an assistant secretary of state.

Answers
1. Francis Bacon, 2. Elmer Rice, 3. Edgar Lee Masters, 4. Robert Louis Stevenson, 5. Wallace Stevens, 6. Richard Henry Dana, Jr., 7. George V. Higgins, 8. William Cullen Bryant, 9. James Boswell, 10. Erle Stanley Gardner, 11. John Galsworthy, 12. Sir Walter Scott, 13. Nikos Kazantzakis, 14. Royall Tyler, 15. Archibald MacLeish

■ READ ALL ABOUT IT! JOURNALISM —FACT AND FICTION

The Craft
David Halberstam, *The Powers That Be* (1979)
A. J. Liebling, *The Press* (1961)
Lillian Ross, *Reporting* (1964)
Gay Talese, *The Kingdom and the Power* (1969)
Tom Wicker, *On Press* (1978)

15 Journalists Remember
Edward Behr, *Bearings: A Foreign Correspondent's Life Behind the Lines* (1978)
Margaret Bourke-White, *Portrait of Myself* (1963)
James Cameron, *Point of Departure: An Attempt at Autobiography* (1968)

Francis Hackett, *American Rainbow: Early Reminiscences* (1971)
Arthur Krock, *Sixty Years on the Firing Line* (1968)
H. L. Mencken, *Newspaper Days, 1899–1906* (1941)
Malcolm Muggeridge, *Chronicles of Wasted Time* (1973)
Henry Wood Nevinson, *Fire of Life* (1935)
William Shirer, *Twentieth-Century Journey* (1976)
Lincoln Steffens, *Autobiography* (1931)
C. L. Sulzberger, *Seven Continents and Forty Years: A Concentration of Memoirs* (1977)
Sir John Wheeler-Bennett, *Knaves, Fools and Heroes in Europe Between the Wars* (1977)
Theodore H. White, *In Search of History* (1978)
William Allen White, *Autobiography* (1946)
Leonard Woolf, *Autobiography* (1960–69)

5 Journalists Remembered
Gene Fowler, *Timberline: A Story of Bonfils and Tammen* (1933)
Dale Kramer, *Ross and the New Yorker* (1951)
Marion K. Sanders, *Dorothy Thompson: A Legend in Her Time* (1973)
H. Allen Smith, *The Life and Legend of Gene Fowler* (1977)
W. A. Swanberg, *Citizen Hearst* (1961)

Headlines: 10 Novels About Journalists
John Brooks, *The Big Wheel* (1949)
Richard Condon, *Some Angry Angel* (1960)
Clyde Brion Davis, *The Great American Novel* (1938)
Michael Frayn, *Against Entropy* (1967)
Ben Hecht, *Erik Dorn* (1921)
Guy de Maupassant, *Bel-Ami* (1885)
Richard Stern, *Natural Shocks* (1978)
Evelyn Waugh, *Scoop* (1938)
Nathanael West, *Miss Lonelyhearts* (1933)
Tom Wicker, *Facing the Lions* (1973)

By-Lines: 15 Novels by Journalists
Jimmy Breslin, *World Without End Amen* (1973)
Ned Calmer, *Anchorman* (1970)
Charles Collingwood, *The Defector* (1970)

Janet Flanner, *The Cubical City* (1926)
David Halberstam, *One Very Hot Day* (1968)
Pete Hamill, *Flesh and Blood* (1977)
Smith Hempstone, *A Tract of Time* (1966)
Roger Kahn, *But Not to Keep* (1979)
Marvin Kalb and Ted Koppel, *In the National Interest* (1977)
Edwin Newman, *Sunday Punch* (1979)
Drew Pearson, *The Senator* (1968)
Harrison E. Salisbury, *The Gates of Hell* (1975)
Gail Sheehy, *Love Sounds* (1970)
C. L. Sulzburger, *The Tooth Merchant* (1973)
Jules Witcover, *The Main Chance* (1979)

■ TELLING TALES OUT OF SCHOOL

Readin', Writin', and Rememberin': 20 Teachers' True Tales
Sylvia Ashton-Warner, *Teacher* (1963)
E. R. Braithewaite, *To Sir, With Love* (1960)
Mike Cherry, *Train Whistle Blues* (1978)
Pat Conroy, *The Water Is Wide* (1971)
George Dennison, *The Lives of Children: The Story of the First
    Street School* (1969)
Kit Elliott, *An African School: A Record of Experience* (1970)
Daniel Fader, *The Naked Children* (1971)
Jim Haskins, *Diary of a Harlem Schoolteacher* (1970)
James Herndon, *How to Survive in Your Native Land* (1971)
Myrliss Hershey, *Teacher Was a White Witch* (1973)
Anne Hobbs, as told to Robert Specht, *Tisha, The Story of a
    Young Teacher in the Alaska Wilderness* (1976)
John Holt, *How Children Learn* (1969)
Herbert R. Kohl, *Thirty-Six Children* (1968)
Jonathan Kozol, *Death at an Early Age* (1967)
Leslie Lacy, *Native Daughter* (1974)
Mary MacCracken, *A Circle of Children* (1974)
A. S. Neil, *Summerhill: A Radical Approach to Child Raising*
    (1960)
Richard Piro, *Black Fiddler* (1971)
Esther P. Rothman, *The Angel Inside Went Sour* (1971)
Jesse Stuart, *The Thread That Runs So True* (1949)

10 Novels of Teaching

Sylvia Ashton-Warner, *Spinster* (1958)
Alan Dennis Burke, *Fire Watch* (1980)
Edward Eggleston, *The Hoosier Schoolmaster* (1871)
Peter Fisher and Marc Rubin, *Special Teachers/Special Boys* (1979)
James Hilton, *Good-Bye, Mr. Chips* (1934)
Bel Kaufman, *Up the Down Staircase* (1964)
Frances Gray Patton, *Good Morning, Miss Dove* (1954)
Benjamin Siegel, *The Principal* (1963)
Feodor Sologub, *The Petty Demon* (1907)
Muriel Spark, *The Prime of Miss Jean Brodie* (1961)

10 Boarding-School Novels

Boys at School

James Kirkwood, *Good Times/Bad Times* (1968)
John Knowles, *A Separate Peace* (1959)
Robert Musil, *Young Törless* (1906)
Richard Yates, *A Good School* (1978)

Girls at School

Wendy Owen, *The Education of Winnie D.* (1968)
Monica Stirling, *Dress Rehearsal* (1952)
Antonia White, *Frost in May* (1933)

British Public School

Arthur Calder-Marshall, *Dead Centre* (1935)
Pamela Hansford Johnson, *The Honours Board* (1970)
Iris Murdoch, *The Sandcastle* (1957)

■ DON AND PROF.: THE UNIVERSITY NOVEL

Tales of the Don: 10 "Oxbridge" Novels

Oxford

Max Beerbohm, *Zuleika Dobson* (1911)
Winston J. Churchill, *Running in Place* (1973)

L. P. Hartley, *The Sixth Heaven* (1946)
Philip Larkin, *Jill* (1946)
Compton MacKenzie, *Sinister Street* (1913)
J. I. M. Stewart, *A Staircase in Surrey Series* (1975)

THE ORIGINAL: Thomas Hughes, *Tom Brown At Oxford* (1861)

Cambridge

E. M. Forster, *The Longest Journey* (1907)
Rosamond Lehmann, *Dusty Answer* (1927)
Tom Sharpe, *Porterhouse Blue* (1974)
Andrew Sinclair, *My Friend Judas* (1959)

Professorial Prose: 15 Academic Novels
Kingsley Amis, *Lucky Jim* (1958)
Stringfellow Barr, *Purely Academic* (1958)
Malcolm Bradbury, *Stopping Westward* (1965)
Willa Cather, *The Professor's House* (1925)
Gail Godwin, *The Odd Woman* (1974)
Janet Hoyt, *Wings of Wax* (1929)
Randell Jarrell, *Pictures from an Institution* (1954)
Mary McCarthy, *The Groves of Academe* (1952)
Robie Macauley, *The Disguises of Love* (1952)
Vladimir Nabokov, *Pnin* (1957)
Joyce Carol Oates, *Unholy Love* (1979)
J. B. Priestley, *The Image Men* (1969)
May Sarton, *The Small Room* (1961)
Gladys Schmitt, *A Small Fire* (1956)
C. P. Snow, *The Masters* (1951)

Getting the First Degree: 10 Novels of College Student Life
Ron Carlson, *Betrayed by F. Scott Fitzgerald* (1977)
Jason Epstein, *Wild Oats* (1979)
Richard Fariña, *Been Down So Long It Looks Like Up to Me* (1966)
F. Scott Fitzgerald, *This Side of Paradise* (1920)
Shirley Jackson, *Hangsaman* (1951)
Meredith Marsh, *Eating Cake* (1979)

William Maxwell, *The Folded Leaf* (1945)
John Nichols, *The Sterile Cuckoo* (1965)
George Weller, *Not to Eat, Not to Love* (1934)
Calder Willingham, *End as a Man* (1947)

First American "College Novel": Nathaniel Hawthorne,
   Fanshawe (1828)

■ MORE WHOSE WHAT

Complete the title of each novel by matching a word from
the first column with a word from the middle column; when
you have put the title together, match it with its author in
the third column.

1. *Humboldt's*	A. *People*	a. William Gass
2. *Swann's*	B. *End*	b. Erskine Caldwell
3. *Gulliver's*	C. *Lives*	c. Anthony Burgess
4. *Enderby's*	D. *Little Acre*	d. Philip Roth
5. *Portnoy's*	E. *Gift*	e. Bernard Malamud
6. *Dubin's*	F. *Luck*	f. John LeCarré
7. *Omensetter's*	G. *Way*	g. Saul Bellow
8. *Morgan's*	H. *Complaint*	h. Anne Tyler
9. *Smiley's*	I. *Travels*	i. Jonathan Swift
10. *God's*	J. *Passing*	j. Marcel Proust

Answers
1–E–g, 2–G–j, 3–I–i, 4–B–c, 5–H–d, 6–C–e, 7–F–a, 8–J–h, 9–A–f,
10–D–b

■ DRAMATIS PERSONAE

Dramatic Lives: 10 Biographies
Denis Bablet, *Edward Gordon Craig* (1966)
William Embodean, *Sarah Bernhardt* (1975)
Gene Fowler, *Good Night Sweet Prince: The Life and Times of
   John Barrymore* (1944)
John Lahr, *Prick Up Your Ears: The Biography of Joe Orton*
   (1978)

Scott Meredith, *George S. Kaufman and His Friends* (1974)
Richard Moody, *Edwin Forrest* (1960)
Tad Mosel with Gertrude Macy, *Leading Lady: The World and Theatre of Katherine Cornell* (1978)
Tom Prideaux, *Love or Nothing: The Life and Times of Ellen Terry* (1975)
Eleanor Ruggles, *Prince of Players: Edwin Booth* (1953)
Cornelia Otis Skinner, *Madam Sarah* (1967)

24 Theatrical Remembrances
George Abbott, *Mister Abbott* (1963)
Enid Bagnold, *Enid Bagnold's Autobiography* (1970)
Colly Cibber, *Apology for Life* (1740)
Cheryl Crawford, *One Naked Individual* (1977)
John Gielgud, *Gielgud: An Actor and His Time, A Memoir* (1980)
Max Gordon, *Max Gordon Presents* (1963)
Ruth Gordon, *Myself Among Others* (1970)
Maxim Gorky, *Autobiography* (1913–23)
Tyrone Guthrie, *My Life in the Theatre* (1959)
Uta Hagen, *Respect for Acting* (1973)
Jed Harris, *A Dance on the High Wire* (1979)
Moss Hart, *Act One* (1959)
Helen Hayes, *On Reflection: An Autobiography* (1968)
Lillian Hellman, *An Unfinished Woman: A Memoir* (1970)
John Houseman, *Run-Through: A Memoir* (1973)
Jo Mielziner, *Designing for the Theatre: A Memoir and a Portfolio* (1965)
Ethel Merman with George Eells, *Merman: An Autobiography* (1978)
José Quintero, *If You Don't Dance They Beat You* (1974)
Michael Redgrave, *Mask or Face: Reflections in an Actor's Mirror* (1958)
Marion Seldes, *The Bright Lights: A Theatre Life* (1978)
Walter Slezak, *What Time's the Next Swan?* (1962)
Constantin Stanislavski, *My Life in Art* (1924)
Emlyn Williams, *Emlyn* (1974)
Blanche Yurka, *Bohemian Girl: Blanche Yurka's Theatrical Life* (1970)

Stage Whispers: 10 Different Views
Brooks Atkinson, *The Lively Years* (1973)
Eric Bentley, *What Is Theatre* (1968)
Max Beerbohm, *A Selection from "Around Theatres"* (1960)
John Mason Brown, *Dramatis Personae: A Retrospective Show* (1963)
Walter Kerr, *Journey to the Center of the Theatre* (1979)
Mary McCarthy, *Sights and Spectacles, 1937–1956* (1956)
George Jean Nathan, *The Magic Mirror* (1960)
Sean O'Casey, *Green Crow* (1956)
Lillian and Helen Ross, *The Player: A Profile of an Art* (1962)
Kenneth Tynan, *Curtains* (1961)

Shtik Figures: 5 Comedians
Steve Allen, *The Funny Men* (1956)
Albert Goldman, *Ladies and Gentlemen, Lenny Bruce* (1974)
Walter Kerr, *The Silent Clowns* (1975)
Harpo Marx, *Harpo Speaks* (1961)
Robert Lewis Taylor, *W. C. Fields: His Follies and His Fortunes* (1967)

Caught in the Act: 15 Theatre Novels
E. F. Benson, *Travail of Gold* (1933)
Richard Bissell, *Say, Darling* (1956)
Mikhail Bulgakov, *Black Snow* (1965)
Ilka Chase, *Island Players* (1956)
Noel Coward, *Star Quality* (1951)
Clemence Dane, *Broome Stages* (1931)
Fitzroy Davis, *Quicksilver* (1942)
Margaret Drabble, *The Garrick Year* (1964)
Daphne DuMaurier, *Parasites* (1949)
Bamber Gascoigne, *The Heyday* (1973)
Pamela Hansford Johnson, *Catherine Carter* (1951)
John P. Marquand, *Woman and Thomas Harrow* (1960)
Elmer L. Rice, *The Show Must Go On* (1949)
Monica Stirling, *Some Daring Folly* (1956)
Magda Szabo, *The Fawn* (1963)

■ AT THE BARRE: THE WORLD OF DANCE

The Dance and Dancing
Richard Buckle, *Buckle at the Ballet* (1980)
Arlene Croce, *Afterimages* (1977)
Edwin Denby, *Dancers, Buildings and People in the Streets* (1965)
John Gruen, *The Private World of Ballet* (1975)
Arnold L. Haskell, *The Beauty of Ballet* (1961)
Lincoln Kirstein, *Movement and Metaphor: Four Centuries of Ballet* (1970)
Joseph Mazo, *Dance Is a Contact Sport* (1974)
Don McDonagh, *How to Enjoy Ballet* (1978)
Marcia B. Siegel, *Watching the Dance Go By* (1977)
Marshall and Jean Stearns, *Jazz Dance* (1966)

The Dancers and Dance Makers
Katherine Dunham, *A Touch of Innocence* (1959)
Michael Fokine, *Fokine: Memoirs of a Ballet Master* (1961)
Margot Fonteyn, *Autobiography* (1976)
Martha Graham, *The Notebooks of Martha Graham* (1973)
Doris Humphrey, *Doris Humphrey: Artist First* (1972)
Alicia Markova, *Giselle and I* (1961)
Marie Rambert, *Quicksilver: An Autobiography* (1972)
Lydia Sokolova, *Dancing for Diaghilev* (1960)
Walter Terry, *Ted Shawn: Father of American Dance* (1976)
Mary Wigman, *The Mary Wigman Book: Her Writings* (1975)

5 Russians' Memoirs
Tamara Karsavina, *Theatre Street* (1961)
Matilda Kschessinka, *Dancing in Petersburg* (1960)
Natalia Makarova, *A Dance Autobiography* (1979)
Rudolph Nureyev, *Nureyev* (1963)
Valery Panov, *To Dance* (1978)

Write on Pointe: 5 Ballet Novels
Rumer Godden, *Candles for St. Jude* (1948)
Darrell Husted, *Louisa Brancusi* (1980)
Tom Murphy, *Ballet* (1978)

Francis Pollini, *Excursion* (1965)
Edward Stewart, *Ballerina* (1978)

■ ROCK 'N' ROLL AND ALL THAT JAZZ

Oldies But Goodies: Ten Best Rock 'n' Roll Hits
Nik Cohn, *Rock from the Beginning* (1969)
Myra Friedman, *Buried Alive: The Biography of Janis Joplin* (1973)
Reebie Garofalo, *Rock 'n' Roll Is Here to Stay* (1978)
Charles Gillett, *The Sound of the City: The Rise of Rock and Roll* (1972)
Bob Greene, *Billion Dollar Baby* (1974)
David Henderson, *Jimi Hendrix: Hoodoo Child of the Aquarian Age* (1978)
Michael Lydon, *Rock Folk* (1971)
Greil Marcus, *Mystery Train: Images of America in Rock and Roll Music* (1975)
Arnold Shaw, *Honkers and Shouters: The Rhythm and Blues Years* (1978)
Geoffrey Stokes, *Star-Making Machinery: The Odyssey of an Album* (1976)

20 Best Books on Blues and Jazz
Chris Albertson, *Bessie* (1973)
Whitney Balliett, *American Singers* (1979)
Joachim-Ernst Berendt, *Jazz: A Photo History* (1979)
Ralph Berton, *Remembering Bix: A Memoir of the Jazz Age* (1974)
Rudi Blesch and Harriet Janis, *They All Played Ragtime* (1950)
Samuel Charters, *Country Blues* (1959)
Duke Ellington, *Music Is My Mistress* (1974)
Dizzy Gillespie with Al Fraser, *To Be or Not . . . to Bop: Memoirs* (1979)
Hampton Hawes and Don Asher, *Raise Up Off Me* (1975)
Nat Hentoff, *The Jazz Life* (1961)
Billie Holiday with William Duffy, *Lady Sings the Blues* (1958)
LeRoi Jones, *Blues People* (1963)

Alan Lomax, *Mister Jelly Roll* (1950)
Mezz Mezzrow with Bernard Wolfe, *Really the Blues* (1946)
Charles Mingus, *Beneath the Underdog* (1971)
Paul Oliver, *Living with the Blues* (1965)
Ross Russell, *Bird Lives* (1973)
Willie the Lion Smith with George Holfer, *Music in My Mind* (1964)
A. B. Spellman, *Four Lives in the Bebop Business* (1966)
J. C. Thomas, *Chasin' the Trane* (1975)

Riff Raps: 10 Best Jazz Novels
Dorothy Baker, *Young Man with a Horn* (1938)
Nat Hentoff, *Jazz Country* (1965)
John Clellon Holmes, *The Horn* (1959)
Albert Murray, *Train Whistle Guitar* (1974)
Michael Ondaatje, *Coming Through Slaughter* (1976)
Ross Russell, *The Sound* (1961)
Robert Simmons, *Man Walking on Eggshells* (1962)
Harold Sinclair, *Music of Dixie* (1952)
Josef Skvorecky, *The Bass Saxophone* (1979)
John A. Williams, *Night Song* (1961)

■ CLASSICAL WORKS

Composers: 10 Biographies
Jacques Barzun, *Berlioz and his Century* (1956)
Robert Craft, *Stravinsky* (1972)
Marcia Davenport, *Mozart* (1932)
Hans Gal, *Johannes Brahms* (1963)
Paul Henry Lang, *George Frederic Handel* (1966)
Hans and Rosaleen Moldenhauer, *Anton von Webern* (1979)
Maynard Solomon, *Beethoven* (1977)
J. W. N. Sullivan, *Beethoven: His Spiritual Development* (1927)
Alexander Wheelock Thayer, *Life of Beethoven* (rev. 1967)
W. J. Turner, *Mozart: The Man and His Works* (rev. 1966)

Composers: 10 Memoirs
Hector Berlioz, *Memoirs of Hector Berlioz* (1969)
Charles A. Ives, *Memos* (1972)

Darius Milhaud, *Notes Without Music* (1952)
Sergei Prokofiev, *Prokofiev by Prokofiev: A Composer's Memoir* (1979)
Dmitri Shostakovich, *Testimony: The Memoirs of Dmitri Shostakovich as Related to and Edited by Solomon Volkov* (1979)
Ethel Smythe, *Impressions That Remained* (1919)
Richard Strauss, *Recollections and Reflections* (1953)
Igor Stravinsky, *Themes and Episodes* (1966)
Virgil Thomson, *Virgil Thomson* (1966)
Richard Wagner, *My Life* (trans. 1911)

5 Performers
Walter Damrosch, *My Musical Life* (1926)
Erich Leinsdorf, *Cadenza: A Musical Career* (1976)
Yehudi Menuhin, *Unfinished Journey* (1976)
Ignace Jan Paderewski, *The Paderewski Memoirs* (1938)
Arthur Rubinstein, *My Younger Years* (1973)

Aria of Concern: 10 Opera Memoirs
Rudolph Bing, *5,000 Nights at the Opera* (1972)
Boris Chaliapin, *Pages from My Life* (1926)
Geraldine Ferrar, *Geraldine Ferrar: The Story of an American Singer* (1916)
Kirsten Flagstad, *The Flagstad Manuscripts* (1952)
Mary Garden and Louis Brancolli, *Mary Garden's Own Story* (1951)
Giulio Gatti-Casuzza, *Memories of the Opera* (1941)
Lotte Lehmann, *Midway in My Song* (1938)
Jules Massenet, *My Recollections* (1919)
Nellie Melba, *Melodies and Memories* (1925)
Beverly Sills, *Bubbles: A Self-Portrait* (1976)

■ WORDS INTO MUSIC

15 Operas from Fiction
Billy Budd (Britten): Herman Melville, *Billy Budd* (post. 1924)
Carmen (Bizet): Prosper Merimée, *Carmen* (1852)

Cavalleria Rusticana (Mascagni): Giovanni Verga, "Cavalleria Rusticana" (1883)

Eugene Onegin (Tschaikovsky): Alexander Pushkin, *Eugene Onegin* (1833)

La Bohème (Puccini): Henri Murger, *La Vie De Bohème* (1848)

Lakmé (Delibes): Pierre Loti, *The Marriage of Loti* (1880)

La Traviata (Verdi): Alexandre Dumas, fils, *La Dame Aux Caméllias* (1852)

Lucia Di Lamermoor (Donizetti): Sir Walter Scott, *The Bride of Lamermoor* (1819)

Manon (Massenet): Abbé Prévost, *Manon Lescaut* (1731)

Porgy and Bess (Gershwin): DuBose Heyward, *Porgy* (1925)

Rienzi (Wagner): Edward Bulwer-Lytton, *Rienzi, The Last of the Tribunes* (1835)

Rigoletto (Verdi): Victor Hugo, *Le Roi S'Amuse* (1832)

Tales of Hoffman (Offenbach): E. T. A. Hoffman, *Weird Tales* (1815)

Thaïs (Massenet): Anatole France, *Thaïs* (1890)

Werther (Massenet): Johann Wolfgang von Goethe, *The Sorrows of Young Werther* (1774)

15 Musicals from Fiction

Cabaret: Christopher Isherwood, *Berlin Stories* (1935–39)

Camelot: T. H. White, *The Once and Future King* (1958)

Damn Yankees: Douglas Wallop, *The Year the Yankees Lost the Pennant* (1954)

Fiddler on the Roof: Sholom Aleichem, *Tevye's Daughter* (Trans. 1949)

Flower Drum Song: C. Y. Lee, *Flower Drum Song* (1957)

Guys and Dolls: Damon Runyon, "The Idyll of Miss Sarah Brown" (1932)

Lost in the Stars: Alan Paton, *Cry the Beloved Country* (1948)

Mame: Patrick Dennis, *Auntie Mame* (1955)

Oliver: Charles Dickens, *Oliver Twist* (1837–39)

Pal Joey: John O'Hara, *Pal Joey* (1940)

Show Boat: Edna Ferber, *Showboat* (1926)

Man of La Mancha: Miguel Cervantes, *Don Quixote* (1605)

The Pajama Game: Richard Bissell, *7½¢* (1953)

The Wiz: L. Frank Baum, *The Wonderful Wizard of Oz* (1900)

Wonderful Town: Ruth McKenney, *My Sister Eileen* (1938)

> *Music into Words*
> Herman Raucher based his 1976 novel, *Ode to Billy Joe*, on the popular song of the same title. Actually, the book was a novelization of the movie of the same title, which in turn was a cinematization of the song's lyrics, themselves a versification by Bobbie Gentry.

■ TINSEL TOWN: THE HOLLYWOOD NOVEL

4-Star Classics
Joan Didion, *Play It As It Lays* (1970)
F. Scott Fitzgerald, *The Last Tycoon* (1941)
Norman Mailer, *The Deer Park* (1955)
Budd Schulberg, *What Makes Sammy Run?* (1941)
Nathanael West, *The Day of the Locust* (1939)
Harry Leon Wilson, *Merlin of the Movies* (1922)

The Bs: Serious Attempts and High Trash
Ludwig Bemelmans, *Dirty Eddie* (1947)
Richard Brooks, *The Producer* (1951)
Robert Carson, *The Image Lantern* (1952)
Henry Blake Fuller, *Not on the Screen* (1930)
Gavin Lambert, *Inside Daisy Clover* (1963)
Anita Loos, *The Better Things of Life* (1941)
Larry McMurtry, *Somebody's Darling* (1978)
Darcy O'Brien, *A Way of Life, Like Any Other* (1978)
Elmer Rice, *A Voyage to Purilia* (1930)
Bernard Wolfe, *Come On Out, Daddy* (1963)

Guilty-Pleasure Reading
Rona Barrett, *The Lovomaniacs* (1972)
Joyce Haber, *The Users* (1976)
Harold Robbins, *The Inheritors* (1969)
Irving Shulman, *The Velvet Knife* (1959)
Jacqueline Susann, *Valley of the Dolls* (1966)

A good columnist is like a good sketch artist, like Daumier, for example, but it takes fiction to get inside someone's head. You can't go there in journalism, even though I know a number of guys—and some of them are friends of mine—tried. . . . There ought to be more reporting in novels. The great novelists of the past were also great reporters—Dickens and Balzac, for example, Today there are a lot of novelists who seem to be writing to be reviewed, not read.

—PETE HAMILL, INTERVIEW, 1978

The Reel McCoys: Oscar Winners Based on Fictional Works

1929–30: *All Quiet on the Western Front* (Erich Maria Remarque, 1929)

1930–31: *Cimarron* (Edna Ferber, 1930)

1931–32: *Grand Hotel* (Vicki Baum, 1928)

1934: *It Happened One Night* ("Night Bus," Samuel H. Adams, 1933)

1935: *Mutiny on the Bounty* (Charles Nordhoff and James Norman Hall, 1932)

1939: *Gone With the Wind* (Margaret Mitchell, 1936)

1940: *Rebecca* (Daphne DuMaurier, 1938)

1941: *How Green Was My Valley* (Richard Llewellyn, 1940)

1942: *Mrs. Miniver* (Jan Struthers, 1939)

1945: *The Lost Weekend* (Charles Jackson, 1943)

1946: *The Best Years of Our Lives (Glory for Me*, Mackinlay Kantor, 1945)

1947: *Gentlemen's Agreement* (Laura Z. Hobson, 1947)

1949: *All the King's Men* (Robert Penn Warren, 1946)

1953: *From Here to Eternity* (James Jones, 1951)

1956: *Around the World in Eighty Days* (Jules Verne, 1873)

1957: *The Bridge Over the River Kwai* (Pierre Boulle, 1952)

1958: *Gigi* (Colette, 1945)

1963: *Tom Jones* (Henry Fielding, 1749)

1967: *In the Heat of the Night* (John Ball, 1965)

1969: *Midnight Cowboy* (James Leo Herlihy, 1965)

1972: *The Godfather* (Mario Puzo, 1969)

1974: *The Godfather II* (Mario Puzo, 1969)

1975: *One Flew Over the Cuckoo's Nest* (Ken Kesey, 1962)

1979: *Kramer vs. Kramer* (Avery Corman, 1977)

> *Never judge a book by its movie.*
>
> —ANONYMOUS

Lost It at the Movies: 20 Title Changes

Each of these novels underwent a change of title when it was transformed into a film. Some had already shifted titles when, before being filmed, they were the bases of dramas; others changed at the whim of their producers; yet others were made into films more than once.

Edward Abbey, *The Brave Cowboy* (1958): *Lonely Are the Brave* (1962)

James Agee, *A Death in the Family* (1957): *All the Way Home* (1963)

Emile Ajar, *Momo* (trans. 1978): *Madame Rosa* (1978)

Ann Beattie, *Chilly Scenes of Winter* (1976): *Head Over Heels* (1979)

Joseph Conrad, *The Secret Agent* (1907): *Sabotage* (1939)

Pietro DiDonato, *Christ in Concrete* (1939): *Give Us This Day* (1949)

Theodore Dreiser, *An American Tragedy* (1925): *A Place in the Sun* (1951)

William Faulkner, *Pylon* (1935): *Tarnished Angels* (1957)

———, *The Hamlet* (1940): *The Long Hot Summer* (1957)

Graham Greene, *The Power and the Glory* (1940): *The Fugitive* (1947)

Ernest Hemingway, *To Have and Have Not* (1937): *The Breaking Point* (1950)

Henry James, *The Aspern Papers* (1888): *The Lost Moment* (1947)

———, *Washington Square* (1881): *The Heiress* (1949)

Ken Kesey, *Sometimes a Great Notion* (1964): *Never Give an Inch* (1972)

Larry McMurtry, *Horseman, Pass By* (1961): *Hud* (1963)

Robert Stone, *A Hall of Mirrors* (1966): *W.U.S.A.* (1970)

———, *Dog Soldiers* (1974): *Who'll Stop the Rain* (1978)

Nathanael West, *Miss Lonelyhearts* (1933): *Advice to the Lovelorn* (1933)

John A. Williams, *Night Song* (1961): *Sweet Love, Bitter* (1968)
Calder Willingham, *End as a Man* (1947): *The Strange One* (1957)

Names Below the Title: 15 Novels by Screen Actors

Johanna Barnes, *Who Is Carla Hart?* (1973)
Joan Blondell, *Center Door Fancy* (1972)
Dirk Bogarde, *A Gentle Occupation* (1980)
Tony Curtis, *Kid Andrew Cody and Julie Sparrow* (1977)
Jean Harlow, *Today is Tonight* (post. 1965)
Sterling Hayden, *Voyage* (1977)
Adam Kennedy, *Just Like Humphrey Bogart* (1978)
Lilli Palmer, *The Red Raven* (1978)
Michael Redgrave, *The Mountebank's Tale* (1959)
Robert Shaw, *The Sun Doctor* (1961)
Sylvester Stallone, *Paradise Alley* (1977)
Tom Tryon, *Crowned Heads* (1976)
Peter Ustinov, *Krumnagel* (1971)
Orson Welles, *Mr. Arkadian* (1956)
Mae West, *Pleasure Man* (1975)

Names Above the Title: 20 Screenplays by Novelists

James Agee, *The African Queen* (1951)
Ray Bradbury, *Moby Dick* (1956)
Truman Capote, *Beat the Devil* (1954)
James Clavell, *To Sir, With Love* (1967)
Roald Dahl, *You Only Live Twice* (1967)
William Faulkner, *The Big Sleep* (1946)
F. Scott Fitzgerald, *Three Comrades* (1938)
Dashiell Hammett, *Watch on the Rhine* (1943)
Aldous Huxley, *A Woman's Vengeance* (1947)
Christopher Isherwood, *Rage in Heaven* (1941)
Tom McGuane, *Rancho Deluxe* (1976)
John O'Hara *Moontide* (1942)
Irwin Shaw, *Desire Under the Elms* (1958)
Leon Uris, *Gunfight at the O.K. Corral* (1957)
Gore Vidal, *Last of the Mobile Hot-Shots* (1969)
Jerome Weidman, *The Eddie Cantor Story* (1953)
Jessamyn West, *Stolen Hours* (1963)

Nathanael West, *Born to be Wild* (1938)
Thornton Wilder, *Shadow of a Doubt* (1943)
Herman Wouk, *Slattery's Hurricane* (1949)

■ FILM-FLAM: THE REAL TINSEL

Reel Lives: 10 Most Literate Autobiographies of the Seventies
Mary Astor, *A Life on Film* (1971)
Lauren Bacall, *By Myself* (1979)
Dirk Bogarde, *A Postillion Struck by Lightning* (1977)
James Cagney, *Cagney by Cagney* (1975)
Joan Fontaine, *No Bed of Roses* (1978)
Pola Negri, *Memoirs of a Star* (1970)
David Niven, *The Moon's a Balloon* (1972)
Lilli Palmer, *Change Lobsters and Dance* (1975)
Gene Tierney, *Self-Portrait* (1979)
Peter Ustinov, *Dear Me* (1977)

Five Best Bios of the Seventies
Nathanial Benchley, *Humphrey Bogart* (1975)
Patricia Bosworth, *Montgomery Clift* (1978)
Gerold Frank, *Judy* (1975)
Sheridan Morley, *Marlene Dietrich* (1976)
Lyn Tornabene, *Long Live the King: A Biography of Clark Gable* (1977)

Behind the Camera: 5 Directors
Arthur Calder-Marshall, *The Innocent Eye: The Life of Robert J. Flaherty* (1966)
Frank Capra, *The Name Above the Title* (1971)
Thomas Quinn Curtiss, *Von Stroheim* (1971)
Jean Renoir, *My Life and My Films* (1974)
Eric Rohmer and Claude Chabrol, *Hitchcock: The First 44 Films* (trans. 1979)

Typewriter Casting: 10 Film Biographies of Writers
The Loves of Edgar Allan Poe (1942): Shepperd Strudwick
Beloved Infidel (1959): Gregory Peck as F. Scott Fitzgerald
Oscar Wilde (1960): Robert Morley

Hans Christian Andersen (1952): Danny Kaye
The Life of Émile Zola (1937): Paul Muni
Devotion (1946): Olivia de Havilland and Ida Lupino as the
 Brontë sisters
Jack London (1943): Michael O'Shea
Heartbeat (1979): John Heard as Jack Kerouac
The Adventures of Mark Twain (1944): Fredric March
The Bad Lord Byron (1948): Dennis Price

Charles Champlin's List of Basic Movie Books

In the *Los Angeles Times'* film critic's *The Flicks* (1977), he
included a "desert island treasury of the film books I would
not want to be without."

James Agee, *Agee on Film* (1964)
Rudy Behlmer, *Memo from David O. Selznick* (1972)
Kevin Brownlow, *The Parade's Gone By* (1958)
Frank Capra, *The Name Above the Title: An Autobiography*
 (1977)
Bosley Crowther, *The Lion's Share: The Story of an
 Entertainment Empire* (1957)
————, *Hollywood Rajah: The Life and Times of Louis B. Mayer*
 (1960)
Leslie Halliwell, *The Filmgoer's Companion* (1974)
Sydney W. Head, *Broadcasting in America, A Survey of
 Television and Radio* (1972)
Molly Haskell, *From Reverence to Rape: The Treatment of
 Women in the Movies* (1973)
Arthur Knight, *The Liveliest Art* (1957)
Pauline Kael, any of her books
Pierre Leprohon, *The Italian Cinema* (1972)
Mickey Rooney, *I.E., An Autobiography* (1965)
Norma Rosen, *Popcorn Venus: Women, Movies and the
 American Dream* (1973)
Leonard Q. Ross, *Hollywood, The Movie Colony, The Movie
 Makers* (1941)
Andrew Sarris, *The American Cinema* (1968)
Daniel Spoto, *The Art of Alfred Hitchcock* (1976)
Jack Vizzard, *See No Evil: Life Inside a Hollywood Censor*
 (1970)

Raoul Walsh, *Each in His Own Time* (1974)
William Wellman, *A Short Time for Insanity* (1974)
Basil Wright, *The Long View* (1974)

A Star is Born Again . . . and Again . . . and Again . . .
Whether or not you are a proponent of the Big Bang Theory, there seems little doubt that stars, like other cosmic phenomena, are born and not made. Here is proof: the opening lines of some stellar autobiographies. Can you guess who wrote them?

1. "I was born in Harlem on December 18, 1925."
2. "I was born on April 16, 1889, at eight o'clock at night, in East Lane, Walworth."
3. "I was born into a cliché-loving middle-class Virginia family."
4. "I was born in a small hospital in Tokyo. Momma says she remembers two things: A mouse came running across the floor, which she took as a sign of good luck. A nurse bending down and whispering apologetically: 'I'm afraid it's a girl. Would you prefer to inform your husband yourself?'"
5. "I was born in Weatherford, Texas, on December 1, 1913."
6. "I was born in 1905.*"
7. "I tore out of my mother's body on a hot Thursday before Labor Day weekend, four years before the 1929 stock market crash."
8. "I was born in Santiago de Cuba on March 2, 1917. (I had to be born someplace!)"
9. "My first road began in the charity ward of New Orleans' Hotel Dieu hospital on a very cold December 10, 1914."
10. "I was born in Miami, Florida on the evening of February 10, 1927."

A. Liv Ullman, *Changing*
B. Anne Jackson, *Early Stages*
C. Sammy Davis, Jr., *Yes I Can*
D. Mary Martin, *My Heart Belongs*
E. Sidney Poitier, *This Life*
F. Shirley Maclaine, *Don't Fall Off the Mountain*
G. Dorothy Lamour, *My Side of the Road*
H. Desi Arnaz, *A Book*
I. Marion Davies, *The Times We Had*
J. Charles Chaplin, *Autobiography*

*She was actually born in 1897.

Answers
1–C, 2–J, 3–F, 4–A, 5–D, 6–I, 7–B, 8–H, 9–G, 10–E

■ GAMES SOME PEOPLE PLAY

Hallowed Be Thy Game: The Best Sports Overviews
Robert Lipsyte, *Sports World* (1975)
James A. Michener, *Sports in America* (1976)
Michael Novak, *The Joy of Sports* (1976)
Skip Rozin, *One Step From Play: On the Fringes of Professional Sports* (1979)
Leonard Schechter, *The Jocks* (1970)

Forgive Us Our Press Passes: The Best Sports Journalism
Dave Anderson, *Sports of Our Times* (1979)
Heywood Hale Broun, *Tumultuous Merriment* (1979)
Heywood Broun, *Collected Edition* (1941)
Jimmy Cannon, *Nobody Asked Me But . . . The World of Jimmy Cannon* (1979)
Paul Gallico, *A Farewell to Sport* (1938)
Arthur Haley, *Sports of the Times: The Arthur Haley Years* (1975)
W. C. Heinz, *Once They Heard the Cheers* (1979)
Jerome Holtzman, *No Cheering in the Press Box* (1974)
John Kieran, *The American Sporting Scene* (1941)
John Lardner, *The World of John Lardner* (1961)
Ring Lardner, *The Portable Ring Lardner* (1946)
Larry Merchant, *Ringside Seat at the Circus* (1976)
Grantland Rice, *The Best of Grantland Rice* (1963)
Red Smith, *Strawberries in the Wintertime* (1974)
Herbert Warren Wind, *The Golden Age of Sport* (1961)

True Sports Stories

Bases of Truth: Baseball

Roger Angell, *The Summer Game* (1972)
Eliot Asinof, *Eight Men Out: The Black Sox and the 1919 World Series* (1963)
Jim Brosnan, *The Long Season* (1961)

Ty Cobb with Al Stump, *My Life in Baseball: The True Record* (1961)

Robert Creamer, *Babe* (1974)

Jimmy Dykes and Charles Dexter, *You Can't Steal First Base* (1967)

James T. Farrell, *My Baseball Diary* (1957)

Lee Gutkind, *The Best Seat in Baseball, But You Have to Stand! The Game as Umpires See It* (1975)

Donald Honig, *Baseball When the Grass Was Real* (1975)

Pat Jordan, *The Suitors of Spring* (1973)

Roger Kahn, *The Boys of Summer* (1972)

Fred Lieb, *Baseball As I Have Known It* (1977)

Lawrence Ritter, *The Glory of Their Times* (1966)

Bill Veeck with Ed Linn, *Veeck as in Wreck* (1962)

Ted Williams, *My Turn at Bat* (1969)

Ring of Truth: Boxing

Muhammad Ali, *The Greatest: My Own Story* (1975)

A. J. Liebling, *The Sweet Science* (1956)

Sugar Ray Robinson, *Sugar Ray* (1970)

Everett Skebran, *Rocky Marciano: The Brother of the First Son* (1977)

Gene Tunney, *Arms for Living* (1941)

Hole Truth: Golf

Bernard Darwin, *Mostly Golf: A Bernard Darwin Anthology* (1976)

Colman McCarthy, *The Pleasures of the Game* (1977)

Henry Longhurst, *The Best of Henry Longhurst* (1978)

Robert T. Jones, Jr., and O. B. Keeler, *Down the Fairway* (1927)

Dan Jenkins, *The Dogged Victims of Inexorable Fate* (1970)

Sideline Reading

Blue Lines: Hockey

Bobby Hull, *Hockey Is My Game* (1967)

George ("Punch") Imlach with Scott Young, *Hockey Is a Battle* (1970)

Neil D. Isaacs, *Checking Back* (1977)

Keith Magnuson with Robert Bradford, *None Against!* (1973)

Bobby Orr, *Orr On Ice* (1971)

Foul Lines: Basketball

Pete Axthelm, *The City Game* (1970)

Bill Bradley, *Life on the Run* (1976)

Wilt Chamberlain with David Shaw, *Wilt: Just Like Any Other Seven-Foot Black Millionaire Who Lives Next Door* (1973)

Red Holzman with Leonard Lewin, *A View From the Bench* (1980)

Pat Jordan, *Chase the Game* (1979)

John McPhee, *A Sense of Place* (1965)

Charles Rosen, *God, Man and Basketball Jones* (1979)

Bill Russell and Taylor Branch, *Second Wind: The Memoirs of an Opinionated Man* (1979)

Rick Telander, *Heaven is a Playground* (1976)

David Wolf, *Foul! The Connie Hawkins Story* (1972)

Goal Lines: Football

Dan Jenkins, *Saturday's America* (1970)

Bill Libby, *Life in the Pits: The Deacon Jones Story* (1970)

Y. A. Tittle as told to Don Smith, *Pass!* (1964)

Roy Blount, Jr., *About Three Bricks Shy of a Load* (1974)

Jerry Kramer and Dick Schapp, *Instant Replay* (1968)

Vince Lombardi with W. C. Heinz, *Run to Daylight* (1963)

Dave Meggyesy, *Out of Their League* (1970)

George Plimpton, *Paper Lion* (1966)

Amos Alonzo Stagg as told to Wesley Stout, *Touchdown!* (1927)

John Wiebusch, *More Than a Game* (1974)

Base Lines: Tennis

Dave Anderson, *The Return of a Champion: Pancho Gonzales' Golden Year, 1964* (1973)

Don Budge, *A Tennis Memoir* (1967)
Althea Gibson with Ed Fitzgerald, *I Always Wanted To Be Somebody* (1958)
Billie Jean King with Kim Chapin, *Billie Jean* (1974)
Jack Kramer with Frank Deford, *The Game: My 40 Years in Tennis* (1979)
John McPhee, *Levels of the Game* (1970)
Marty Riessen and Richard Evans, *Match Point: A Candid View of Life on the International Tour Circuit* (1973)
Bill Tilden, *My Story: A Champion's Memoirs* (1948)
Herbert Warren Wind, *Game, Set and Match: The Tennis Boon of the 1960s and 1970s* (1979)

Table Tennis:

Marty Reisman, *The Money Player* (1974)

■ GREAT SPORTS FICTION

The Baseball Novel: 18 Smash Hits

Write Off the Bat: 9 All-Stars

Eliot Asinof, *Man on Spikes* (1955)
William Brashler, *The Bingo Long Traveling All Stars and Motor Kings* (1973)
Jerome Charyn, *The Seventh Babe* (1979)
John Craig, *Chappie and Me* (1978)
Valentine Davies, *It Happens Every Spring* (1947)
Paul Hemphill, *Long Gone* (1979)
Donald Honig, *The Last Great Season* (1979)
Philip O'Connor, *Stealing Home* (1979)
John Sayles, *Pride of the Bimbos* (1975)

3 Hall of Famers

Mark Harris, *Henry A. Wiggen's Books* (1956–78)
Ring Lardner, *You Know Me, Al* (1916)
Bernard Malamud, *The Natural* (1952)

3 Slow Curves: Baseball Allegories

Barry Berkham, *Runner Mack* (1972)

Robert Coover, *The Universal Baseball Association, J. Henry Waugh, Prop.* (1968)

Philip Roth, *The Great American Novel* (1973)

3 Screwballs

Jay Cronley, *Screwballs* (1980)

H. Allen Smith, *Rhubarb* (1946)

Douglas Wallop, *The Year the Yankees Lost the Pennant* (1954)

Adventures in the Pigskin Trade: 11 Football Novels

Bernard Brunner, *Six Days to Sunday* (1975)

Jay Crowley, *Fall Guy* (1978)

Robert Daley, *Only A Game* (1967)

Don DeLillo, *End Zone* (1972)

Pete Gent, *North Dallas Forty* (1973)

Dan Jenkins, *Semi-Tough* (1972)

Jack Jones, *The Animals* (1975)

Norman Keifetz, *Welcome Sundays* (1979)

Jack Olsen, *Alphabet Jackson* (1974)

Joseph Pellitteri, *Two Hours on Sunday* (1971)

James Whitehead, *Joiner* (1971)

Tall Stories: Basketball Novels

Robert Greenfield, *Haymon's Crowd* (1978)

Walter Kaylin, *The Power Forward* (1979)

Bob Levin, *The Best Ride to New York* (1978)

Jay Neugeborn, *Big Man* (1966)

Jack Olsen, *Massy's Game* (1975)

Charles Rosen, *A Mile Above the Rim* (1976)

Lawrence Shainberg, *One on One* (1970)

Todd Walton, *Inside Moves* (1978)

Love Stories: Tennis Novels

Robert Barker, *Love Forty* (1975)

Jane and Burt Boyer, *World Class* (1975)

Russell Braddon, *The Finalist* (1977)

Peter Brennan, *Sudden Death* (1978)
William Brinkley, *Breakpoint* (1978)
Ralph M. Demers, *The Circuit* (1976)
Edwin Fadiman, Jr., *The Professional* (1973)
Arthur Hoppe, *The Tiddling Tennis Theorem* (1977)
Douglas Wallop, *Mixed Singles* (1977)

Best Tennis Stories by a Tennis Immortal
William Tilden, *It's All in the Game* (1922)

Whole Other Ball Games
On the Beach (Volleyball): Ron Bernstein, *Straight Down* (1977)
Off the Wall (Handball): Tom Alibrandi, *Killshot* (1979)
In the Saddle (Polo): Jerzy Kosinski, *Passion Play* (1979)
Over the Fence: (Horse Show): Leigh Brown, *The Show Gypsies* (1975)
At the Bars (Bicycle Racing): Ralph Hume, *The Yellow Jersey* (1973)
By the Green(Golf): Donald McDougall, *Davie* (1977)

Worth Another Rook: 5 Novels of Chess
Robert Bernhard, *The Ullmann Code* (1975)
Jerome Charyn, *Going to Jerusalem* (1967)
John Keckhut, *The Dublin Pawn* (1977)
Frances Parkinson Keyes, *The Chess Players* (1961)
Stefan Zweig, *The Royal Game* (1941)

The Grand Master
Vladimir Nabokov, *The Defense* (1964)

■ TALES TO TRANSPORT YOU

The Art of Plane Speaking: 15 Pilot Memoirs
Richard Bach, *Stranger to the Ground* (1963)
Brent Balchen, *Come North With Me* (1958)
"Pappy" Boyington, *Baa, Baa Black Sheep* (1958)
Rene Fonck, *Ace of Aces* (1967)
Ernest K. Gann, *Fate is the Hunter* (1961)

Richard Hilary, *Falling through Space* (1942)
Anne Morrow Lindbergh, *North to the Orient* (1931)
Charles A. Lindbergh, *The Spirit of St. Louis* (1953)
Tom Mayer, *Climb for the Evening Star* (1974)
Charles Nordhoff, *The Fledgling* (1919)
Edward Park, *Nanette* (1977)
Antoine de Saint-Exupéry, *Flight to Arras* (1942)
Robert Lee Scott, Jr., *God is My Co-Pilot* (1943)
Sheila Scott, *Barefoot in the Sky* (1974)
Ernst Udet, *The Ace of the Iron Cross* (1970)

Sky Writing: 15 Aviation Novels
Richard Bach, *Bi-Plane* (1966)
David Beaty, *The Wing Off the Sea* (1962)
Martin Caiden, *Whip* (1976)
Pierre Closterman, *Flames in the Sky* (1951)
Len Deighton, *Bomber* (1970)
Richard Frede, *The Pilots* (1978)
Gerd Gaiser, *The Last Squadron* (1953)
Ernest K. Gann, *In the Company of Eagles* (1966)
Richard Hough, *Wings Against the Sky* (1979)
Jules Roy, *The Navigator* (1954)
Antoine de Saint-Exupéry, *Night Flight* (1931)
James Salter, *The Hunters* (1955)
Robert J. Serling, *Wings* (1978)
Craig Thomas, *Firefox* (1978)
Arch Whitehouse, *Squadron Forty-Four* (1965)

■ SALTY SAGAS

5 Classics
Humphrey Barton, *Atlantic Adventurers: Voyages in Small
    Craft* (1953)
Frank Thomas Bullen, *The Cruise of the Chachalot* (1898)
Francis Chichester, *Gypsy Moth Circles the World* (1968)
Richard Henry Dana, *Two Years Before the Mast* (1840)
Joshua Slocum, *Sailing Alone Around the World* (1900)

15 True-Blue Sea Yarns

Robin Lee Graham and Derek L. T. Gill, *Dove* (1972)

Eric C. Hiscock, *Sou'west in* Wanderer IV (1973)

Naomi James, *Alone Around the World* (1979)

Tristan Jones, *Saga of a Wayward Sailor* (1979)

Robin Knox-Johnston, *A World of Our Own: The Single-Handed Non-Stop Circumnavigation of the World in* Suhaili (1970)

Frank Page, *Sailing Solo to America* (1973)

Douglas Robertson, *Survive the Savage Sea* (1973)

Hal Roth, *Two Against the Horn* (1979)

Mike Saunders, *The Walkabouts* (1975)

Tim Severin, *The Brendan Voyage* (1978)

William Snaith, *On the Wind's Way: The Story of an Atlantic Race* (1973)

H. M. Tilman, *Triumph and Tibulation* (1979)

Nicholas Tomalin and Ron Hale, *The Strange Last Voyage of Donald Crowhurst* (1970)

Roger Vaughan, *Fastnet: One Man's Voyage* (1980)

Alan J. Villiers, *By Way of Cape Horn* (1930)

Hitting the High Seas: The Nautical Novel

The Classics

Joseph Conrad, *Typhoon and Other Tales* (1902)

James Fenimore Cooper, *The Pilot* (1823)

Charles Kingsley, *Westward Ho!* (1855)

Alexander Laing, *The Sea Witch* (1933)

Jack London, *The Sea Wolf* (1904)

Frederick Maryatt, *Mr. Midshipman Easy* (1836)

Herman Melville, *Moby Dick* (1851)

Charles Nordhoff and James Hall, *The Bounty Trilogy* (1932–34)

Morgan Robertson, *Spun Yarn* (1898)

Michael Scott, *Cruise of the Midge* (1836)

B. Traven, *The Death Ship* (1926)

Jules Verne, *20,000 Leagues Under the Sea* (1869)

The Moderns

Edward Beach, *Run Silent, Run Deep* (1955)
Lothor Gunther Buckheim, *The Boat* (1975)
Jan De Hartog, *The Captain* (1966)
Richard Duprey, *Duel on the Wind: A Novel of the America's Cup Challenge* (1976)
Marcus Goodrich, *Delilah* (1941)
James Hanley, *Boy* (1932)
Richard Hughes, *In Hazard* (1938)
Hammond Innes, *The Wreck of the Mary Deare* (1956)
Richard Jessup, *Sailor* (1969)
Nicholas Monsaratt, *The Cruel Sea* (1951)
Patrick O'Hara, *The Look of the Lonely Sea* (1966)
Sloan Wilson, *Ice Brothers* (1979)

The Series

C. S. Forester (Horatio Hornblower): *Capt. Horatio Hornblower* (1939)
Alexander Kent (Richard Bolitho): *In Glory We Steer* (1968)
Patrick O'Brian (Capt. Jack Aubrey): *Master and Commander* (1969)
C. Northcote Parkinson (Richard Delancey): *Devil to Pay* (1973)
Dudley Pope (Nicholas Ramage): *Ramage* (1965)
Simon White (Capt. Jonathan Cockerell Penhalizon): *The English Captain* (1977)

There is no Frigate like a Book
To take us Lands away
Nor any Coursers like a Page
Of prancing Poetry—
This Traverse may the poorest take
Without oppress of Toll—
How frugal is the Chariot
That bears the Human soul.   —EMILY DICKINSON

■ ON THE ROAD

Kicks on Route 66: 5 Road Novels
Josh Greenfield and Paul Mazursky, *Harry and Tonto* (1975)
Jack Kerouac, *On the Road* (1957)
Charles Portis, *Norwood* (1966)
Clancy Sigal, *Going Away* (1962)
Robert Lewis Taylor, *The Travels of Jamie McPheeters* (1958)

In No Sense Abroad: On the Road in America—15 True Accounts
William Attwood, *Still the Most Exciting Country* (1955)
Peter Beagle, *I See By Your Outfit* (1965)
Erskine Caldwell, *Afternoon in Mid-America* (1976)
Peter Jenkins, *A Walk Across America* (1979)
Charles Kuralt, *Dateline America* (1979)
Henry Miller, *The Air-Conditioned Nightmare* (1948)
Bill Moyers: *Listening to America: A Traveller Rediscovers His Country* (1971)
Gurney Norman, *Divine Right's Trip* (1972)
Charlton Ogburn, Jr., *The Continent in Our Hands* (1971)
Harrison Salisbury, *Travels Around America* (1976)
William Saroyan, *Short Drive, Sweet Chariot* (1966)
John Steinbeck, *Travels With Charley in Search of America* (1962)
Edwin Way Teale, *Autumn Across America* (1956)
Mark Twain, *Roughing It* (1875)
Leonard Wibberly, *Voyage by Bus* (1971)

■ ROLL OUT THE PERILS: GREAT TRUE ADVENTURE NARRATIVES

L. D. Brongersman and G. F. Venema, *To the Mountains of the Stars* (1963)
Capt. Edward L. Beach, *Around the World Submerged: The Voyage of the* Triton (1962)
Michael Collins, *Carrying the Fire* (1974)

Ted Falcon-Barker, *Devil's Gold* (1969)

Colin Fletcher, *The Man Who Walked Through Time* (1967)

Thor Heyerdahl, *Kon-Tiki: Across the Pacific by Raft* (1948)

John Dunn Hunter, *Memories of a Captivity Among the Indians of North America* (1823)

Wally Herbert, *Across the Top of the World: The Last Great Journey on Earth* (1971)

Dana and Ginger Lamb, *Quest for the Lost City* (1951)

Albert Lisi, *Machaquili: Through the Mayan Jungle to a Lost City* (1968)

George Lowe, *From Everest to the South Pole* (1961)

Peter Matthiessen, *Oomingmak: The Expedition to the Musk Ox Island in the Bering Sea* (1967)

Michel Peissel, *The Lost World of Quintana Roo* (1963)

Carl Raswan, *Drinkers of the Wind* (1961)

Eric and Tim Ryback, *The Ultimate Journey: Canada to Mexico Down the Continental Divide* (1973)

Gene Savoy, *Antisuyo: The Search for the Lost Cities of the Amazon* (1970)

Lloyd Sumner, *The Long Ride* (1978)

■ GREAT TALES OF EXPLORATION

Everett S. Allen, *Arctic Odyssey: The Life of Rear Admiral Donald B. MacMillan* (1962)

Pat Barr, *A Curious Life for a Lady: The Story of Isabelle Bird* (1970)

J. C. Beaglehole, *The Life of Captain James Cook* (1974)

Peter Brent, *Captain Scott and the Antarctic Tragedy* (1977)

Fawn M. Brodie, *The Devil Drives: A Life of Sir Richard Burton* (1967)

Cmdr. Edward Ellsberg, *Hell on Ice: The Saga of the* Jeanette (1938)

Fernand Fournier-Aubry, *Don Fernando* (1974)

Richard Hall, *Stanley: An Adventure Explored* (1975)

Rolant Huntford, *Scott and Amundsen* (1980)

Alfred Lansing, *Endurance: Shackelton's Incredible Voyage* (1959)

Luree Miller, *On Top of the World: Five Women Explorers in Tibet* (1976)

Alan Moorehead, *Cooper's Creek* (1964)

Samuel Eliot Morison, *Admiral of the Ocean Sea: A Life of Christopher Columbus* (1942)

Michael Ross, *Cross the Great Desert* (1977)

George Gaylord Simpson, *Attending Mercies: A Patagonian Journal* (1934)

Memoirs of the Polar Explorers

Roald Amundsen, *South Pole* (1912)

Richard Byrd, *Alone* (1938)

Fridtjof Nansen, *In Night and Ice* (1897)

Robert E. Peary, *The North Pole: Its Discovery in 1909* (1910)

Finn Ronne, *Antarctica, My Destiny* (1979)

Robert Falcon Scott, *Scott's Last Expedition: Journals and Reports* (1913)

■ AN EYRIE FEELING: MOUNTAINS AND MOUNTAINEERS

Ascents of History

Ronald W. Clark, *The Day the Rope Broke: The Story of the First Ascent of the Matterhorn* (1965)

Heinrich Harrer, *The White Spider: The History of the Eiger's North Face* (1959)

Eric Newby, *Great Ascents: A Narrative History of Mountaineering* (1977)

Lowell Thomas, *Book of the High Mountains* (1964)

John Muir, *The Mountains of California* (1894)

10 Best Climb and Tell Books

Jeremy Bernstein, *Mountain Passages* (1978)

Chris Bonington, *The Ultimate Challenge* (1973)

Robert W. Craig, *Storm and Sorrow in the High Pamirs* (1978)

Maurice Herzog, *Annapurna* (1952)

Edmund Hilary, *High in the Cold Air* (1961)

John Hunt, *The Conquest of Everest* (1954)

Reinhold Messner, *The Challenge* (1977)
David Roberts, *Deborah: A Wilderness Narrative* (1970)
William Woodrow Sayre, *Four Against Everest* (1964)
Norgay Sherpa Tenzing with James Ramsay Ullmann, *Tiger of the Snows* (1955)

Peak Experiences: 5 Mountaineering Novels
Roger Frison-Roche, *First on the Rope* (1950)
Charles Gaines, *Dangler* (1979)
Roger Hubank, *North Wall* (1978)
James Salter, *Solo Faces* (1979)
James Ramsey Ullmann, *And Not to Yield* (1970)

■ POLES APART: THE GREAT WHITE NOVELS

The Arctic
Jane and Paul Annixter, *The Great White* (1966)
Edward Ellsberg, *Hell on Ice* (1938)
Peter Freuchen, *White Man* (1946)
James Houston, *The White Dawn* (1971)
Alexander H. Leighton, *Come Near* (1971)
Alexander Knox, *Night of the White Bear* (1971)
Farley Mowat, *The Snow Walker* (1975)
C. W. Nicol, *The White Shaman* (1979)
Hans Ruesch, *Back to the Top of the World* (1973)

Antarctica
Graham Billings, *Forbush and the Penguins* (1966)
Ian Cameron, *The White Ship* (1975)
Kare Holt, *The Race* (1976)
Thomas Keneally, *Victim of the Aurora* (1978)
David Stevens, *White for Danger* (1979)

■ The White Stuff

The answer to each of the following questions contains the word "white." See if you can guess the white answers.

1. What is the title of Robert Graves' anthropological-mythological study of the ancient female deity?
2. Who wrote *The Making of the President* series?
3. What is the title of the Joan Didion work named after a sixties Beatles disc?
4. What is the name of Alan Moorehead's 1960 account of the nineteenth-century exploration of Africa's longest river?
5. Who was the early *Life* photographer whose inspiring autobiography is *Portrait of Myself?*
6. Who is the essayist and humorist long associated with *The New Yorker* and author of several classic children's books?
7. What is the title of the memoirs of a German-born recent secretary of state?
8. Who was the long-time editor of the Emporia (Ka.) *Gazette* whose autobiography won the Pulitzer Prize in 1947?
9. Who was the modern English philosopher and mathematician who coauthored *Principia Mathematica* with Bertrand Russell?
10. What is the title of Eisenhower's presidential memoirs?

Answers
1. *The White Goddess,* 2. Theodore H. White, 3. *The White Album,* 4. *The White Nile,* 5. Margaret Bourke-White, 6. E. B. White, 7. *White House Years,* 8. William Allen White, 9, Alfred North Whitehead, 10. *The White House Years*

■ ENDURING READING

10 Sagas of Survival
Maurice and Marily Bailey, *Staying Alive!* (1974)
Leonard Bickel, *Mawson's Will: The Greatest Survival Story Ever Written* (1977)
F. S. Chapman, *The Jungle Is Neutral* (1949)
Lauren Elder with Shirley Streshinsky, *And I Alone Survived* (1978)
Rob and Sarah Elder, *Crash* (1977)

Piers Paul Read, *Alive: The Story of the Andes Survivors* (1974)
Douglas Robertson, *Survive the Savage Sea* (1973)
Monika Schwinn and Bernhard Diehl, *We Came to Help* (1976)
Robert Trumbull, *The Raft* (1942)
Barry Wynne, *The Man Who Refused to Die: Telhu Makimare's 2,000-Mile Drift in an Open Boat Across the South Seas* (1966)

10 Fittest of the Survival Novels
John Buell, *Playground* (1976)
James Dickey, *Deliverance* (1970)
Robert Flynn, *The Sounds of Rescue, The Signs of Hope* (1970)
Pat Frank, *Alas, Babylon* (1959)
William Golding, *Lord of the Flies* (1955)
James Hanley, *The Ocean* (1941)
James Vance Marshall, *A Walk to the Hills of the Dreamtime* (1970)
Muriel Spark, *Robinson* (1958)
Michel Tournier *Friday* (1967)
Patrick White, *A Fringe of Leaves* (1976)

The Greatest Survivor
Daniel Defoe, *Robinson Crusoe* (1719)

■ ESCAPIST READING

Fugitive Glimpses: 10 True Escapes
Paul Brickhill, *The Great Escape* (1950)
Henri Charrière, *Papillon* (1970)
Dieter Dengler, *Escape from Laos* (1979)
Clark Howard, *Six Against the Rock* (1977)
E. M. Jones, *The Road to Endor* (1919)
Airey Neave, *They Have Their Exits* (1953)
Roul Tunley, *Ordeal by Fire* (1966)

When G. K. Chesterton was asked what books he would want to have with him if he were stranded on a desert island, he replied, "Thomas's Guide to Practical Shipbuilding."

Ethel Vance, *Escape* (1939)
Eric Williams, *The Tunnel* (1960)
E. E. Williams, *The Wooden Horse* (1950)

A Test of Survival: Great Escapes of Fiction
Can you identify the character and the novel associated with the following escapes?

1. From a dungeon, by sewing himself into the burial sack intended for a dead fellow prisoner.
2. From the Huron Indians, after the Delaware chief, Chingachook, cut his bonds.
3. From the cave of the Cyclops, by hiding himself under the belly of a ram.
4. From a slave trader named Haley, in a flight across river ice floes.
5. From the noose, because the hangman's incompetence spared this incorrigible optimist.

Answers
1. *The Count of Monte Cristo;* 2. Natty Bumppo, *The Deerslayer;* 3. Odysseus, *The Odyssey;* 4. Eliza, *Uncle Tom's Cabin;* 5. Dr. Pangloss, *Candide*

Lives of a Cell: Prison and Prisoners
Ben H. Bagdikian, *Caged: Eight Prisoners and Their Keepers* (1976)
Brendan Behan, *Borstal Boy* (1959)
James Blake, *The Joint* (1971)
Malcolm Braly, *False Starts: A Memoir of San Quentin and Other Prisons* (1975)
Thomas E. Gaddis, *Birdman of Alcatraz* (1955)
Bill Sands, *My Shadow Ran Fast* (1964)
Edgar Smith, *Brief Against Death* (1968)
Tommy Trantino, *Lock the Lock* (1974)
Tom Wicker, *A Time to Die* (1975)

Prose and Cons: Prison Novels
Brendan Behan, *The Scarperer* (1964)
H. C. Bosman, *Cold Stone Jug* (1948)

Malcolm Braly, *On the Yard* (1967)
Edward Bunker, *The Animal Factory* (1979)
John Cheever, *Falconer* (1977)
Ben Greer, *Slammer* (1975)
Chester Himes, *Cast the First Stone* (1952)
James McLendon, *Deathwork* (1977)
Derek Maitland, *Breaking Out* (1979)
Albert Maltz, *A Long Day in a Short Life* (1957)

Long ago I discovered the value of books. Every prison has a library, and prison wardens, knowing that you can't file through steel bars with a copy of Tom Sawyer, *gladly let you have all the books you want. I've been reading for 30 years; I've given myself a pretty fair education, good enough to enable me to appreciate decent literature. Reading? Everyone has a crutch of some sort to lean on. With some it's whiskey or drugs. There are luckier ones who have the crutch of real faith to hold them up when they start to sag. My crutch? Books.*

I'll spend the rest of my life reading, and because I'd rather read than do anything else, I don't look forward to years of hopeless, black despair. Most men who are in for life are filled with bitterness and hatred for the unkind fate that led them to such a horrible end. My reading has given me the ability to judge my life, my actions and my present situation with a considerable degree of detachment. I can't repeat often enough that there is not a soul in the world I can blame for what happened to me. . . .

QUENTIN REYNOLDS, *I, Willie Sutton* (1970)

■ THE ANNALS OF CRIME

Best Fact Crime Books: The Edgar Winners
The Mystery Writers of America annually present an Edgar Allan Poe Award for the best nonfiction work dealing with crime.

1954: Charles Boswell and Lewis Thompson, *The Girl with the Scarlet Brand*
1955: Manly Wade Wellman, *Dead and Gone*
1956: Charles and Louise Samuels, *Night Fell on Georgia*

1957: Harold R. Danforth and James D. Horan, *The D.A.'s Man*

1958: Wenzell Brown, *They Died in the Chair*

1959: Thomas Gallagher, *Fire at Sea*

1960: Miriam Alled deFord, *The Overbury Affair*

1961: Barrett Prettyman, Jr., *Death and the Supreme Court*

1962: Francis Russell, *Tragedy in Dedham*

1963: Gerold Frank, *The Deed*

1964: Anthony Lewis, *Gideon's Trumpet*

1965: Truman Capote, *In Cold Blood*

1966: Gerold Frank, *The Boston Strangler*

1967: Victoria Lincoln, *A Private Disgrace*

1968: John Walsh, *Poe, The Detective*

1969: Herbert B. Ehrmann, *The Case That Will Not Die*

1970: Mildred Savage, *A Great Fall*

1971: Sandor Frankel, *Beyond A Reasonable Doubt*

1972: Stephen Fay, Lewis Chester, and Magnus Linkletter, *Hoax*

1973: Barbara Levy, *Legacy of Violence*

1974: Vincent Bugliosi and Curt Gentry, *Helter Skelter*

1975: Tom Wicker, *A Time to Die*

1976: Thomas Thompson, *Blood and Money*

1977: George Jonas and Barbara Amiel, *By Persons Unknown*

1978: Vincent Bugliosi and Ken Hurwitz, *Til Death Do Us Part*

1979: Robert Lindsey, *The Falcon and the Snowman*

15 True Crime Stories

Harvey Aronson, *The Killing of Joey Gallo* (1973)

Donald Bain, *War in Illinois: An Incredible True Story from the Roaring Twenties* (1978)

Sybille Bedford, *The Trials of Dr. Adams* (1957)

Alastair Cooke, *A Generation on Trial* (1950)

Lillian de la Torre, *Elizabeth Is Missing* (1945)

Jonathan Goodman, *The Killing of Julia Wallace* (1969)

Ludovic Kennedy, *Ten Rillington Place* (1961)

William M. Kunstler, *The Minister and the Choir Singer* (1964)

Raymond Paul, *Who Murdered Mary Rogers* (1971)

Piers Paul Read, *The Train Robbers* (1978)

Gay Talese, *Honor Thy Father* (1971)
Robert Tannenbaum and Philip Rosenberg, *Bridge of the Assassin* (1979)
Peter Van Slingerland, *Something Terrible Has Happened* (1966)
George Waller, *Kidnap* (1961)
Joseph Wambaugh, *The Onion Field* (1973)

Inside Dope: Drug Merchant Princes
Richard Berdin, *Code Name Richard* (1974)
David Durk and Ira Silverman, *The Pleasant Avenue Connection* (1976)
Donald Goddard, *Easy Money* (1978)
Robert Sabbag, *Snow Blind: A Brief Career in the Cocaine Trade* (1976)
Richard Woodley, *Dealer: Portrait of a Cocaine Merchant* (1971)

■ BEST LITERARY NATURALISTS: WINNERS OF BURROUGHS MEDAL

Offered by the John Burroughs Memorial Association, American Museum of Natural History, the Burroughs Medal is awarded annually for a work combining literary merit with accuracy of statement, with the emphasis on "literature of power" rather than "literature of knowledge." In the years not listed below, no award was given.

1926: William Beebe, *Pheasants of the World*
1927: Ernest Thompson Seton, *Lives of Game Animals*
1928: John Russel McCarthy, *Nature Poems*
1929: Frank M. Chapman, *Handbook of North American Birds*
1930: Archibald Rutledge, *Peace in the Heart*
1932: Frederick S. Dellenbaugh, *A Canyon Voyage*
1933: Oliver P. Medsgar, *Spring; Summer; Fall; Winter*
1934: W. W. Christman, *Wild Pasture Pine*
1936: Charles Crawford Ghorst, *Recordings of Bird Calls*
1938: Robert Cushman Murphy, *Oceanic Birds of South America*
1939: T. Gilbert Pearson, *Adventures in Bird Protection*

1940: Arthur Cleveland Bent, *Life Histories of North American Birds*

1941: Louis J. Halle, Jr., *Birds Against Man*

1942: Edward Armstrong, *Birds of The Gray Wind*

1943: Edwin Way Teale, *Near Horizons*

1945: Rutherford Platt, *This Green World*

1946: Francis Lee and Florence P. Jacques, *Snowshoe Country*

1948: Theodora Stanwell-Fletcher, *Driftwood Valley*

1949: Allan D. and Helen G. Cruickshank, *Flight Into Sunshine*

1950: Roger Tory Peterson, *Birds Over America*

1952: Rachel Carson, *The Sea Around Us*

1953: Gilbert Klingel, *The Bay*

1954: Joseph Wood Krutch, *The Desert Year*

1955: Wallace B. Grange, *Those of the Forest*

1956: Guy Murchie, *Song of the Sky*

1957: Archie Carr, *Windward Road*

1958: Robert Porter Allen, *On the Trail of Vanishing Birds*

1960: John Kieran, *A Natural History of New York City*

1961: Loren C. Eiseley, *The Firmament of Time*

1962: George Miksch Sutton, *Iceland Summer*

1963: Adolph Murie, *A Naturalist in Alaska*

1964: John Hay, *The Great Beach*

1965: Paul Brooks, *Roadless Area*

1966: Louis Darling, *The Gull's Way*

1967: Charlton Ogburn, Jr., *The Winter Beach*

1968: Hal Borland, *Hill Country Harvest*

1969: Louise deKiriline Lawrence, *The Lovely and the Wild*

1970: Victor B. Scheffer, *The Year of the Whale*

1971: John K. Terres, *From Laurel Hill to Siler's Bog*

1972: Robert Arbib, *The Lord's Woods*

1973: Elizabeth Barlow, *The Forests and Wetlands of New York City*

1974: Sigurd F. Olson, *Wilderness Days*

1976: Ann Haymond Zwinger, *Run, River, Run*

1977: Aldo Leopold, *A Sand County Almanac*

1978: Ruth Kirk, *Desert, The American Southwest*

1979: Barry Holstun Lopez, *Of Wolves and Men*

■ GREAT MODERN NATURE WRITING

William H. Amos, *The Life of the Seashore* (1966)
William Ashworth, *The Woallowas: Coming of Age in the Wilderness* (1978)
Wendell Berry, *The Long-Legged House* (1971)
Henry Beston, *The Outermost House* (1928)
Paul Brooks, *Roadless Areas* (1964)
Norman Carr, *Return to the Wild: A Story of Two Lions* (1962)
Sally Carrighar, *One Day on Beetle Rock* (1944)
Dale Rex Corman, *The Endless Adventure* (1972)
Annie Dillard, *Pilgrim at Tinker Creek* (1974)
Frank Frazer-Darling, *A Naturalist on Rona* (1939)
Frank Graham, Jr., *Where the Place Called Morning Lies* (1973)
John Graves, *Hard Scrabble* (1974)
Hazel Heckman, *Island in the Sound* (1967)
John Hillaby, *Journey Through Love* (1977)
Russ Hutchins, *Hidden Valley of the Smokies: With a Naturalist to North Great Smoky Mountains* (1971)
John Janovy, Jr., *Keith County Journal* (1979)
Joseph Wood Krutch, *The Best Nature Writings of Joseph Wood Krutch* (1970)
Stephen Levine, *Planet Steward: Journal of a Wildlife Sanctuary* (1974)
Dudley Cammett Lunt, *The Woods and the Sea* (1965)
John McPhee, *The Survival of the Bark Canoe* (1975)
Alexandra Marshall, *Still Waters* (1978)
Peter Matthiessen, *The Cloud Forest: A Chronicle of the South American Wilderness* (1961)
Louis J. and Margery Milne, *The Valley* (1963)
C. W. Nicol, *From the Roof of Africa* (1972)
Anita Nygaard, *Earthclock* (1976)
Sigurd F. Olson, *Open Horizons* (1969)
Donald Culross Peattie, *Road of a Naturalist* (1941)
Humphrey Phelps, *Just Across the Fields* (1977)
Russell Peterson, *Another View of the City* (1967)
Marsha Reben, *A Sharing of Joy* (1963)
Jack Rudloe, *The Living Docks at Panacea* (1977)
Franklin Russell, *Watchers of the Pond* (1961)

Calvin Rustrun, *Once Upon a Wilderness* (1973)

Alexander F. Skutch, *A Naturalist on a Tropical Farm* (1980)

Ian Starange, *The Bird Man* (1976)

R. D. Symons, *Silton Seasons: From the Diary of a Country Man* (1975)

John and Mildred Teal, *Life and Death of the Salt Marsh* (1969)

Edwin Way Teale, *Wandering Through Winter* (1965)

T. H. Watkins, *On the Shore of the Sundown Sea* (1974)

Mary Theilgaard Watts, *Reading the Landscape* (1957)

Peggy Wayburn, *Edge of Life: The World of the Estuary* (1972)

Anne Zwinger, *Wind on the Rock* (1978)

Beneath the Sea

William Beebe, *Half-Mile Down* (1934)

Rachel Carson, *The Sea Around Us* (1951)

Arthur C. Clarke, *The Coast of Coral* (1956)

Jacques Yves Cousteau and Frederic Dumas, *The Silent World* (1953)

Philippe Diole, *4,000 Years Under the Sea* (1954)

Frederic Dumas, *30 Centuries Under the Sea* (1976)

Alistair Hardy, *Great Waters* (1968)

Hans Hass, *Diving To Adventure: The Daredevil Story of Hunters Under the Sea* (1951)

In the Jungle

William Beebe, *High Jungle* (1949)

Stanley Brock, *Jungle Cowboy* (1972)

Adrian Cowell, *The Heart of the Forest* (1961)

Julian Duguid, *Green Hell: Adventures in the Mysterious Jungles of Eastern Bolivia* (1931)

Jean-Pierre Hallet, *Congo Kitabu* (1966)

Friedrich Morton, *In the Land of the Quetzal Feather* (1960)

Gordon Young, *Tracks of an Intruder* (1971)

Just Deserts

Edward Abbey, *Desert Solitude* (1968)

Mary Austin, *The Land of Little Rain* (1903)

Burton Bernstein, *Sinai: The Great and Terrible Wilderness* (1979)

Mildred Cable and Francesca French, *The Gobi Desert* (1944)
Raymond B. Cowles, *Reflections of a Naturalist* (1977)
David F. Costello, *The Desert World* (1972)
Uwe Georgi, *In the Deserts of This Earth* (1978)
W. Eugene Hollon, *The Great American Desert: Then and Now* (1966)
Philip Keller, *Under Desert Skies* (1970)
Joseph Wood Krutch, *The Voice of the Desert: A Naturalist's Interpretation* (1955)
Barry Lopez, *Desert Notes* (1976)
Geoffrey Moorhouse, *The Fearful Void* (1974)
Guy Mountfort, *Portrait of a Desert: The Story of an Expedition to Jordan* (1965)
Ann Woodin, *Home is the Desert* (1964)

◼ CONSCIOUSNESS-OF-STREAM WRITING

Riparian Writers: 15 River Books
L. T. C. Bolt, *The Thames* (1951)
Ben Lucien Burman, *Look Down That Winding River: An Informal Profile of the Mississippi* (1973)
Peter Forbath, *The River Congo: The Discovery, Exploration and Exploitation of the World's Most Dramatic River* (1977)
Sanche de Granmont, *The Strong Brown God: The Story of the Niger River* (1965)
John Graves, *Goodbye to a River* (1960)
Paul Horgan, *Great River: The Rio Grande in North American History* (1970)
Barry Lopez, *River Notes: The Dance of Herons* (1977)
Alan Moorehead, *The White Nile* (1961), *The Blue Nile* (1962)
Guy Mountfort, *The Wild Danube: A Portrait of a River* (1962)
Milton Osborne, *River Road to China: The Mekong River Expedition, 1866–1873* (1975)
Edward Rice, *The Ganges: A Personal Encounter* (1974)
Alex Shoumatoff, *The Rivers Amazon* (1978)
Gaylord Staveley, *Broken Waters Sing: Rediscovering Two Great Rivers of the West* (1971)

Henry David Thoreau, *A Week on the Concord and Merrimack Rivers* (1849)

Mark Twain, *Life on the Mississippi* (1883)

From Allegheny to Yazoo: A Monumental Series
The fifty volume *The Rivers of America* edited by Carl Cranmer

---

Rod 'N' Reel People: 10 Best Fish Stories
Ray Bergman, *Trout* (1944)
Zane Grey, *Tales of Fishing* (1925)
Roderick Haig-Brown, *Fishermen's Summer* (1959)
William Humphrey, *My Moby Dick* (1978)
Dana S. Lamb, *Where the Pools Are Bright and Deep* (1973)
Nick Lyons, *The Seasonable Angler* (1970)
John McDonald, *Quill Gordon* (1973)
Alfred W. Miller, *Fishless Days, Angling Nights by Sparse Grey Hackle* (1971)
Steve Raymond, *The Year of the Angler* (1973)
Red Smith, *Red Smith on Fishing Around the World* (1963)

The Best Lines
Izaak Walton, *The Compleat Angler* (1653)

■ GAPPING THE BRIDGE

Here are parts of the titles of ten great "bridge" works (*pace* Mr. Goren). Fill in the gaps from the clues provided. You have three minutes to complete this test. Pick up your pencil. Begin.

1. *The Bridges at* _____
   A Korean war novel by James A. Michener.
2. _____ *Bridge*
   Willa Cather's first novel.
3. *A* _____ *From the Bridge*
   Arthur Miller's 1955 drama.
4. _____ *Bridge*
   The major poetic work of Hart Crane.

5. *The Bridge of* _____
Thornton Wilder's Pulitzer Prize-winning novel, set in Peru.
6. *The Bridge in the* _____
Important novel of the mysterious B. Traven.
7. *A Bridge Too* _____
Cornelius Ryan's World War II battle story.
8. *A Bridge on the* _____
Nobel Laureate Ivo Andric's Serbo-Croatian epic.
9. *The Bridge Over The* _____
Pierre Boule's P.O.W. novel made a memorable movie.
10. _____ *Bridge*
Evan S. Connell, Jr.'s, first novel has absolutely nothing to do with bridges.

Answers
1. *Toko-Ri,* 2. *Alexander's,* 3. *View,* 4. *The,* 5. *San Luis Rey,* 6. *Jungle,*
7. *Far,* 8. *Drina,* 9. *River Kwai,* 10. *Mrs.*

■ TAKE ME TO YOUR READER: THE BEST IN SCIENCE FICTION AND FANTASY

Twentieth-Century Science Fiction and Fantasy, a List by Alexei and Cory Panshin

This list is based on a bibliography to appear in *Masters of Space and Time: The Story of Science Fiction* by Alexei and Cory Panshin, to be published by Pocket Books, and is used with permission of the authors.

Aldiss, Brian, *The Long Afternoon of Earth* (1962)
Anderson, Poul and Gordon R. Dickson, *Earthman's Burden* (1957)
———— *Three Hearts and Three Lions* (1961)
———— *The Man Who Counts* (1958)
Asimov, Isaac., ed., *Before the Golden Age* (1974)
———— *The Caves of Steel* (1954)
———— *The Foundation Trilogy* (1951–53)
———— *The Gods Themselves* (1962)
————, ed. *The Hugo Winners, Volumes One and Two* (1962, 1971)

Bester, Alfred, *The Demolished Man* (1953)
―――― *The Stars My Destination* (1957)
Blish, James, *A Case of Conscience* (1958)
―――― *Jack of Eagels* (1952)
Bova, Ben, ed., *The Science Fiction Hall of Fame, Vols. Two A and Two B* (1974)
Brackett, Leigh, *Sword of Rhiannon* (1953)
Bradbury, Ray, *Farenheit 451* (1953)
―――― *The Martian Chronicles* (1950)
Brown, Fredric, *The Best of Fredric Brown* (1972)
―――― *What Mad Universe* (1949)
Burgess, Anthony, *A Clockwork Orange* (1963)
Burroughs, Edgar Rice, *A Princess of Mars* (1917)
Campbell, John W., *The Best of John W. Campbell* (1973)
Capek, Karel, *War With the Newts* (1939)
Clarke, Arthur C., *Childhood's End* (1953)
―――― *The City and the Stars* (1956)
―――― *Rendezvous With Rama* (1973)
Clement, Hal, *Mission of Gravity* (1954)
de Camp, L. Sprague and Fletcher Pratt, *The Compleat Enchanter* (1941)
de Camp, L. Sprague, *Lest Darkness Fall* (1950)
Delany, Samuel R., *Babel-17* (1966)
―――― *Driftglass* (1971)
Dick, Philip K., *The Man in the High Castle* (1962)
―――― *The Three Stigmata of Palmer Eldritch* (1965)
Disch, Thomas M., *Camp Concentration* (1969)
Doyle, Sir Arthur Conan, *The Lost World* (1912)
Eddison, E. R., *The Worm Ouroboros* (1922)
Farmer, Philip José, *To Your Scattered Bodies Go* (1971)
Graves, Robert, *Watch the Northwind Rise* (1949)
Harness, Charles L., *Flight Into Yesterday* (1953)
Healy, Raymond J. and J. Francis McComas, *Adventures in Time and Space* (1946)
Heinlein, Robert A., *Beyond This Horizon* (1948)
―――― *Have Space Suit—Will Travel* (1958)
―――― *The Past Through Tomorrow* (1957)
―――― *Stranger in a Strange Land* (1961)
Herbert, Frank, *The Dragon in the Sea* (1956)
―――― *Dune* (1965)

Huxley, Aldous, *Brave New World* (1932)
Knight, Damon, *Hell's Pavement* (1955)
Kornbluth, C. M., *The Syndic* (1953)
Kuttner, Henry, *The Best of Henry Kuttner* (1975)
Lafferty, R. A., *Fourth Mansions* (1969)
Le Guin, Ursula K., *The Dispossessed* (1974)
——— *The Left Hand of Darkness* (1969)
Leiber, Fritz, *The Best of Fritz Leiber* (1974)
Lewis, C. S., *Out of the Silent Planet* (1938)
Lindsay, David, *A Voyage to Arcturus* (1920)
Malzberg, Barry N., *Beyond Apollo* (1972)
Merritt, A., *The Moon Pool*
Miller, Walter M., Jr., *A Canticle for Leibowitz* (1959)
Moore, C. L., *The Best of C. L. Moore* (1975)
Niven, Larry, *Ringworld* (1970)
Orwell, George, *1984* (1949)
Pangborn, Edgar, *Davy* (1964)
Panshin, Alexei, *Rite of Passage* (1969)
Pohl, Frederik and C. M. Kornbluth, *The Space Merchants* (1953)
——— *Wolfbane* (1959)
Russ, Joanna, *And Chaos Died* (1970)
Russell, Eric Frank, *Wasp* (1957)
Sheckley, Robert, *Mindswap* (1966)
Shiel, M. P., *The Purple Cloud* (1901)
Silverberg, Robert, ed., *The Science Fiction Hall of Fame, Vol. One* (1970)
Silverberg, Robert, *A Time of Changes* (1971)
Simak, Clifford D., *City* (1952)
Smith, Cordwainer, *The Best of Cordwainer Smith* (1975)
——— *Norstrilia* (1975)
Smith, E. E., *Gray Lensman* (1951)
——— *The Skylark of Space* (1947)
Spinrad, Norman, *Bug Jack Barron* (1969)
Spinrad, Norman, ed., *Modern Science Fiction* (1974)
Stapledon, Olaf, *Last and First Men*, (1930), and *Star Maker* (1937)
Stewart, George R., *Earth Abides* (1949)
Sturgeon, Theodore, *More Than Human* (1953)
Tolkien, J. R. R., *The Lord of the Rings* (1954–56)
van Vogt, A. E., *Slan* (1946)

———— *The World of Null-A* (1948)
Vance, Jack, *The Dying Earth* (1950)
Vonnegut, Kurt, Jr., *Player Piano* (1952)
———— *The Sirens of Titan* (1959)
Weinbaum, Stanley G., *The Best of Stanley G. Weinbaum* (1974)
Wells, H. G., *Seven Famous Novels* (1934)
Williamson, Jack, *The Humanoids* (1949)
———— *The Legion of Space* (1947)
Wright, S. Fowler, *The World Below* (1930)
Wyndham, John, *Re-Birth* (1955)
Zamyatin, Eugene, *We* (1924)
Zelazny, Roger, *Four for Tomorrow* (1967)
———— *Lord of Light* (1967)

Fans' Favorite Novels: The Hugo Award Winners

This award, named after Hugo Gernsback, one of the fathers of modern science fiction, is determined by popular vote of science fiction fans. It is awarded at the annual World Science Fiction Convention.

1952: Alfred Bester, *The Demolished Man*
1953: No award
1954: Mark Clifton and Frank Riley, *They'd Rather Be Right*
1955: Robert Heinlein, *Double Star*
1956: No award
1957: Fritz Leiber, *The Big Time*
1958: James Blish, *A Case of Conscience*
1959: Robert A. Heinlein, *Starship Troopers*
1960: Walter M. Miller, Jr., *A Canticle for Leibowitz*
1961: Robert A. Heinlein, *Stranger in a Strange Land*
1962: Philip K. Dick, *The Man in the High Castle*
1963: Clifford Simak, *Way Station*
1964: Fritz Leiber, *The Wanderer*
1965: Frank Herbert, *Dune*
      Roger Zelazny, *And Call Me Conrad*
1966: Robert A. Heinlein, *The Moon Is a Harsh Mistress*
1967: Robert Zelazny, *Lord of Light*
1968: John Brunner, *Stand on Zanzibar*
1969: Ursula K. Le Guin, *The Left Hand of Darkness*

1970: Lary Niven, *Ringworld*
1971: Philip José Farmer, *To Your Scattered Bodies Go*
1972: Isaac Asimov, *The Gods Themselves*
1973: Arthur C. Clarke, *Rendezvous With Rama*
1974: Ursula K. Le Guin, *The Dispossessed*
1975: Joe Haldeman, *The Forever War*
1976: Kate Wilhelm, *Where Late the Sweet Birds Sang*
1977: Frederik Pohl, *Gateway*
1978: Vonda N. McIntyre, *Dreamsnake*
1979: Arthur C. Clarke, *The Fountain of Paradise*

20 Sci-Fi Novels by Mainstream Writers
Thomas Berger, *Regiment of Women* (1973)
Anthony Burgess, *A Clockwork Orange* (1963)
Hortense Calisher, *Journey from Ellipsia* (1965)
E. L. Doctorow, *Big As Life* (1966)
Lawrence Durrell, *Tunc* (1968)
Howard Fast, *The Edge of Tomorrow* (1961)
Romain Gary, *The Gasp* (1973)
Herman Hesse, *The Glass Bead Game* (1943)
Aldous Huxley, *Brave New World* (1932)
John Hersey, *My Petition for More Space* (1974)
William Melvin Kelley, *A Different Drummer* (1962)
Doris Lessing, *Shikasta* (1979)
Ira Levin, *This Perfect Day* (1970)
Vladimir Nabokov, *Ada* (1969)
Walker Percy, *Love In the Ruins* (1971)
Thomas Pynchon, *Gravity's Rainbow* (1973)
Ayn Rand, *Anthem* (1937)
Gore Vidal, *Kalki* (1978)
Evelyn Waugh, *Love Among The Ruins* (1953)
Herman Wouk, *The 'Lomokome' Papers* (1949)

Writers' Favorite Novels: The Nebula Award Winners
　　Winners of this prestigious award are chosen by their peers—the members of the Science Fiction Writers of America. A trophy is presented to the winners of each category at the annual Nebula Awards Banquet. The winners of the best novella, novelette, and short story awards are published

each year in a special collection. Below are the winners in the best novel category.

1965: Frank Herbert, *Dune*
1966: Samuel R. Delany, *Babel-17*
      Daniel Keyes, *Flowers for Algernon*
1967: Samuel R. Delany, *The Einstein Intersection*
1968: Alexei Panshin, *Rite of Passage*
1969: Ursula K. Le Guin, *The Left Hand of Darkness*
1970: Larry Niven, *Ringworld*
1971: Robert Silverberg, *A Time of Changes*
1972: Isaac Asimov, *The Gods Themselves*
1973: Arthur C. Clarke, *Rendezvous With Rama*
1974: Ursula K. Le Guin, *The Dispossessed*
1975: Joe Haldeman, *The Forever War*
1976: Frederik Pohl, *Man Plus*
1977: Frederik Pohl, *Gateway*
1978: Vonda N. McIntyre, *Dreamsnake*
1979: Arthur C. Clarke, *The Fountain of Paradise*

■ CHOICE OF HOBBIT: THE BEST FANTASIES

The Classic Fantasies

English

E. R. Eddison, *The Worm Ouroboros* (1922)
C. S. Lewis, *The Perelandra Trilogy* (1944)
Mervyn Peake, *The Gormenghast Trilogy* (1946–59)
J. R. R. Tolkien, *The Lord of the Rings* (1954–55)
T. H. White, *The Once and Future King* (1958)

American

Edgar Rice Burroughs, *The Princess of Mars* (1912)
James Branch Cabell, *Jurgen* (1919)
Fritz Leiber, *Fafhrd and Gray Mouser Saga* (1936)
H. P. Lovecraft, *The Dream Quest of Unknown Kadath* (1926)

August Derleth Fantasy Award
Awarded annually by the British Fantasy Society.

1972: Michael Moorcock, *The Knight of the Sword*
1973: Michael Moorcock, *The King of the Sword*
1974: Poul Anderson, *Hrolf Kraki's Saga*
1975: Michael Moorcock, *The Sword and the Stallion*
1976: Michael Moorcock, *The Hollow Lands*
1977: Gordon R. Dickson, *The Dragon and the George*
1978: Stephen R. Donaldson, *The Chronicles of Thomas Covenant the Unbeliever*

5 Great Modern Fantasy Series
Lloyd Alexander, *Chronicles of Prydain* (1964–68)
Susan Cooper, *The Dark Is Rising* (1966–77)
Ursula K. Le Guin. *Earthsea Trilogy* (1968–72)
Patricia A. McKillip, *Riddle-Master Trilogy* (1976–)
Evangeline Walton, *Mabinogion Tetralogy* (1936–74)

5 Classic Modern Fantasies
Poul Anderson, *The Broken Sword* (1954)
Peter Beagle, *The Last Unicorn* (1968)
Joy Chant, *Red Moon and Black Mountain* (1970)
Alan Garner, *The Weirdstone of Brisingamen* (1960)
Jack Vance, *The Dying Earth* (1950)

World Fantasy Award
Awarded at the annual World Fantasy Convention.

1975: Patricia A. McKillip, *The Forgotten Beasts of Eld*
1976: Richard Matheson, *Bid Time Return*
1977: William Kotzwinkle, *Doctor Rat*
1978: Fritz Leiber, *Our Lady of Darkness*

■ LOOKS DOWN THAT LOATHSOME ROAD

The Novel of Manors: The Gothic Classics
William Beckford, *Vathek* (1786)
Wilkie Collins, *The Woman in White* (1886)

Nathaniel Hawthorne, *The House of the Seven Gables* (1851)
Matthew Lewis, *The Monk* (1796)
Charles Robert Maturin, *Melmoth the Wanderer* (1820)
Ann Radcliffe, *The Mysteries of Udolpho* (1794)
Mary Shelley, *Frankenstein* (1818)
Bram Stoker, *Dracula* (1897)

The Original Gothic Horror
Horace Walpole, *The Castle of Otranto* (1764)

The First American Gothic Tale
Charles Brockden Brown, *Wieland* (1798)

The Clot Thickens: 10 Best (Post-*Dracula*) Vampire Novels
Stephen King, *Salem's Lot* (1975)
John Linssen, *Tabitha Ffoulkes: A Love Story About a Reformed Vampire and his Favorite Lady* (1978)
Marc Lovell, *An Enquiry Into the Existence of Vampires* (1974)
Richard Matheson, *I Am Legend* (1954)
Anne Rice, *Interview with the Vampire* (1976)
Raymond Rudorff, *The Dracula Archives* (1971)
Theodore Sturgeon, *Some of Our Blood* (1961)
Peter Tremayne, *Bloodright* (1979)
Colin Wilson, *The Space Vampires* (1976)
Chelsea Quinn Yarbro, *Hotel Transylvania: A Novel of Forbidden Love* (1978)

Sons of Frankenstein
Brian Aldiss, *Frankenstein Unbound* (1977)
Robert J. Myers, *The Cross of Frankenstein* (1975)

Of Wolves and Wolfmen: 5 Howling Successes
Alexandre Dumas, *The Wolf-Leader* (1857)
Franklin Gregory, *White Wolf* (1941)
Jack Mann, *Gray Shapes* (1938)
Whitley Strieber, *The Wolfen* (1979)
Jack Williamson, *Darker Than You Think* (1948)

The Classic
Guy Endore, *The Wolf-Man of Paris* (1938)

Occult Following: 10 Supernatural Classics
Ray Bradbury, *The October Country* (1955)
H. Rider Haggard, *She* (1887)
Shirley Jackson, *The Haunting of Hill House* (1959)
Sheridan Le Fanu, *The House by the Churchyard* (1863)
H. P. Lovecraft, *The Dunwich Horror* (1963)
Arthur Machen, *The Hill of Dreams* (1907)
Dennis Wheatley, *The Devil Rides Out* (1935)
Oscar Wilde, *The Picture of Dorian Gray* (1891)
Charles Williams, *Descent Into Hell* (1949)
Colin Wilson, *The Mind Parasites* (1967)

Weird and Uncanny Tales: 5 Masters
Ambrose Bierce, *Can Such Things Be?* (1893)
Algernon Blackwood, *Tales of the Uncanny and Supernatural* (1949)
Walter De la Mare, *On the Edge* (1932)
Fitz-James O'Brien, *What Was It?* (1859)
Edgar Allan Poe, *Tales of the Grotesque and Arabesque* (1840)

A Ghostly Era: 10 Masters of the Ghost Story
Elizabeth Bowen, *The Demon Lover and Other Stories* (1945)
Walter De la Mare, *Ghost Stories* (1952)
Charles Dickens, *The Christmas Books* (1923)
L. P. Hartley, *The Travelling Grave and Other Stories* (1951)
Henry James, *The Ghostly Tales of Henry James* (1948)
M. R. James, *The Collected Ghost Stories of M. R. James* (1931)
Sheridan Le Fanu, *Green Tea and Other Ghost Stories* (1947)
Oliver Onions, *Ghosts in Daylight* (1924)
Akinari Ueda, *Tales of Moonlight and Rain* (1972)
Edith Wharton, *The Ghost Stories of Edith Wharton* (1973)

5 Modern Masters of the Macabre
Robert Aickman, *Painted Devils* (1979)
John Collier, *The John Collier Reader* (1972)
Roald Dahl, *Tales of the Unexpected* (1979)
Henry Kuttner, *The Best of Henry Kuttner* (1975)
Richard Matheson, *Hell House* (1971)

■ DAYS OF PAST AND FUTURE GLORY

Favorite Past Times: 10 Time Travelers' Tales of the Past
Daphne DuMaurier, *The House on the Strand* (1969)
Sumner Locke Elliott, *The Man Who Got Away* (1972)
Jack Finney, *Time and Again* (1970)
Henry James, *A Sense of the Past* (1917)
Richard Matheson, *Bid Time Return* (1975)
Michael Moorcock, *Behold the Man* (1970)
Ward Moore, *Bring the Jubilee* (1953)
Rob Swigart, *The Time Trap* (1979)
L. Sprague de Camp, *Lest Darkness Fall* (1942)
Wilson Tucker, *The Lincoln Hunters* (1958)

Future Perfect Tense: 10 Best Utopian Novels

Utopia

Edward Bellamy, *Looking Backwards* (1888)
B. F. Skinner, *Walden II* (1948)
H. G. Wells, *A Modern Utopia* (1905)
Franz Werfel, *Star of the Unborn* (1945)
Austin Wright, *Islandia* (1942)

Dystopia
Samuel Butler, *Erewhon* (1872)
Aldous Huxley, *Brave New World* (1932)
David Karp, *One* (1953)
George Orwell, *1984* (1949)
Yevgeni Zamyatin, *We* (1924)

■ CURIOUSER AND CURIOUSER: 20 NOVELS OF FANTASY

Dark Carnivals and Strange Sideshows
Ray Bradbury, *Something Wicked Comes This Way* (1962)
Robertson Davies, *World of Wonders* (1975)
Charles Finney, *The Circus of Dr. Lao* (1935)

William Lindsay Gresham, *Nightmare Alley* (1946)
Tom Kearney, *Blind Voices*(1978)

You Bring Out the Beast in Me: 5 Tales of Metamorphosis
Lucius Apuleius, *The Golden Ass* (second century, A.D.)
John Collier, *His Monkey Wife* (1930)
David Garnett, *Lady Into Fox* (1922)
Franz Kafka, *The Metamorphosis* (1915)
Vercors, *Sylva* (1961)

Miscellanea Fantasia: 10 Fantastic Novels
Peter Beagle, *A Fine and Private Place* (1960)
Leonora Carrington, *The Hearing Trumpet* (1976)
Margharita Laski, *The Victorian Chaise Lounge* (1954)
Jean Malaquais, *The Joker* (1953)
Brian Moore, *The Great Victorian Collection* (1975)
Donald Newlove, *Eternal Life* (1979)
T. F. Powys, *Mr. Weston's Good Wine* (1927)
Bonnie Jones Reynolds, *The Truth About Unicorns* (1972)
Thorne Smith, *Topper* (1926)
Sylvia Townsend Warner, *Lolly Willowes* (1926)

■ THE CASE OF THE BOOKSELLER'S FAVORITE MYSTERIES

Jennifer Castro, proprietor of Cloak & Dagger, sellers of books of mystery and suspense in Santa Barbara, California, offers her favorites in a few categories. The author has officiously added his favorites.

7 Favorite School Mysteries
Nicholas Blake, *A Question of Proof* (1935)
Amanda Cross, *The Theban Mysteries* (1971)
Michael Gilbert, *The Night of the Twelfth* (1976)
John LeCarré, *A Murder of Quality* (1962)
Peter Lovesey, *Swing, Swing Together* (1976)
Charlotte McLeod, *Rest You Merry* (1978)
Josephine Tey, *Miss Pym Disposes* (1948)

6 Favorite Methodical Detectives

Martin Beck in Maj Sjöwall and Per Wahlöö, *Roseanna* (1967)

Sergeant Cribb in Peter Lovesey, *Waxwork* (1978)

Judge Dee in Robert van Gulik, *The Chinese Bell Murders* (1951)

Sherlock Holmes in Sir Arthur Conan Doyle, *The Adventures of Sherlock Holmes* (1892)

Commissaire Jules Maigret in Georges Simenon, *Versus Inspector Maigret* (1960)

Inspector Wexford in Ruth Rendell, *Murder Being once Done* (1972)

7 Favorite Clerical Crime Solvers

Father Bredder in Leonard Holton, *The Saint Maker* (1959)

Father Brown in G. K. Chesterton, *The Innocence of Father Brown* (1911)

Father Dowling in Ralph McInerny, *Her Death of Cold* (1977)

Rev. Bob Koesler in William X. Kienzle, *Death Wears a Red Hat* (1980)

Rabbi Small in Harry Kemmelman, *Friday The Rabbi Slept Late* (1974)

Rev. Randolph in Charles Merril Smith, *Rev. Randolph and the Fall From Grace* (1978)

Sister Mary Ursula, O.M.B., in H. H. Holmes, *Nine Times Nine* (1940)

7 Favorite Female Sleuths

Modesty Blaise in Peter O'Donnell, *Pieces of Modesty* (1972)

Sarah Chayse in Lynn Meyer, *Paperback Thriller* (1975)

Kate Fansler in Amanda Cross, *The Question of Max* (1976)

Julia Hayes in Dorothy Salisbury Davis, *Scarlet Night* (1980)

Miss Jane Marple in Agatha Christie, *Sleeping Murder* (1976)

Sharon McCone in Marcia Muller, *Edwin of the Iron Shoes* (1977)

Arlette Van der Valk in Nicholas Freeling, *The Widow* (1979)

■ WHOPUNITS

No other genre of literature so abounds in witty and whimsical titles as does crime fiction. Both cunning and punning are helpful in marketing mysteries. Here is a sampling of the least execrable puns and double-meaning titles.

The Top 10
Morgue the Merrier
Half-Past Mortem
3 Short Biers
Dewey Decimated
Remains to be Seen
Widow's Pique
A Time to Prey
Board Stiff
Corpse de Ballet
Bones of Contention

The Runners-Up
Abracadaver
Murder Has Its Points
Reclining Figure
Stab in the Dark
What A Body!
Slay Ride
Too Long Endured
Having Wonderful Crime
You Leave Me Cold
Lucky Stiff
If the Shroud Fits
Some Like 'em Shot
Up to the Hilt
Just Killing Time

Trial and Terror
Trio for Blunt Instruments
For Old Crime's Sake

Dead to Writes: The 10 Best
The Dead of Winter
Never Wake a Dead Man
Portrait of the Artist as a
*   Dead Man*
Deadly Beloved
Dead Reckoning
Dead to the World
Funny, Jonas, You Don't
*   Look Dead*
Over My Dead Body
Dead Man's Float
Dead Giveaway

Dying the Good Death: The 5 Best
One Good Death Deserves
*   Another*
They Died Laughing
Sudden Death
Died in the Wool
Death Is Skin Deep

Whodunit? The Writer Did It
The term "whodunit" appears to have been first used by Wolfe Kaufman in a piece in, you guessed it, *Variety*, the New York show biz newspaper famous for its imaginative

diminutions of words and phrases. Since its coinage in 1928, it has enjoyed continued use.

The detective story is the normal recreation of noble minds.
—PHILIP GUEDALLA

■ THE BEST CRIME NOVELS: EDGAR ALLAN POE AWARD WINNERS AND NOMINEES

Each year the Mystery Writers of America present an Edgar Award for the best novel of the preceding year. The winners and the nominees for each year are:

1953
Charlotte Jay, *Beat Not the Bones*

1954
Raymond Chandler, *The Long Goodbye*

1955
Margaret Millar, *Beast in View*

The Gordons, *The Case of the Talking Bug*
Patricia Highsmith, *The Talented Mr. Ripley*

1956
Charlotte Armstrong, *A Dram of Poison*

Margot Bennett, *The Man Who Didn't Fly*

1957
Ed Lacy, *Room to Swing*

Bill Ballinger, *The Longest Second*
Marjorie Carleton, *The Night of the Good Children*
Arthur Upfield, *The Bushman Who Came Back*

1958
Stanley Ellin, *The Eighth Circle*

David Alexander, *The Madhouse in Washington Square*
Lee Blackstock, *Woman in the Woods*
Dorothy Salisbury Davis, *A Gentleman Called*

1959
Celia Fremlin, *The Hours Before Dawn*

Philip MacDonald, *The List of Adrian Messenger*

1960
Julian Symons, *Progress of a Crime*

Herbert Brean, *The Traces of Brilihart*
Peter Curtis, *The Devil's Own*
Geoffrey Household, *The Watcher in the Shadows*

1961
J. J. Marric, *Gideon's Fire*

Anne Blaisdell, *Nightmare*
Suzanne Blanc, *The Green Stone*
Lionel Davidson, *The Night of Wenceslas*
Ross MacDonald, *The Wycherly Woman*

1962
Ellis Peters, *Death of the Joyful Woman*

Ross MacDonald, *The Zebra-Sriped Hearse*
Mark McShane, *Seance*
Jean Potts, *The Evil Wish*
Dell Shannon, *Knave of Hearts*
Shelly Smith, *The Ballad of the Running Man*

1963
Eric Ambler, *The Light of Day*

Elizabeth Fenwick, *The Make-Believe Man*
Stanton Forbes, *Grieve for the Past*

Dorothy B. Hughes, *The Expendable Man*
Ellery Queen, *The Player on the Other Side*

1964

John LeCarré, *The Spy Who Came in from the Cold*

Hans Hellmut Kirst, *The Night of the Generals*
Margaret Millar, *The Fiend*
Mary Stewart, *This Rough Magic*

1965

Adam Hall, *The Quiller Memorandum*

Len Deighton, *Funeral in Berlin*
Dorothy Salisbury Davis, *The Pale Betrayer*
H. R. F. Keating, *The Perfect Murder*
Ross MacDonald, *The Far Side of the Dollar*
Mary Stewart, *Airs Above the Ground*

1966

Nicholas Freeling, *The King of the Rainy Country*

Dick Francis, *Odds Agains*
Ngaio Marsh, *Killer Dolphin*
Donald E. Westlake, *The Busy Body*

1967

Donald E. Westlake, *God Save the Mark*

Charlotte Armstrong, *Lemon in the Basket*
———, *The Gift Shop*
George Baxt, *A Parade of Cockeyed Creatures*
Dick Francis, *Flying Finish*
Ira Levin, *Rosemary's Baby*

1968

Jeffrey Hudson, *A Case of Need*

Heron Carvic, *Picture Miss Seeton*
Dorothy Salisbury Davis and Jerome Ross, *God Speed the
   Night*
Peter Dickinson, *The Glass-Spider Ants' Nest*

Stanley Ellin, *The Valentine Estate*
Dick Francis, *Blood Sport*

1969
Dick Francis, *Forfeit*

Dorthy Salisbury Davis, *The Dark Streets Go*
Peter Dickinson, *The Old English Peep Show*
Shaun Herron, *Miro*
Chester Himes, *Blind Man with a Pistol*
Emma Lathan, *When in Greece*

1970
Maj Sjöwall and Per Wahloö, *The Laughing Policeman*

Shaun Herron, *The Hound and the Fox and the Harper*
Margaret Millar, *Beyond This Point Are Monsters*
Patricia Moyes, *Many Deadly Returns*
Donald E. Westlake, *The Hot Rock*

1971
Frederick Forsyth, *The Day of the Jackal*

Tony Hillerman, *The Fly on the Wall*
P. D. James, *Shroud for a Nightingale*
G. F. Newman, *Sir, You Bastard*
Arthur Wise, *Who Killed Enoch Powell?*

1972
Warren Kiefer, *The Lingala Code*

John Ball, *Five Pieces of Jade*
Ngaio Marsh, *Tied Up In Tinsel*
Hugh C. Rae, *The Shooting Gallery*
Martin Smith, *Canto for a Gypsy*

1973
Tony Hillerman, *Dance Hall of the Dead*

Victor Canning, *The Rainbird Pattern*
Francis Clifford, *Amigo, Amigo*

P. D. James, *An Unsuitable Job for a Woman*
Jean Stubbs, *Dear Laura*

1974
Jon Cleary, *Peter's Pence*

Malcolm Bosse, *The Man Who Loved Zoos*
Francis Clifford, *Goodbye and Amen*
Paul E. Erdman, *The Silver Bears*
Andrew Garve, *The Lester Affair*

1975
Brian Garfield, *Hopscotch*

Marvin Albert, *The Gargoyle Conspiracy*
Maggie Rennert, *Operation Alcestic*
Gerald Seymour, *Harry's Game*
Ross Thomas, *The Money Harvest*

1976
Robert Parker, *Promised Land*

Thomas Gifford, *The Cavanaugh Quest*
Richard Neeley, *Madness of the Heart*
Trevanian, *The Main*

1977
William Hallahan, *Catch Me: Kill Me*

William McIlvanney, *Laidlaw*
Martin Cruz Smith, *Nightwing*

1978
Ken Follett, *The Eye of the Needle*

John Godey, *The Snake*
Tony Hillerman, *Listening Woman*
Ruth Rendell, *A Sleeping Life*
Jack S. Scott, *The Shallow Grave*

1979
Arthur Maling, *The Rheingold Route*
134

Robert Barnard, *Death of a Mystery Writer*
Frank Parrish, *Fire in the Barley*
Ruth Rendell, *Make Death Love Me*
C. P. Snow, *A Coat of Varnish*

■ CLASSIC CRIMES

Crooks & Grannies: 5 Great Little Old Lady Sleuths
Miss Marple in Agatha Christie, *Murder at the Vicarage* (1930)
Miss Seeton in Heron Carvic, *Picture Miss Seeton* (1968)
Miss Silver in Patricia Wentworth, *Miss Silver Deals with Death* (1943)
Mrs. Pollifax in Dorothy Gilman, *The Unexpected Mrs. Pollifax* (1966)
Minnie Santangelo in Anthony Mancini, *Minnie Santangelo's Mortals* (1975)

Shooting Stars: 5 Hollywood Mysteries
Andrew Bergman, *Hollywood and Levine* (1975)
Thomas Gifford, *Hollywood Gothic* (1979)
Stuart Kaminsky, *Murder on the Yellow Brick Road* (1977)
Charles Larson, *Muir's Blood* (1976)
Max Wilk, *The Moving Picture Boys* (1978)

Who-Don-Its: 5 Best Oxford Mysteries
Edmund Crispin, *The Moving Toyshop* (1946)
Joan Fleming, *How to Live Dangerously* (1975)
Michael Innes, *Old Hall, New Hall* (1956)
Dorothy L. Sayers, *Gaudy Night* (1935)
Margaret Yorke, *Grave Matters* (1973)

Courtroom Battles: 5 Best English Law Mysteries
Michael Gilbert, *Smallbone Deceased* (1950)
Edward Grierson, *Reputation for a Song* (1952)
Cyril Hare, *Tragedy at Law* (1942)
Francis Noyes Hart, *The Bellamy Trial* (1927)
Edgar Lustgarten, *A Case to Answer* (1947)

**Writing Holmes for Money or Sherlock
You Survived: 10 Best**

Randall Collins, *The Case of the Philosopher's Stone* (1978)
Adrian Conan Doyle and John Dickson Carr, *The Exploits of Sherlock Holmes* (1954)
Loren Estleman, *Dr. Jekyll & Mr. Holmes* (1979)
Robert L. Fish, *The Incredible Shlock Homes* (1964)
William S. Baring-Gould, *Sherlock Holmes of Baker Street* (1962)
John Gardner, *The Return of Moriarty* (1974)
Michael Harrison, *I, Sherlock Holmes* (1977)
Robert Lee Hall, *Exit Sherlock Holmes* (1978)
Michael Hodel and Sean Wright, *Enter the Case* (1979)
Nicholas Meyer, *The Seven Per Cent Solution* (1974)
Fred Saberhagen, *The Holmes-Dracula File* (1978)
Vincent Starrett, *The Private Life of Sherlock Holmes* (1933)

■ DETECTO-GRAM: THE BEST DETECTIVE SERIES

I. The English

Scotland Yard

Author	Detective	Representative Work
Catherine Aird	Insp. Sloan	*The Stately Home Murders* (1970)
Michael Allen	Supt. Ben Spence	*Spence at the Blue Bazaar* (1979)
Frank Branston	Sgt. Richie	*Sgt. Richie's Conscience* (1978)
W. J. Burley	Supt. Wycliffe	*Wycliffe in Paul's Court* (1980)
John Creasey	Roger West	*Inspector West Takes Charge* (1942)
Freeman Will Crofts	Insp. Joseph French	*The Purple Sickle Murders* (1929)
Colin Dexter	Insp. Morse	*Last Bus to Woodstock* (1975)
Peter Dickinson	Supt. Pibble	*The Glass-Sided Ants' Nest* (1968)
Michael Gilbert	Insp. Hazelrigg	*Accent on Murder* (1958)

Author	Detective	Representative Work
Peter Hill	Cmdr. Allan Dice	*The Fanatic* (1978)
Alan Hunter	Chf. Supt. Gently	*Gently in an Omnibus* (1966)
J. B. Hilton	Simon Kentworthy	*Death in Midwinter* (1969)
Michael Innes	John Appleby	*The Crabtree Affair* (1962)
P. D. James	Adam Dalgliesh	*Death of an Expert Witness* (1977)
Michael Kenyon	Harry Peckover	*The Molehill File* (1978)
Peter Lovesey	Sgt. Cribb and Constable Thackery (Victorian)	*Wobble to Death* (1970)
Victor MacClure	Insp. Archie Burford	*Death Behind the Door* (1933)
J. J. Marric	Cmdr. George Gideon	*Gideon's River* (1968)
Ngaio Marsh	Insp. Roderick Alleyn	*Overture to Death* (1936)
Patricia Moyes	Supt. Tibbet	*Johnny Under Ground* (1965)
Gil North	Sgt. Caleb Cluff	*Sergeant Cluff Stands Firm* (1960)
Joyce Porter	Insp. Wilfred Dover	*Dead Easy for Dover* (1979)
Ruth Rendell	Insp. Reginald Wexford	*Wolf to the Slaughter* (1968)
Jack S. Scott	Sgt. Howes	*Poor Old Lady's Dead* (1976)
Francis Selwyn	Sgt. Clarence Verity (Victorian)	*Cracksman on Velvet* (1975)
Josephine Tey	Insp. Alan Grant	*The Singing Sands* (1953)
June Thompson	Insp. Rudd	*Death Cap* (1977)
John Wainright	Supt. Lennox	*Square Dance* (1971)
Colin Watson	Insp. Purbright (small town)	*Hopjoy Was Here* (1962)
Pauline Glen Winslow	Supt. Merle Capricorn	*Copper Gold* (1978)
Margery Allingham	Albert Campion (gentleman)	*The Fashion in Shrouds* (1938)
Josephine Bell	Dr. David Wintringham (physician)	*Murder in Hospital* (1937)

Author	Detective	Representative Work
Simon Brett	Charles Paris (actor)	*Star-Trip* (1977)
Leo Bruce	Carolus Deene (schoolmaster)	*Nothing Like Blood* (1962)
John Dickson Carr	Dr. Gideon Fell (physician)	*The Mad Hatter Mystery* (1933)
Clyn Carr	Abercrombie Lewker (actor-mountaineer)	*Death Finds a Foothold* (1961)
Agatha Christie	Hercule Poirot (gentleman)	*The Mysterious Affair at Styles* (1920)
Leslie Charteris	The Saint (Simon Templar, adventurer)	*Enter the Saint* (1930)
Edmund Crispin	Gervase Fen (Oxford professor)	*The Moving Toyshop* (1946)
John Creasey	The Toff (Richard Rollison, gentleman)	*Introducing the Toff* (1938)
Elizabeth Daly	Henry Gamadge (*literateur*)	*Death and Letters* (1950)
Carter Dickson	Sir Henry Merrivale	*Unicorn Murder* (1935)
Antonia Fraser	Jemima Shore	*Quiet as a Nun* (1977)
Anthony Gilbert	Arthur Crook (lawyer)	*Spy for Mr. Crook* (1944)
Jonathan Gash	Lovejoy (antique dealer)	*The Judas Pair* (1977)
Anne Morice	Tessa Crichton (actress)	*Scared to Death* (1977)
Dorothy Sayers	Lord Peter Wimsey	*Strong Poison* (1930)
Mignon Warner	Mrs. Charles (clairvoyant)	*A Medium for Murder* (1977)
Sara Woods	Anthony Maitland (barrister)	*Error of the Moon* (1963)

Author	Detective	Representative Work
Nicholas Blake	Nigel Strange-ways (private investigator)	*A Question of Proof* (1935)
Christopher Bush	Ludovic Travers (London private eye)	*Case of the Jumbo Sandwich* (1965)
Mike Fredman	Willie Holliday (private eye)	*You Can Always Blame the Rain* (1979)
Bartholomew Gill	Chief Insp. McGarr (Irish cop)	*McGarr on the Cliffs of Moher* (1978)
Dick Francis	Sid Halley (ex-jockey, private eye)	*Odds Against* (1965)
Tim Heald	Simon Bognor (Board of Trade)	*Unbecoming Habits* (1973)
Michael Kirk	Insp. Laird (Scottish insurance investigator)	*Salvage Job* (1979)
Bill Knox	Webb Carrick (Scottish Fisheries Protection Service)	*Witchrock* (1977)
	Colin Thane (Glasgow C.D.)	*Pilot Error* (1977)
Donald Mackenzie	John Raven (formerly of Scotland Yard)	*Zaleksi's Revenge* (1975)
Noah Webster	Jonathan Gault (Queen's Remembrancer)	*An Incident in Iceland* (1979)

5 Best-Written Modern English Series
Simon Brett: *Charles Paris*
Jonathan Gash: *Lovejoy*
Tim Heald: *Simon Bognor*
Jack Scott: *Sgt. Howes*
Colin Watson: *Insp. Purbright*
  et al.

II. The Americans

Cops

Author	Detective	Representative Work
New York		
George Bagby	Insp. Schmidt	*The Tough Get Going* (1977)
Thomas Chastain	Insp. Max Kauffman	*High Voltage* (1979)
Ed McBain	87th Precinct Squad	*Fuzz* (1968)
Helen McCloy	Dr. Basil Willing (medical assistant to D.A.)	*Dance of Death* (1938)
Lillian O'Donnell	Norah Mulcahaney	*No Business Being A Cop* (1979)
Shephard Rifkin	McQuaid	*McQuaid in August* (1979)
Southern California		
John Crowe	Sheriff Beckett (Buena Vista)	*Crooked Shadows* (1975)
John Ball	Virgil Tibbs (Pasadena)	*In the Heat of the Night* (1965)
E. V. Cunningham	Masao Masuto (Beverly Hills)	*The Case of the Threepenny Orange* (1977)
Lange Lewis	Insp. Richard Tuck (LAPD)	*The Building Murder* (1945)
Elizabeth Linington	Lt. Mendoza (LAPD)	*Cold Trail* (1978)
San Francisco		
Bill Pronzini	Nameless detective	*Blowback* (1977)

Author	Detective	Representative Work
Colin Wilcox	Lt. Hastings	*Aftershock* (1975)
In between		
Rex Burns	Gabriel Wager (Denver)	*Speak for the Dead* (1978)
Tony Hillerman	Lt. Joe Leaphorn (Navaho, New Mexico)	*The Blessing Way* (1970)
Jon A. Jackson	Det. Sgt. Mulheisen (Detroit)	*The Diehard* (1977)
Steve Knickmeyer	Steve Cranmer (Oklahoma City)	*Straight* (1976)
Hillary Waugh	Chief Fred Fellows (Stockford, Connecticut)	*The Con Game* (1968)

The Hardest-Boiled Shamuses

Edwin Gage	Daniel Falconer	*Phoenix No More* (1978)
Dashiell Hammett	The Continental Op	*Real Harvest* (1929)
Anthony Lyons	Jacob Asch	*Castles Burning* (1979)
Ross MacDonald	Lew Archer	*Moving Target* (1949)
Robert Parker	Spenser	*The Godwulf Manuscript* (1973)
Jonathan Valin	Harry Stoner	*The Lime Pit* (1980)
Brad Solomon	Charles Quinlan	*The Open Shadow* (1979)
Raymond Chandler	Phillip Marlowe	*The Big Sleep* (1939)

New York Sleuths

Arthur Maling	Brock Potter (stockbroker)	*The Koberg Link* (1979)
Lawrence Block	Bernie Rhodenbarr (burglar)	*Burglars Can't Be Choosers* (1977)
J. F. Burke	Samuel Moses Kelly (private eye)	*Kelly Among the Nightingales* (1979)

Author	Detective	Representative Work
M. E. Chaber	Milo March (insurance investigator)	*The Bonded Dead* (1971)
James P. Wohl	Sam Gross (insurance investigator)	*The Blind Trust Kills* (1979)
Tucker Coe	Mitch Tobin (ex-cop)	*A Jade in Aries* (1970)
R. R. Irvine	Robert Christopher (TV newsman)	*Horizontal Hold* (1979)
Emma Lathan	John Putnam Thatcher (banker)	*Banking on Death* (1961)
Hugh Pentecost	Pierre Chambrun (hotelier)	*The Fourteen Dilemma* (1971)
Ellery Queen	Ellery Queen (amateur sleuth)	*The Roman Hat Mystery* (1929)
S. S. Van Dine	Philo Vance (dilettante)	*The Benson Murder Case* (1926)
Rex Stout	Nero Wolfe (private eye)	*Fer-de-Lance* (1934)

San Franciscans

Author	Detective	Representative Work
Charles Alverson	Joe Goodey (private eye)	*Goodey's Last Stand* (1975)
Joe Gores	Dan Kearney (skip-tracer)	*Dead Skip* (1972)
Stephen Greenleaf	John Marshall Tanner (private eye)	*Grave Error* (1979)

L. A. Dicks

Author	Detective	Representative Work
James Crumley	Sughrue	*The Last Good Kill* (1978)
A. A. Fair	Bertha Cool and Donald Lam	*Bigger They Come* (1939)

Author	Detective	Representative Work
Peter Israel	B. F. Cage	*Hush Money* (1974)
Timothy Harris	Thomas Kyd	*Good Night and Good-Bye* (1979)
Kin Platt	Max Roper	*The Screwball King* (1978)
Stuart Kaminsky	Toby Peters	*The Howard Hughes Affair* (1979)
Roger L. Simon	Moses Wine	*The Big Fix* (1973)
Brett Halliday	Mike Shayne (Miami)	*Private Practice of Michael Shayne* (1940)
Janice Law	Anne Peters (Washington, D.C.)	*The Big Payoff* (1977)
Michael Z. Lewin	Alberi Samson (Indianapolis)	*Ask the Right Question* (1971)
John MacDonald	Travis McGee (Florida)	*Deep Blue Good Bye* (1964)
James Mac-Dougall	David Stuart (Cleveland)	*Death and the Maiden* (1978)

Journalists

George Harmon Coxe	Jack "Flashgun" Casey (Boston press photographer)	*Silent Are the Dead* (1942)
Pete Hamill	Sam Briscoe (New York City ex-re-porter)	*Dirty Laundry* (1978)
Lucille Kallen	C. B. Greenfield (suburban New York editor)	*Introducing C. B. Greenfield* (1979)
Gregory Mac-Donald	Fletch (freelance writer)	*Fletch* (1975)

Author	Detective	Representative Work

Lawyers and Lawmakers

Author	Detective	Representative Work
Joe L. Hensley	Donald Robank (small-town lawyer)	*Minor Murder* (1979)
Paul Kruger	Phil Kramer (Colorado attorney)	*The Cold Ones* (1972)
R. B. Dominic	Ben Scafford (Congressman)	*The Attending Physician* (1979)
Erle Stanley Gardner	Perry Mason (lawyer)	*The Case of the Velvet Claws* (1933)

Detectives—With a Twist

All these detectives were created with a little something extra to make them memorable.

Author	Detective	Representative Work
Ernest Bramah	Max Carrados (blind amateur sleuth)	*Eyes of Max Carrados* (1923)
Timothy Childs	Peter Stokes (one-armed investigator)	*Cold Turkey* (1979)
Michael Collins	Dan Fortune (one-armed private eye)	*Act of Fear* (1967)
George C. Chesbro	Dr. Bob Frederickson (dwarf criminologist)	*City of Whispering Stone* (1978)
Michael Delving	Dave Cannon (antiques dealer)	*No Sign of Life* (1979)
Edith Pinero Green	Deborah V. Pinch (old rascal)	*Rotten Apples* (1978)

Author	Detective	Representative Work
Joseph Hansen	Dave Brandstetter (gay insurance investigator)	*Fadeout* (1970)
Baynard H. Kendrick	Duncan McLain (blind private eye)	*Frankinscence and Murder* (1961)
Judson Phillips	Peter Styles (one-legged magazine columnist)	*Murder by the Book* (1963)

The Most Literary Sleuth

Amanda Cross	Professor Kate Fansler	*The Question of Max* (1976)

Continental Detectives

Georges Simenon	Inspector Maigret	*Maigret Mystified* (1932)
Nicholas Freeling	Inspector Van der Valk (Amsterdam)	*Love in Amsterdam* (1962)
Nicholas Freeling	Henri Castang (France)	*The Night Lords* (1978)
Per Wahloö and Maj Sjöwall	Martin Beck (Sweden)	*Roseanna* (1967)
Janwillian van de Wetering	Gripetra and de-Gier (Amsterdam)	*The Corpse on the Dike* (1976)
Paul Orun	Jonas Morck (Denmark)	*Scapegoat* (1974)
Vincent McConnor	Inspector Damiot (France)	*The Provence Puzzle* (1980)
Pierre Aubemars	M. Pinaud (Paris)	*Now Dead Is Any Man* (1980)

Some Exotic Locales

Arthur Upfield	Insp. Napoleon "Bony" Bonaparte (half-caste Australian)	*The New Shoe* (1951)
James McClure	Lt. Tramp Kramer and Sgt. Mickey Zondi (South African cops)	*The Steam Pig* (1972)
H. R. F. Keating	Inspector Ghote (Bombay P.D.)	*Inspector Ghote's Good Crusade* (1966)
William Marshall	Insp. Harry Feiffer (Hong King)	*Skullduggery* (1979)
Robert L. Fish	Captain DaSilva (Brazil)	*Isle of the Snakes* (1963)
John Wylie	Dr. Quarshie (West Africa)	*The Butterfly Flood* (1975)
Robert van Gulik	Judge Dee (ancient China)	*The Chinese Bell Murders* (1951)
Ivor Drummond	Jenny, Cotty, and Sandro (international crime busters)	*The Man With the Tiny Head* (1969)

■ PRIVATE EYE Q. TEST

1. Who was Sam Spade's late partner?
2. What are Lord Peter Wimsey's middle names?
3. Which private eyes are associated with these fictional locales: (a) Wrightsville, Connecticut; (b) Santa Teresa; (c) Bay City?
4. What is the name of Nick and Nora Charles' dog?
5. What is the name of Travis McGee's houseboat?
6. What is the name of Pierre Chambrun's hotel?
7. Who is the "Sherlock Holmes of Praed Street" created by August Derleth?

8. What is the title of the first Perry Mason novel?

9. What is the name of the sleuth in a series created by the writers of Ellery Queen under the pseudonym of Barnaby Ross?

10. What is the name of the narrator of the Nero Wolfe series?

Answers

1. Miles Archer, 2. Death Bredon, 3. (a) Ellery Queen, (b) Lew Archer, (c) Phillip Marlowe, 4. Asta, 5. *The Busted Flush*, 6. Beaumont, 7. Solar Pons, 8. *The Case of the Velvet Claws*, 9. Drury Lane, 10. Archie Goodwin

Julian Symons' Personal Pantheon

Julian Symons is one of the most respected writers of crime fiction, and is the author of *Mortal Consequences* (1972), one of the most readable histories of mysteries. This list is from an article in *Publishers Weekly* (March 13, 1978).

In the Beginning

Caleb Williams, *William Godwin* (1794)

Edgar Allen Poe, *Dupin Stories, The Gold Bug, Thou Art the Man* (1840s)

Charles Felix, *The Notting Hill Mystery* (1862)

Emile Gaborieau, *Monsieur Lecoq* (1869)

Wilkie Collins, *The Woman in White* (1860), *The Moonstone* (1894)

Sherlock and the Short Story

Sir Arthur Conan Doyle, *The Adventures of Sherlock Holmes* (1892), *The Memoirs of Sherlock Holmes* (1894)

Jacques Futrelle, *The Thinking Machine* (1907)

G. K. Chesterton, *The Innocence of Father Brown* (1911)

A. E. W. Mason, *At the Villa Rose* (1910)

The Golden Age

Agatha Christie, *The Murder of Roger Ackroyd* (1926), *10 Little Indians* (1939)

Margery Allingham, *Tiger in the Smoke* (1952)

Ngaio Marsh, *Opening Night* (1951)

Rex Stout, *Fer-de-Lance* (1934)
Michael Innes, *Hamlet, Revenge* (1937)
S. S. Van Dine, *The Bishop Murder Case* (1929)
Ellery Queen, *The Greek Coffin Mystery* (1932), *The Adventures of Ellery Queen* (1935)
John Dickinson Carr, *The Three Coffins* (1935)
Edmund Crispin, *The Moving Toyshop* (1946)

The Hard Men

Dashiell Hammett, *The Glass Key* (1931), *Red Harvest* (1929)
Raymond Chandler, *The Long Goodbye* (1953)
Ross MacDonald, *The Zebra-Striped Hearse* (1962)

The Thriller

W. Somerset Maugham, *Ashenden: Or The British Agent* (1928)
Graham Greene, *This Gun For Hire* (1936)
Eric Ambler, *The Mask of Dimitrios* (1939), *Doctor Frigo* (1974)
John LeCarré, *The Spy Who Came in from the Cold* (1963)
Len Deighton, *The Billion Dollar Brain* (1965)

The Crime Novel

Francis Iles, *Malice Aforethought* (1931)
John Franklin Bardin, *Devil Take the Blue-Tail Fly* (1948)
Patricia Highsmith, *The Two Faces of January* (1964)
Margaret Millar, *How Like An Angel* (1962)
Ira Levin, *A Kiss Before Dying* (1954)
Georges Simenon, *The Stain on the Snow* (1948), *My Friend Maigret* (1949)
Stanley Ellin, *Mystery Stories* (1956)

The Police Procedural

Ed McBain, *Like Love* (1962)
Hillary Waugh, *Last Seen Wearing* (1960)

Noms de Crime: Blowing Their Cover

For a variety of motives, many writers have chosen to use assumed names for their criminal lucubrations, thus shrouding in mystery the real culprit whodunit. Now at last you can detect the perpetrators of these literary crimes as we reveal the true names behind the aliases.

Catherina Aird	a/k/a	Kim Hamilton McIntosh
George Bagby		Aaron Marc Stein
Josephine Bell		Doris Bell
Anthony Berkeley		A. B. Cox
Charity Blackstock		Ursula Torday
Leslie Charteris		Leslie Yin
Edmund Crispin		Bruce Montgomery
A. A. Fair		Erle Stanley Gardner
E. X. Ferrars		Morna Brown
Nicholas Freeling		F. R. Nicholas
Andrew Garve		Paul Winnerton
Anthony Gilbert		Lucy Beatrice Malleson
Brett Halliday		Davis Dressler
Ross MacDonald		Kenneth Millar
J. J. Marric		John Creasey
Hugh Pentecost		Judson Philips
Ellis Peters		Edith Pargeter
Dell Shannon		Elizabeth Linington
Josephine Tey		Elizabeth MacKintosh
S. S. Van Dine		Willard H. Wright

A Real Switch

Agatha Christie's "criminal record" was so well known that she had to take another name in order to go straight. Thus she used "Mary Westmacott" as a pen name for her "straight" novels.

Accomplices Before the Fact

Each of these aliases is a front for two clever criminal masterminds. Their "m.o." is to work with an accomplice. So watch out; they may be in your bookstore next.

Francis Beeding	a/k/a	John L. Palmer and Hilary St. George Saunders
Manning Coles		Cyril H. Coles and Adelaide F. Manning
Jeffrey Campbell		Jeffrey Caine and Campbell Black
Emma Lathan		Mary J. Latis and Martha Hennissart
Ellery Queen		Frederic Dannay and Manfred Lee

They Led 2 Lives
These writers had one pen dipped in the mainstream and another pseudonymously dipped in a criminal tributary. Let's unmask these two-faced, duplicitous, bi-nomial double-dealers.

Edgar Box	a/k/a	Gore Vidal
Nicholas Blake		C. Day Lewis
Leo Bruce		Rupert Croft-Cook
Amanda Cross		Carolyn Heilbrun
E. V. Cunningham		Howard Fast
Matthew Head		John Canaday
Leonard Holton		Leonard Wibberly
Michael Innes		J. I. M. Stewart
David Keith		Francis Steegmuller
Ed McBain		Evan Hunter
Glen Trevor		James Hilton

■ ENGLISH MAINSTREAM CONTRIBUTIONS

Aside from the writers cited earlier who have penned crime fiction pseudonymously, other English writers, either for fun or profit, have attempted its commission unmasked and in plain sight. Probably the most famous work is Charles Dickens' unfinished *The Mystery of Edwin Drood*. Here are ten who followed in that tradition.

Phyllis Bentley, *The House of Moreys* (1953)
Anthony Burgess, *Tremor of Intent* (1966)
C. S. Forester, *Payment Deferred* (1926)
Antonia Fraser, *Island-in-Waiting* (1979)
Roy Fuller, *With My Little Eye* (1948)
Graham Greene, *This Gun for Hire* (1936)
A. A. Milne, *The Red House Mystery* (1922)
J. B. Priestley, *The Old Dark House* (1928)
C. P. Snow, *A Coat of Varnish* (1979)
Frank Swinnerton, *On the Shady Side* (1970)

■ THE GRAND MASTERS

Since 1954 the Mystery Writers of America have periodically selected a writer to join the pantheon of "Grand Masters," in tribute to his or her body of work over the years.

Eric Ambler
W. R. Burnett
James M. Cain
George Harmon Coxe
John Dickson Carr
Agatha Christie
John Creasey
Daphne duMaurier
Mignon G. Eberhart
Erle Stanley Gardner
Graham Greene

Dorothy B. Hughes
Baynard Kendrick
John D. MacDonald
Ross MacDonald
Ngaio Marsh
Judson Philips
Ellery Queen
Georges Simenon
Vincent Starrett
Aaron Marc Stein
Rex Stout

■ SCENES OF THE CRIME

Final Curtain: Backstage Mysteries
Simon Brett, *A Comedian Dies* (1979)
Ngaio Marsh, *False Scent* (1959)
Lillian O'Donnell, *Falling Star* (1979)
Barbara Paul, *The Fourth Wall* (1979)
Bob Randall, *The Fan* (1977)

My theory is that people who don't like mystery stories are anarchists.

—REX STOUT

Best Mystery By an Ecdysiast
Gypsy Rose Lee, *The G-String Murder* (1941)

Danse Macabre: Ballet Mysteries
Edgar Box, *Death in the Fifth Position* (1952)

Caryl Brahms, *A Bullet in the Ballet* (1938)
Cornelius Conyn and Jon C. Martin, *The Bali Ballet Murders* (1961)
Lucy Cores, *Corpse de Ballet* (1944)
Andrew Garve, *Came the Dawn* (1949)

Bass Motives: Mysteries of the Opera
Robert Barnard, *Death on the High C's* (1979)
Carter Brown, *The Savage Salomé* (1961)
Fred G. Jarvis, *Murder at the Met* (1971)
Gladys Mitchell, *Death at the Opera* (1934)
Chelsea Quinn Yarbro, *Music When Sweet Voices Die* (1979)

Best Mystery By a Soprano
Helen Traubel, *The Metropolitan Opera Murders* (1951)

Brush with Death: Art World Mysteries
Richard Cox, *The Botticelli Madonna* (1979)
Michael Innes, *One-Man Show* (1952)
Lawrence Sanders, *The Second Deadly Sin* (1977)
Dorothy L. Sayers, *Five Red Herrings* (1931)
Clarissa Watson, *The Bishop in the Back Seat* (1979)

■ UNDERCOVER TALES

25 Especially Good Modern Espionage Novels
Ted Allbeury, *A Choice of Enemies* (1971)
Desmond Bagley, *The Enemy* (1978)
Victor Canning, *Birdcage* (1979)
Francis Clifford, *The Naked Runner* (1967)
James Coltrane, *Talon* (1978)

A good detective story is the answer to Lowell's question, "What is so rare as a day in June?"

—FRANKLIN DELANO ROOSEVELT

Kenneth Follett, *Eye of the Needle* (1978)
Frederick Forsyth, *The Odessa File* (1972)
Brian Freemantle, *The Man Who Wanted Tomorrow* (1975)
Philip Friedman, *The Termination Order* (1979)
Sarah Gainham, *Night Falls on the City* (1967)
Brian Garfield, *Hopscotch* (1974)
Jack Higgins, *Day of Judgment* (1979)
Peter Hill, *The Fanatics* (1978)
John Howlett, *The Christmas Spy* (1975)
Charles McCarry, *The Tears of Autumn* (1975)
Wilson McCarthy, *The Detail* (1974)
Helen MacInnes, *The Salzburg Connection* (1968)
George Markstein, *The Goering Testament* (1979)
Joe Poyer, *The Chinese Agenda* (1972)
Robert Rosenblum, *The Mushroom Cave* (1973)
Gerald Seymour, *Harry's Game* (1975)
Douglas Terman, *First Strike* (1979)
Ross Thomas, *The Eighth Dwarf* (1979)
Trevanian, *The Eiger Sanction* (1973)
Edward Weissmiller, *The Serpent Sleeping* (1962)

5 Classic Spy Stories
Eric Ambler, *The Mask of Dimitrios* (1939)
John Buchan, *Hunting Tower* (1922)
Erskine Childers, *The Riddle of the Sands* (1903)
W. Somerset Maugham, *Ashenden: The British Agent* (1927)
E. Phillips Oppenheim, *The Great Impersonator* (1920)

10 Best Spy Series

Author	Agent	Representative Work
William Buckley, Jr.	Blackford Oakes	*Saving the Queen* (1975)
James Grady	Ronald Malcolm	*Six Days of the Condor* (1974)
Ian Fleming	James Bond	*Casino Royale* (1953)
Kenneth Follett	Philis	*Bishop's Pawn* (1979)
Adam Hall	Quiller	*The Quiller Memorandum* (1965)
Joseph Hone	Marlow	*The Private Sector* (1971)
James Mitchell	Callan	*Death in Bright Water* (1974)

Hugh McLeave	Paul Brodie	*A Borderline Case* (1978)
Ritchie Perry	Marcus Aurelius Farrow	*The Manchester Thing* (1972)
Angus Ross	Piers Roper	*The Shakeout* (1970)

Spy Novel Instant Title Kit

Simply take one word from each of the columns below and, behold, you have a title guaranteed to appeal to the most discerning spy-thriller fan. All the words, incidentally, are from actual recent titles.

The	*Midas*	*Consequence*
	Caesar	*Code*
	Obelisk	*Conspiracy*
	Rhineman	*Exchange*
	Scarlatti	*Inheritance*
	Kobra	*Manifesto*
	Coventry	*Option*
	Hamlet	*Warning*
	Gemini	*Contenders*
	Quiller	*Memorandum*
	Tangent	*Objective*
	Borman	*Brief*
	Lansing	*Legacy*
	Rheingold	*Route*
	Alpha	*List*
	Carnellian	*Circle*
	Osterman	*Weekend*
	Alvarez	*Journal*
	D'artagnan	*Signature*
	Kermanshah	*Transfer*
	Lasko	*Tangent*
	Telemann	*Touch*
	Ipcress	*File*
	Kilroy	*Gambit*
	Hawkeland	*Cache*
	Ludlum	*Formula*

> *Anyone who hopes that in time it may be possible to abolish war should give serious thought to the problem of satisfying harmlessly the instincts that we inherit from long generations of savages. For my part I find a sufficient outlet in detective stories, where I alternately identify myself with the murderer and the huntsman-detective.*
>
> —BERTRAND RUSSELL

■ CONSORTS IN CRIME

Marriage Partners in Crime-Solving: 5 Favorite Couples
Ivor and Sue Maddox: Elizabeth Linington, *Consequence of Crime* (1980)

Peter and Iris Duluth: Patrick Quentin, *Puzzle for Fools* (1936)

Tuppence and Tommy Beresford: Agatha Christie, *Secret Adversary* (1922)

Pamela and Jerry North: Richard & Francis Lockridge, *Norths Meet Murder* (1940)

Lyn and Bea Wentworth: Richard Forrest, *The Death in the Willows* (1979)

Marriage Partners in Crime-Writing
The Gordons, *The Night Before the Wedding* (1969)

The Hanshews, *The Amber Junk* (1924)

Nan and Ivan Lyons, *Someone Is Killing the Great Chefs of Europe* (1978)

Richard and Frances Lockridge, *With Option to Die* (1967)

Maj Sjöwall and Per Wahloö, *The Locked Room* (1973)

Marriage Partners of Crime Solvers
Match each of the detectives in the first column with his spouse in the opposite column.

1. Chief Insp. Roderick Alleyn   A. Miriam
2. Sgt. Cribb   B. Emmy
3. Cmdr. Gideon   C. Arlette

4. David Small   D. Dora
5. John Appleby   E. Agatha Troy
6. Insp. Van der Valk   F. Amanda Fitton
7. Lord Peter Wimsey   G. Millie
8. Chief Insp. Tibbett   H. Kate
9. Albert Campion   I. Judith Raven
10. Insp. Wexford   J. Harriet Vane

Answers
1–E, 2–G, 3–H, 4–A, 5–I, 6–C, 7–J, 8–B, 9–F, 10–D

Her Winn-Some Best

Dilys Winn, perpetrator of *Murder, Ink* and *Murderess, Ink*, both published by Workman Publishing Company, prepared this list of mystery reading recommendations as part of the promotion of her books.

Margery Allingham, *The Tiger in the Smoke* (1952)
John Dickson Carr, *The Three Coffins* (1935)
Raymond Chandler, *The Lady in the Lake* (1943)
Agatha Christie, *The Pale Horse* (1961)
Wilkie Collins, *The Woman in White* (1860)
Sir Arthur Conan Doyle, *The Sign of Four* (1890)
Nicholas Freeling, *The King of the Rainy Country* (1966)
Graham Greene, *The Confidential Agent* (1939)
Dashiell Hammett, *The Glass Key* (1931)
P. D. James, *Shroud for a Nightingale* (1971)
Ross McDonald, *The Chill* (1964)
John MacDonald, *The Girl, The Gold Watch, and Everything* (1962)
Ngaio Marsh, *Vintage Murder* (1937)
Dorothy L. Sayers, *The Documents in the Case* (1930)
Georges Simenon, *Maigret and the Headless Corpse* (1968)
Maj Sjöwall & Per Wahloö, *Roseanna* (1967)
Josephine Tey, *Brat Farrar* (1949)
Ross Thomas, *The Cold War Swap* (1966)
Donald E. Westlake, *The Hot Rock* (1970)

5 Best Murder Novels
From Dilys Winn, *Murder, Ink* (1977)

L. P. Davies, *Who Is Lewis Pindar?* (1965)
Jack Finney, *Time and Again* (1970)
Dashiell Hammett, *The Glass Key* (1931)
Julian Symons, *The 31st of February* (1950)
Josephine Tey, *The Daughter of Time* (1951)

Future Felonies: 5 Sci-Fi Detective Novels
David Bear, *Keeping Time* (1979)
Lloyd Biggle, Jr., *All the Colors of Darkness* (1975)
Lee Killough, *The Doppelgänger Effect* (1979)
Wilson Tucker, *Tomorrow Plus X* (1970)
Ian Wallace, *The Sign of the Mute Medium* (1977)

■ MORE OF THE BEST: THE DAGGER WINNERS

The British Crime Writers Association annually presents its Gold Dagger Award to the best British crime novel of the year. Since 1969 it has presented The Silver Dagger to the runner-up. Between 1964 and 1969, the runner-up was merely named the best British or foreign crime novel as the case may have been. The Gold Dagger winners are listed first after each date below.

1955: Winston Graham, *The Little Walls*
1956: Edward Grierson, *The Second Man*
1957: Julian Symons, *The Colour of Murder*
1958: Margot Bennett, *Someone From the Past*
1959: Eric Ambler, *A Passage of Arms*
1960: Lionel Davidson, *The Night of Wenceslas*
1961: Mary Kelly, *The Spoilt Kill*
1962: Joan Fleming, *When I Grow Rich*
1963: John LeCarré, *The Spy Who Came in From the Cold*
1964: H. R. F. Keating, *The Perfect Murder*
Patricia Highsmith, *The Two Faces of January* (best foreign)

1965: Ross McDonald, *The Far Side of the Dollar*
       Gavin Lyall, *Midnight Plus One* (best British)
1966: Lionel Davidson, *A Long Way to Shiloh*
       John Ball, *In the Heat of the Night* (best foreign)
1967: Emma Lathan, *Murder Against the Grain*
       Eric Ambler, *Dirty Story* (best British)
1968: Peter Dickinson, *Skin Deep*
       Sebastien Japrisot, *The Lady in the Car* (best foreign)
1969: Peter Dickinson, *A Pride of Heroes*
       Francis Clifford, *Another Way of Dying*
       Rex Stout, *The Father Hunt* (best foreign)
1970: Joan Fleming, *Young Man, I Think You're Dying*
       Anthony Price, *The Labyrinth Makers*
1971: James McClure, *The Steam Pig*
       P. D. James, *Shroud for a Nightingale*
1972: Eric Ambler, *The Levanter*
       Victor Canning, *The Rainbird Pattern*
1973: Gwen Butler: *A Coffin for Pandora*
       Robert J. Littell, *The Defection of A. J. Lewinter*
1974: Anthony Price, *Other Paths to Glory*
       Francis Clifford, *The Grosvenor Square Goodbye*
1975: Nicholas Meyer, *The Seven Percent Solution*
       P. D. James, *The Black Tower*
1976: Ruth Rendell, *Demon in My View*
       James McClure, *Rogue Eagle*
1979: John LeCarré, *The Honourable Schoolboy*
       William McIlvanney, *Laidlaw*
1978: Lionel Davidson, *The Chelsea Murders*
       Peter Lovesey, *Waxwork*
1979: Audrey Williamson, *The Mystery of the Princes*
       Harry Hawkes, *The Capture of the Black Panther*
1980: Dick Francis, *Whip Hand*
       Colin Dexter, *Service of All the Dead*

■ MODERN GOTHIC ROMANCES

The original gothic novel has bred with *Jane Eyre* to produce the Gothic Romance—visible at every supermarket checkout stand. Although a goodly proportion of these efforts seem to have been computer-written according to a very old program, nevertheless occasionally a fresh and fine volume is produced. Here are fifteen that a Gothic-devotée friend recommends.

5 Best Historical Gothics
Susan Howatch, *Cashelmara* (1974)
Barbara Michaels, *Greygallows* (1972)
Anya Seton, *Green Darkness* (1972)
Sandra Shulman, *The Brides of Devil's Leap* (1968)
Sylvia Thorpe, *Stranger on the Moor* (1955)

5 Best Sentimental Gothics
Elizabeth Cadell, *Brimstone in the Garden* (1950)
Glenda Carrington, *Master of Greystone* (1977)
Elsie Cromwell, *Ivorstone Manor* (1970)
Cecily Crowe, *Northwater* (1968)
Erica Lindley, *The Brackenroyd Inheritance* (1975)

5 Best Romantic Suspense Novels
Madeleine Brent, *Moonraker's Bride* (1973)
Evelyn Berckman, *The Heir of Starvelings* (1967)
Joy Ann Blackwood, *The Ghost at Lost Lovers Lake* (1973)
Jacqueline LaTourette, *The Pompeii Scroll* (1975)
Phyllis Whitney, *Black Amber* (1964)

We romantic authors are there to make people feel and not think. A historical romance is the only kind of book where chastity really counts.

—BARBARA CARTLAND

Pagan Raptures of Passion or The Sweet/Savage Sell
The Gothic Romance formula calls for a title with certain time-honored words that will subliminally press the "buy" button of the Gothic consumer. Here are some favorites, all real and contemporary.

Love's Pagan Heart	*Tears of Passion*	*Savage Fancy*
With Rapture Bound	*Rapture*	*Sweet Savage Love*
Stolen Rapture	*A Splendid Passion*	*A Feast of Passions*
Blaze of Passion	*Savage Love*	*The Dark Side of Passion*
Desert Rapture	*Passion Star*	*The Passionate Savage*
The Eden Passion	*Royal Savage*	*The Savage Eden*
Love's Sweet Agony	*Sweet Nemesis*	*The Savage Aristocrat*
Ports of Passion	*Savage Possession*	*Passion's Blazing Triumph*

The perfect hostess will see to it that the works of male and female authors are properly separated on her bookshelves. Their proximity, unless they happen to be married, should not be tolerated.

—BOOK OF ETIQUETTE (1863)

■ HISTORICAL FICTION

Egypt: 5 Nileistic Novels
Allen Drury, *A God Against the Gods* (1976)
Howard Fast, *Moses* (1958)
Pauline Gedge, *Child of the Morning* (1977)
Jacquetta Hawkes, *King of the Two Lands* (1966)
Mika Waltari, *The Egyptian* (1954)

Greece: A Dekalist
Alfred Duggan, *Besieger of Cities* (1963)
Robert Graves, *Hercules, My Shipmate* (1945)
Naomi Mitchison, *The Corn King and the Spring Queen* (1931)
Robert Payne, *Alexander The God* (1954)
Wilder Penfield, *The Torch* (1960)
Martha Rolfheart, *My Name is Sappho* (1974)
Mary Renault, *The King Must Die* (1958)
Gladys Schmitt, *Electra* (1965)
Rosemary Sutcliff, *The Flowers of Adonis* (1970)
Henry Treece, *Jason* (1961)

Rome: Imperial XV
Bryher, *Roman Wall* (1954)
Edward Bulwer-Lytton, *The Last Days of Pompeii* (1834)

Alfred Duggan, *Three's Company* (1958)
Howard Fast, *Spartacus* (1958)
Robert Graves, *I, Claudius* (1934)
John Hersey, *The Conspiracy* (1972)
Vintila Horia, *God Was Born in Exile* (1961)
Arthur Koestler, *The Gladiators* (1939)
Walter Pater, *Marius the Epicurean* (1885)
H. Sienkiewicz, *Quo Vadis?* (1896)
Rosemary Sutcliff, *Eagle of the North* (1954)
Rex Warner, *Young Caesar* (1958)
Thornton Wilder, *The Ides of March* (1942)
John Williams, *Augustus* (1972)
Margaret Yourcenar, *Hadrian's Memoirs* (1954)

Feudal Efforts: 10 Novels of the Middle Ages
Herman Hesse, *Narcissus and Goldmund* (1930)
Cecelia Holland, *The Earl* (1971)
Victor Hugo, *The Hunchback of Notre Dame* (1831)
Hope Muntz, *The Golden Warrior* (1949)
Zoé Oldenbourg, *Destiny of Fire* (1961)
Charles Reade, *The Cloister and the Hearth* (1861)
Sir Walter Scott, *Ivanhoe* (1819)
Sigrid Undset, *Kristan Lavrandsdatter* (1920–22)
Helen Waddell, *Peter Abelard* (1933)
Helen White, *Bird of Fire* (1958)

The Great Novella: Heinrich von Kleist, *Michael Kohlhaas* (1808)

Revival! 10 Novels of the Renaissance

On the Continent: 5 Novels

George Eliot, *Romola* (1863)
Cecelia Holland, *City of God: A Novel of the Borgias* (1979)
Dmitri Merezhkovsky, *The Romance of Leonardo Da Vinci* (1902)
Samuel Shellabarger, *Prince of Foxes* (1947)
Irving Stone, *The Agony and the Ecstacy* (1961)

In Elizabethan England: 5 Novels
Anthony Burgess, *Nothing Like the Sun* (1965)
George Garrett, *Death of the Fox* (1971)
Mary M. Luke, *A Crown for Elizabeth* (1970)
Colin MacInnes, *Three Years to Play* (1969)
Sir Walter Scott, *Kenilworth* (1821)

■ TEST YOUR SENSE OF PLACE

From George Eliot's Middlemarch and Sherwood Anderson's Winesburg, Ohio, to John Steinbeck's Cannery Row and John Cheever's Wapshot, great writers have been able to create living communities. Here is a matching quiz designed to put you through your places.

1. Macondo	A. Fedor Dostoevski *(The Brothers Karamazov)*
2. Gopher Prairie	B. Gustave Flaubert *(Madame Bovary)*
3. Yoknapatawpha County	C. John O'Hara
4. Wessex	D. John Updike
5. Catfish Row	E. Marcel Proust
6. Altamont, Catawba	F. Sinclair Lewis *(Main Street)*
7. West Egg, Long Island	G. William Faulkner
8. Combray	H. Arnold Bennett
9. Tarbox, Mass.	I. Anthony Trollope (the Barsetshire novels)
10. Gibbsville, Pa.	J. F. Scott Fitzgerald *(The Great Gatsby)*
11. Shady Hill	K. Thomas Hardy
12. Yonville	L. Thomas Wolfe
13. Skotoprigonyevski	M. Gabriel García Márquez
14. Five Towns	N. DuBose Heyward *(Porgy)*
15. Barchester	O. John Cheever

■ TALE TEST

Try to tie the twenty tales to their tellers.

1. *A Tale of Two Cities*
2. *The Tale of Genji*
3. *The Tale of a Tub*
4. *Canterbury Tale*
5. *The Old Wives' Tales*
6. *The Piazza Tales*
7. *Tales of the South Pacific*
8. *Twice-Told Tales*
9. *Winter's Tales*
10. *Incredible Tales*
11. *Tales of the Grotesque and Arabesque*
12. *Tales from Shakespeare*
13. *Plain Tales from the Hills*
14. *Tales of a Traveller*
15. *Old Country Tales*
16. *The Leatherstocking Tales*
17. *Tales of the Jazz Age*
18. *Youth and Other Tales*
19. *Tales of the Don*
20. *Roman Tales*

A. Edgar Allan Poe
B. Joseph Conrad
C. Alberto Moravia
D. Charles Lamb (Elia)
E. James Fenimore Cooper
F. Jonathan Swift
G. Rudyard Kipling
H. Charles Dickens
I. F. Scott Fitzgerald
J. Mikhail Sholokhov
K. Herman Melville
L. Washington Irving
M. Murasaki Shikibu
N. Sholem Aleichem
O. Isak Dinesen
P. Arnold Bennett
Q. Saki
R. Geoffrey Chaucer
S. Nathaniel Hawthorne
T. James A. Michener

Answers
1–H, 2–M, 3–F, 4–R, 5–P, 6–K, 7–T, 8–S, 9–O, 10–Q, 11–A, 12–D,
13–G, 14–L, 15–N, 16–E, 17–I, 18–B, 19–J, 20–C

The novel is something that never was before and will not be again.
—EUDORA WELTY

■ MODERN BRITISH NOVELS

The Best Twentieth-Century British Novels
Reprinted from *Good Reading* with permission of R. R. Bowker Company. Copyright © 1978 by the Committee on College Reading.

Kingsley Amis, *Lucky Jim* (1954)
———, *One Fat Englishman* (1964)
Max Beerbohm, *Zuleika Dobson* (1911)
Arnold Bennett, *The Old Wives' Tale* (1908)
Elizabeth Bowen, *The Death of the Heart* (1938)
John Braine, *Room at the Top* (1957)
Anthony Burgess, *A Clockwork Orange* (1962)
Joyce Cary, *The Horse's Mouth* (1944)
Ivy Compton-Burnett, *Bullivant and the Lambs* (1948)
Joseph Conrad, *The Nigger of the Narcissus* (1897)
———, *Lord Jim* (1900)
———, *Heart of Darkness* (1902)
———, *Nostromo* (1904)
Norman Douglas, *South Wind* (1917)
Lawrence Durrell, *Alexandria Quartet* (1957–60)
Ford Madox Ford, *The Good Soldier* (1915)
———, *Parade's End* (1924–28)
E. M. Forster, *The Longest Journey* (1907)
———, *A Passage to India* (1924)
John Fowles, *The Magus* (1966)
John Galsworthy, *The Forsyte Saga* (1906–21)
William Golding, *Lord of the Flies* (1954)
Henry Green, *Loving* (1945)
Graham Greene, *Brighton Rock* (1938)
———, *The Heart of the Matter* (1948)
W. H. Hudson, *Green Mansions* (1904)
Richard Hughes, *A High Wind in Jamaica* (1929)
Aldous Huxley, *Point Counter Point* (1928)
———, *Brave New World* (1932)
Christopher Isherwood, *The Berlin Stories* (1946)
James Joyce, *Portrait of the Artist as a Young Man* (1916)
———, *Ulysses* (1922)

Rudyard Kipling, *Kim* (1901)
D. H. Lawrence, *Sons and Lovers* (1913)
———, *The Rainbow* (1915)
———, *Lady Chatterley's Lover* (1928)
Doris Lessing, *Children of Violence* (1965–69)
Malcolm Lowry, *Under the Volcano* (1947)
W. Somerset Maugham, *Of Human Bondage* (1915)
———, *The Moon and Sixpence* (1919)
Iris Murdoch, *The Flight from the Enchanter* (1956)
———, *A Severed Head* (1961)
V. S. Naipaul, *A House for Mr. Biswas* (1961)
———, *Guerrillas* (1975)
Liam O'Flaherty, *The Informer* (1926)
George Orwell, *Animal Farm* (1945)
———, *1984* (1949)
J. B. Priestley, *The Good Companions* (1929)
Anthony Powell, *Dance to the Music of Time* (1951–73)
Jean Rhys, *Quartet* (1928), *Good Morning, Midnight* (1939),
    Wide Sargasso Sea (1966)
Alan Sillitoe, *Saturday Night and Sunday Morning* (1958)
———, *The Loneliness of the Long-Distance Runner* (1959)
C. P. Snow, *Strangers and Brothers* (1940–70)
Muriel Spark, *Memento Mori* (1959)
J. R. R. Tolkien, *The Lord of the Rings* (1954–56)
Evelyn Waugh, *A Handful of Dust* (1934)
———, *Brideshead Revisited* (1945)
H. G. Wells, *Tono Bungay* (1908)
Patrick White, *Voss* (1957)
Angus Wilson, *Anglo-Saxon Attitudes* (1956)
Virginia Woolf, *To the Lighthouse* (1927)
———, *Orlando* (1928)

Transatlantic Transitions

For reasons not always evident, publishers in the United States have on occasion changed the title of an English novel for the American edition. Here are ten examples; first the English title, then the American title.

Anthony Burgess, *The Malayan Trilogy: The Long Day Wanes*
Arnold Bennett, *The Card: Denry the Audacious*

William Golding, *Pincher Martin: The Two Deaths of Christopher Martin*

Robert Graves, *The Golden Fleece: Hercules, My Shipmate*

Graham Greene, *The Power and the Glory: The Labrynthine Ways*

L. P. Hartley, *The Shrimp and the Anemone: The West Window*

Richard Hughes, *A High Wind in Jamaica: The Innocent Voyage*

Christopher Isherwood, *Mr. Norris Changes Trains: The Last of Mr. Norris*

Pamela Hansford Johnson, *Murder's A Swine: The Grinning Pig*

Colin Wilson, *The Killers: Lingard*

Best British Novels: The Booker Prize

Administered by the National Book League, the prize is offered annually for the best novel published in the United Kingdom during the year of the award. The author must be a citizen of Britain or the British Commonwealth, Ireland, or South Africa. Following are the winners and runners-up since its inception.

1969

P. H. Newby, *Something to Answer For*

Muriel Spark, *The Public Image*
Gordon M. Williams, *From Scenes Like These*
Nicholas Mosley, *The Impossible Object*
Barry England, *Figures In a Landscape*
Iris Murdoch, *The Nice and the Good*

1970

Bernice Rubens, *The Elected Member*

William Trevor, *Mrs. Eckdorf in O'Neill's Hotel*
A. L. Barker, *John Brown's Body*
Elizabeth Bowen, *Eva Trout*
Terence Wheeler, *The Conjunction*
Iris Murdoch, *Bruno's Dream*

1971
V. S. Naipaul, *In a Free State*

Elizabeth Taylor, *Mrs. Palfrey at the Claremont*
Doris Lessing, *Briefing for Descent into Hell*
Thomas Kilroy, *The Big Chapel*
Derek Robinson, *Goshawk Squadron*
Mordecai Richler, *St. Urbain's Horseman*

1972
John Berger, *G*

Thomas Keneally, *The Chant of Jimmy Blacksmith*
David Storey, *Pasmore*
Susan Hill, *Bird of Night*

1973
J. G. Farrell, *The Siege of Krishnapur*

Iris Murdoch, *The Black Prince*
Beryl Bainbridge, *The Dressmaker*
Elizabeth Mavor, *The Green Equinox*

1974
Nadine Gordimer, *The Conservationist*
Stanley Middleton, *Holiday*

Kingsley Amis, *Ending Up*
Beryl Bainbridge, *The Bottle Factory Outing*
C. P. Snow, *In Their Wisdom*

1975
Ruth Prawer Jhabvala, *Heat and Dust*

Thomas Keneally, *Gossip from the Forest*

1976
David Storey, *Saville*

André Brink, *An Instant in the Wind*
R. C. Hutchison, *Rising*

Brian Moore, *The Doctor's Wife*
Julian Rathbone, *King Fisher Lives*
William Trevor, *The Children of Dynmouth*

1977
Paul Scott, *Staying On*

Paul Bailey, *Peter Smart's Confessions*
Caroline Blackwood, *Great Granny Webs*
Jennifer Johnston, *Shadows of Our Skin*
Penelope Lively, *The Road to Lichfield*
Barbara Pym, *Quartet in Autumn*

1978
Iris Murdoch, *The Sea, the Sea*

Kingsley Amis, *Jake's Thing*
André Brink, *Rumours of Rain*
Penelope Fitzgerald, *The Bookshop*
Jane Gardam, *God on the Rocks*
Bernice Rubens, *A Five-Year Sentence*

1979
Penelope Fitzgerald, *Offshore*

Thomas Keneally, *Confederates*
V. S. Naipaul, *A Bend in the River*
Julian Rathbone, *Joseph*
Fay Weldon, *Praxis*

1980
Anthony Burgess, *Earthly Powers*

J. L. Carr, *A Month in the Country*
Anita Desai, *Clear Light of Day*
William Golding, *Rites of Passage*
Alice Munro, *The Beggar Maid*
Julia O'Faolain, *No Country for Young Men*

Read and Gone: 10 Forgotten Modern English Classics
Walter Allen, *All in a Lifetime* (1959)

Jocelyn Brooks, *The Image of a Drawn Sword* (1950)
Cyril Connolly, *The Unquiet Grave* (1945)
William Cooper, *Disquiet and Peace* (1956)
William Gerhardie, *Of Mortal Love* (1936)
Raymer Heppenstall, *The Connecting Door* (1962)
Thomas Hinde, *Mr. Nicholos* (1952)
Rosamond Lehmann, *Dusty Answer* (1927)
May Sinclair, *Mary Olivier: A Life* (1919)
Angus Wilson, *The Old Man at the Zoo* (1961)

The Angry Young Men: 5 Great British Working-Class Novels
Stan Barstow, *A Kind of Loving* (1960)
John Braine, *Room at the Top* (1957)
Alan Sillitoe, *Saturday Night and Sunday Morning* (1958)
David Storey, *The Sporting Life* (1960)
Keith Waterhouse, *Billy Liar* (1960)

Gefilte Fish and Chips: 10 Anglo-Jewish Novels
Chaim Bermant, *The Last Supper* (1973)
Anthony Blond, *Family Business* (1979)
Gerda Charles, *The Crossing Point* (1960)
Louis Golding, *Magnolia Street* (1932)
Bernard Kops, *By the Waters of Whitechapel* (1969)
Emmanuel Litvinoff, *Journey Through a Small Planet* (1972)
Wolf Mankowitz, *A Kid for Two Farthings* (1954)
Frederic Raphael, *The Limits of Love* (1960)
C. P. Snow, *The Conscience of the Rich* (1958)
G. B. Stern, *A Deputy Was King* (1926)

Classic
Israel Zangwill, *Children of the Ghetto* (1892)

The Bards of Wales: 15 Modern Welsh Novels
Alexander Cordell, *The Rape of the Fair Country* (1959)
Rhys Davies, *The Best of Rhys Davies* (1979)
Caradoc Evans, *This Way to Heaven* (1934)
James Hanley, *The Welsh Sonata* (1954)
John L. Hughes, *Before the Crying Ends* (1977)

Glyn Jones, *The Walk Home* (1963)
Gwyn Jones, *The Island of Apples* (1965)
Richard Jones, *The Tower Is Everywhere* (1971)
Barbara Kees, *Prophet of the Wind* (1973)
Richard Llewellyn, *How Green Was My Valley* (1940)
Kate Roberts, *Feet in Chains* (1978)
Haydn Stephens, *Dafydd* (1978)
Gwyn Thomas, *A Wolf at Dusk* (1958)
Hilda Vaughan, *Pardon and Peace* (1943)
Raymond Williams, *Border Country* (1960)

Great Scots: 10 Modern Scottish Novels
Lillian Beckwith, *A Sea for Breakfast* (1926)
George Mackay Brown, *Greenvoe* (1972)
Dominic Cooper, *The Dead of Winter: A Novel of Modern Scotland* (1975)
A. J. Cronin, *A Song of Sixpence* (1964)
Elspeth Davies, *The Night of the Funny Hats* (1980)
Lewis Grassic Gibbon, *A Scots Quair Trilogy* (1932)
Clifford Hanly, *The Hot Month* (1967)
Robin Jenkins, *Fergus Lamont* (1979)
Eric Linklater, *Magnus Merriman* (1934)
David Walker, *Come Back, Geordie* (1966)

Best Novel of Scotland by an American
Joanna Ostrow, . . . *In the Highlands Since Time Immemorial* (1970)

Wild Irish Prose: 10 Irish Short Story Tellers
Patrick Boyle, *A View From Calvary* (1976)
Aidan Higgins, *Asylum and Other Stories* (1978)
Benedict Kiely, *The State of Ireland* (1980)
Mary Lavin, *Collected Stories* (1971)
James McGahern, *Getting Through* (1978)
Eugene McCall, *Heritage* (1978)
Michael McLaverty, *Collected Stories* (1978)
Bryon MacMahon, *The End of the World and Other Stories* (1976)
James Plunkett, *The Trusting and the Maimed* (1959)
William Trevor, *Angels at the Ritz* (1975)

The Most Dedicated Irish Writer

Christy Brown's novel *Down All the Days* was published when the author was thirty-seven years old. One of twenty-two children, he spent his life in a Dublin slum, the scene of the novel. Born with a severe case of cerebral palsy, he has had full use of only one limb, his left foot. With the small toe of that foot, for more than fifteen years, Brown typed the manuscript of his novel.

■ THE CONTINENTAL SHELF: MODERN EUROPEAN FICTION

The Best Twentieth-Century Continental Novels

Reprinted from *Good Reading* with permission of R. R. Bowker Company. Copyright © 1978 by The Committee on College Reading.

Simone de Beauvoir, *The Mandarins* (1955)
Samuel Beckett, *Three Novels: Molloy, Malone Dies,* and *The Unnamable* (1951–53)
———, *Murphy* (1938)
Andrey Biely, *St. Petersburg* (1911)
Heinrich Böll, *Billiards at Half-Past Nine* (1959)
Hermann Broch, *The Sleepwalkers* (1932)
Italo Calvino, *Invisible Cities* (1974)
Albert Camus, *The Stranger* (1946)
———, *The Plague* (1948)
Karel Capek, *War With the Newts* (1937)
Louis Ferdinand Céline, *Journey to the End of the Night* (1932)
———, *Death on the Installment Plan* (1936)
Sidonie Gabrielle Colette, *Six Novels* (1960)
Friedrich Durrenmatt, *The Pledge* (1959)
———, *The Quarry* (1961)
Anatole France, *Penguin Island* (1908)
Jean Genêt, *Our Lady of the Flowers* (1942)
André Gide, *The Counterfeiters* (1927)
———, *The Immoralist* (1902)

Günter Grass, *The Tin Drum* (1959)
————, *Cat and Mouse* (1961)
————, *Dog Years* (1963)
Knut Hamsun, *Growth of the Soil* (1920)
Peter Handke, *The Goalies Anxiety at the Penalty Kick* (1972)
————, *Short Letter, Long Farewell* (1974)
Jaroslav Hasek, *The Good Soldier Schweik* (1923)
Hermann Hesse, *Steppenwolf* (1929)
————, *Siddhartha* (1951)
Franz Kafka, *The Trial* (1937)
————, *The Castle* (1926)
Nikos Kazantzakis, *Zorba the Greek* (1952)
Arthur Koestler, *Darkness at Noon* (1941)
Pär Lagerkvist, *Barabbas* (1951)
Carlo Levi, *Christ Stopped at Eboli* (1945)
André Malraux, *Man's Fate* (1933)
Thomas Mann, *Buddenbrooks* (1901)
————, *The Magic Mountain* (1924)
————, *The Joseph Tetralogy* (1924–44)
François Mauriac, *Therese* (1927)
Alberto Moravia, *The Time of Indifference* (1953)
————, *Two Adolescents* (1950)
Robert Musil, *The Man Without Qualities* (1931–43)
Boris Pasternak, *Dr. Zhivago* (1958)
Cesare Pavese, *The Moon and the Bonfire* (1950)
Marcel Proust, *Remembrance of Things Past* (1913–28)
Erich Maria Remarque, *All Quiet on the Western Front* (1929)
Alain Robbe-Grillet, *The Voyeur* (1958)
Jules Romains, *The Death of a Nobody* (1911)
————, *Men of Good Will* (1932–47)
Nathalie Sarraute, *The Golden Fruits* (1964)
Jean-Paul Sartre, *Nausea* (1938)
Mikhail Sholokhov, *The Silent Don* (1934–41)
Ignazio Silone, *Bread and Wine* (1936)
Aleksandr I. Solzhenitsyn, *The First Circle* (1964, 1968)
————, *Cancer Ward* (1968)
Sigrid Undset, *Kristin Lavransdatter* (1920–22)
Franz Werfel, *The Forty Days of Musa Dagh* (1934)
Yevgeny Zamyatin, *We* (1924)

172

5 Novels of Greece

John Fowles, *The Magus* (1977)
Stratis Haviaris, *When the Tree Sings* (1979)
James Merrill, *The (Diblos) Notebook* (1965)
Wright Morris, *What a Way to Go* (1962)
Glenway Wescott, *Apartment in Athens* (1945)

Venetian Lines: 5 Novels of Venice

Hans Habe, *Palazzo* (1975)
Ernest Hemingway, *Across the River and into the Trees* (1950)
Henry James, *The Aspern Papers* (1888)
Thomas Mann, *Death in Venice* (1913)
Muriel Spark, *Territorial Rights* (1979)

■ OTHER CONTINENTS

India

Sahib Stories: 5 Novels of the Raj

J. G. Farrell, *The Siege of Krishapur* (1973)
E. M. Forster, *A Passage to India* (1924)
Rudyard Kipling, *Kim* (1901)
John Masters, *Bhowani Junction* (1954)
Paul Scott, *The Raj Quartet* (1966–75)

5 Novels of Modern India

Stephen Alter, *Neglected Lives* (1978)
Rumer Godden, *The River* (1946)
Jon Godden, *Ahmed and the Old Lady* (1975)
Ruth Prawer Jhabvala, *Heat and Dust* (1975)
Christine Weston, *Indigo* (1943)

5 Modern Indian Novelists

Anita Desai, *Fire on the Mountain* (1977)
Kamala Markandaya, *Nectar in a Sieve* (1955)
Vyankatesh Madgulkar, *The Village Had No Walls* (1960)
R. K. Narayan, *The Man-Eater of Malgudi* (1961)
Raja Rao, *The Serpent and the Rope* (1960)

China

5 Tales of China

Alexander Cordell, *The Dream and the Destiny* (1975)
John Hersey, *A Single Pebble* (1956)
André Malraux, *Man's Fate* (1933)
Richard McKinna, *The Sand Pebbles* (1962)
Theodore H. White, *The Mountain Road* (1958)

Modern Chinese Fiction

Yuang-tsung Chen, *The Dragon's Village* (1980)
Hsia Chih-yen, *The Coldest Winter in Peking* (1939)
Lu Hsun, *Selected Stories* (1972)
Chen Jo-Hsi, *The Execution of Mayor Yin, and Other Stories
    from the Great Proletarian Cultural Revolution* (1978)
Lao She, *The Drum Singers* (1952)

In Shantung Americans: 5 Recent Reports from China

John Kenneth Galbraith, *A China Passage* (1973)
Arthur Miller and Inge Morath, *Chinese Encounters* (1979)
Robert Payne, *A Rage for China* (1977)
Ross Terrill, *Flowers on an Iron Tree* (1975)
Barbara Tuchman, *Notes from China* (1972)

Japan

5 Tales of Japan

Nibuko Albery, *Balloon Top* (1978)
James Clavell, *Shogun* (1976)
Mona Gardner, *Middle Heaven* (1950)
James E. Michener, *Sayonara* (1954)
Shelley Mydans, *The Vermillion Bridge* (1980)

5 Modern Japanese Novelists

Kobo Abe, *The Woman in the Dunes* (1964)
Shusako Endo, *When I Whistle* (1979)
Yasunari Kawabata, *The Snow Country* (1969)
Yukio Mishima, *The Temple of the Golden Pavilion* (1956)
Junichiro Tanizake, *The Makioka Sisters* (1957)

The Greatest Japanese Novel
The Tale of Genji by Murasaki Shikiou, Heian period
(794–1185). Translated by Arthur Waley (1925–33) and by
Edward Seidensticker (1978).

Promised Landscapes: Israel

5 Novels of Israel
Arthur Koestler, *Thieves in the Night* (1946)
Meyer Levin, *The Settlers* (1972)
James Michener, *The Source* (1965)
Leon Uris, *Exodus* (1960)
Elie Wiesel, *A Beggar in Jerusalem* (1970)

5 Modern Israeli Novels
Aharon Appelfeld, *Badenheim 1939* (1980)
Dahn Ben-Amitz, *To Remember, To Forget* (1973)
Shulamith Hareven, *City of Many Days* (1977)
Uri Orlev, *The Lead Soldiers* (1980)
Amos Oz, *Elsewhere, Perhaps* (1973)

Under Western Eyes: 10 Novels of Africa
Joyce Cary, *Mister Johnson* (1939)
Joseph Conrad, *Heart of Darkness* (1902)
Isak Dinesen, *Shadows in the Grass* (1960)
Graham Greene, *The Heart of the Matter* (1948)
Frederick Forsyth, *The Dogs of War* (1974)
Joseph Kessel, *The Lion* (1962)
V. S. Naipaul, *A Bend in the River* (1979)
Paul Theroux, *The Jungle Lovers* (1971)
John Updike, *The Coup* (1978)
Evelyn Waugh, *Black Mischief* (1932)

Byzantine Stories: 5 Tales of Turkey
Philip Glazebrook, *Byzantine Honeymoon* (1979)
Rose Macauley, *The Towers of Trebizond* (1956)
Richard Reinhardt, *The Ashes of Smyrna* (1971)
Edouard Roditi, *The Delights of Turkey* (1979)
Mary Lee Settle, *Blood Tie* (1977)

The Great Modern Turkish Novel
Yashar Kemal, *Memed, My Hawk* Trilogy (1961)

The Road to Mandalay: 5 Tales of Colonial Southern Asia

Anthony Burgess, *The Long Day Wanes (Malay Trilogy)* (1964)
J. G. Farrell, *The Singapore Grip* (1979)
Robin Jenkins, *The Holy Tree* (1969)
W. Somerset Maugham, *The Casuarina Tree* (1926)
George Orwell, *Burmese Days* (1934)

The Best Novel of Afghanistan
Joseph Kessel, *The Horsemen* (1968)

Tales of the Antipodes

The Great Australian Novel

Henry Handel Richardson, *Fortunes of Richard Mahony* (1917–29)

The Great Historical Novel

Eleanor Dark, *Timeless Land* (1941)

5 Postwar Australian Novels

James Aldridge, *The Untouchable Juli* (1975)
Thomas Keneally, *The Chant of Jimmy Blacksmith* (1972)
James Vance Marshall, *Walkabout* (1959)
Hal Porter, *A Bachelor's Children* (1962)
Patrick White, *The Tree of Man* (1955)

5 Modern New Zealand Novels

Joy Cowley, *Next in a Falling Tree* (1967)
Ian Cross, *The God Boy* (1957)
Janet Frame, *Yellow Flowers in the Antipodean Room* (1969)
Frank Sargeson, *Memoirs of a Peon* (1965)
Sylvia Ashton Warner, *Spinster* (1959)

A novel is a mirror carried along a main road.

—STENDHAL

■ BOOKS THAT CHANGED AMERICA

From *Books That Changed America* by Robert B. Downs (New York: Macmillan Publishing Co., 1970). Copyright © 1970 by Robert B. Downs. Used by permission of Macmillan Publishing Co., Inc.

Jane Addams, *Twenty Years at Hull House* (1910)
Charles Austin Beard, *An Economic Interpretation of the Constitution of the United States* (1913)
William Beaumont, *Experiments and Observations on the Gastric Juice and the Physiology of Digestion* (1833)
Edward Bellamy, *Looking Backward* (1888)
Benjamin Cardozo, *The Nature of the Judicial Process* (1921)
Rachel Carson, *Silent Spring* (1962)
Wilbur Joseph Cash, *The Mind of the South* (1941)
Abraham Flexner, *Medical Education in the United States and Canada* (1910)
John Kenneth Galbraith, *The Affluent Society* (1958)
Oliver Wendell Holmes, *The Contagiousness of Puerperal Fever* (1843)
Meriwether Lewis and William Clark, *History of the Expedition Under the Command of Captains Lewis and Clark* (1814)
Robert Staughton Lynd and Helen Lynd, *Middletown: A Study in Contemporary American Culture* (1929)
Alfred Thayer Mahan, *The Influence of Sea Power Upon History 1660–1783* (1890)
Horace Mann, *Reports* (1837–49)
H. L Mencken, *Prejudices* (1919–27)
Gunnar Myrdal, *An American Dilemma; The Negro Problem and Modern Democracy* (1944)
Thomas Paine, *Common Sense, Addressed to the Inhabitants of America* (1776)
Upton Sinclair, *The Jungle* (1905)
Joseph Smith, *The Book of Mormon* (1830)
Lincoln Steffens, *The Shame of the Cities* (1904)
Harriet Beecher Stowe, *Uncle Tom's Cabin* (1852)
Frederick Winslow Taylor, *The Principles of Scientific Management* (1911)

Henry David Thoreau, *Resistance to Civil Government* (1849)
Alexis de Tocqueville, *Democracy in America* (1835–40)
Frederick Jackson Turner, *The Significance of the Frontier in American History* (1893)

■ METROPOLITAN LIFE

Tales of the Imperial City: New York

Tales of Manhattan: 5 Classic Works of Fiction

John Dos Passos, *Manhattan Transfer* (1928)
O. Henry, *The Four Million* (1906)
William Dean Howells, *A Hazard of New Fortunes* (1890)
Damon Runyon, *The Best of Damon Runyon* (1966)
Edith Wharton, *The Age of Innocence* (1920)

Greenwich Village Romances: 5 Novels

Floyd Dell, *Love in Greenwich Village* (1926)
William Dean Howells, *The Coast of Bohemia* (1893)
James Huneker, *Painted Veils* (1920)
Dawn Powell, *Golden Spur* (1962)
Edmund Wilson, *I Thought of Daisy* (1929)

Harlem Nocturnes: 5 Novels

James Baldwin, *Go Tell It on the Mountain* (1953)
George Cain, *Blueschild Baby* (1971)
Louise Meriwether, *Daddy Was a Numbers Runner* (1970)
Warren Miller, *The Cool World* (1959)
Ann Petry, *The Street* (1946)

5 Paeans to the City

August Heckscher with Phyllis Robinson, *When LaGuardia Was Mayor: New York's Legendary Years* (1979)
Marya Mannes, *The New York I Know* (1961)
Joseph Mitchell, *The Bottom of the Harbor* (1960)
Gay Talese, *New York: A Serendipiter's Journey* (1961)
E. B. White, *Here Is New York* (1949)

Tales of the Second City: Chicago

Written in the Wind: 10 Outstanding Works of Fiction

Nelson Algren, *The Man with the Golden Arm* (1949)
Saul Bellow, *The Adventures of Augie March* (1953)
Theodore Dreiser, *Sister Carrie* (1900)
Stuart Dybek, *Childhood and Other Neighborhoods* (1979)
James T. Farrell, *Studs Lonigan Trilogy* (1932–35)
Henry B. Fuller, *With the Procession* (1895)
Robert Herrick, *Memoirs of an American Citizen* (1905)
Bette Howland, *Blue in Chicago* (1978)
Frank Norris, *The Pit* (1903)
Richard Wright, *Native Son* (1940)

Sweet Home Chicago: 5 Nonfictions

George Abe, *The Chicago Story* (1963)
Nelson Algren, *City on the Make* (1951)
A. J. Liebling, *Chicago: The Second City* (1952)
Mike Royko, *Boss* (1971)
Studs Terkel, *Division Street: America* (1967)

City at Bay: San Francisco

5 San Francisco Novels

Charles Dobie, *Portrait of a Courtesan* (1934)
Joe Gores, *Hammett* (1975)
Ella Leffland, *Love Out of Season* (1974)
Oscar Lewis, *I Remember Christine* (1939)
Frank Norris, *McTeague* (1899)

San Francisco Chronicles: 5 Nonfiction Classics

Herbert Asbury, *The Barbary Coast* (1933)
Herb Caen, *Baghdad-by-the-Bay* (1949)
Jerome Hart, *In Our Second Century* (1931)
John S. Hittell, *A History of the City of San Francisco* (1878)
Oscar Lewis, *The Big Four* (1938)

Never read any book that is not a year old.

—RALPH WALDO EMERSON

---

5 × 5: Tales of 5 Cities

Back Bay Tales: The Bostonians

James Carroll, *Mortal Friends* (1978)
William Dean Howells, *The Rise of Silas Lapham* (1885)
J. P. Marquand, *H. M. Pulham, Esquire* (1941)
Edwin O'Connor, *The Edge of Sadness* (1961)
Jean Stafford, *Boston Adventure* (1944)

Brotherly Writings: The Philadelphia Story

Tom McHale, *Farragan's Retreat* (1971)
Evelyn Wilde Mayerson, *If Birds Are Free* (1980)
S. Weir Mitchell, *Hugh Wynne, Free Quaker* (1897)
Christopher Morley, *Kitty Foyle* (1939)
William Wharton, *Birdy* (1979)

Auto Suggestions: The Detroit Novel

Harriet Arnow, *The Weedkiller's Daughter* (1970)
Elmore Leonard, *City Primeval: High Noon in Detroit* (1980)
Leo E. Litwak, *Waiting for the News* (1969)
Joyce Carol Oates, *Them* (1969)
Al Young, *Snakes* (1970)

L.A.'D Back Reading: Los Angeles Fictions

John Fante, *Ask the Dust* (1939)
Cornelia Jessey, *Teach the Angry* (1949)
Alison Lurie, *The Nowhere City* (1965)
Upton Sinclair, *Oil!* (1927)
Jessamyn West, *The Life I Really Lived* (1979)

Two English Views:

Aldous Huxley, *After Many a Summer Dies the Swan* (1940)
Evelyn Waugh, *The Loved One* (1948)

Bayou Leaves: Novels of New Orleans

George Washington Cable, *The Grandissimes* (1880)
Kate Chopin, *The Awakening* (1899)
Walker Percy, *The Moviegoer* (1961)

Robert Stone, *A Hall of Mirrors* (1967)
John Kennedy Toole, *A Confederacy of Dunces* (1980)

■ COUNTRY WAYS

Back to Basics: 10 Homesteader Narratives
Otis Carney, *New Lease on Life* (1971)
Gilean Douglas, *Silence is My Homeland: Life on Teal River* (1978)
Lisa Hobbs, *Running Towards Life* (1972)
Helen Hoover, *A Place in the Woods* (1969)
Wynant Davis Hubbard, *Ibamba* (1962)
Gregory Jaynes, *Sketches from a Dirt Road* (1977)
Helen and Scott Nearing, *Living the Good Life* (1954)
Samuel R. Ogden, *The Country Life: Making the Most of the Simple Life* (1973)
Charles B. Seib, *The Woods: One Man's Escape to Nature* (1971)
Edwin Way Teale, *A Naturalist Buys an Old Farm* (1974)
Robert Traub, *The Tree Farm* (1977)

The Cold Facts: 10 Narratives of the North Country
Laura Berton, *I Married the Klondike* (1955)
Sally Carrighar, *Moonlight at Midday* (1958)
Edward Hoagland, *Notes from the Century Before* (1969)
Paul Lehmberg, *In the Strong Woods* (1979)
John McPhee, *Coming into the Country* (1977)
Margaret Murie, *Two in the Far North* (1962)
Fridtjof Nansen, *Farthest North* (1897)
Sigurd F. Olson, *Runes of the North* (1963)
Billie Wright, *Four Seasons North* (1973)

Lays of the Land: 10 Rural American Classics
Willa Cather, *My Antonia* (1918)
Hamlin Garland, *Main Travelled Roads* (1891)
Ellen Glasgow, *Barren Ground* (1925)
Curtis Harnack, *Limits of the Land* (1979)
O. E. Rolvaag, *Giants in the Earth Trilogy* (1924–25)

Josephine Johnson, *Now is November* (1934)
Herbert Quick, *Vandemark's Folly* (1922)
Conrad Richter, *The Awakening Land Trilogy* (1940–50)
Ruth Suckow, *Country People* (1924)
John Steinbeck, *The Grapes of Wrath* (1939)

Main Street Scenes: 10 Novels of Small-Town America
Sherwood Anderson, *Winesburg, Ohio* (1919)
Frieda Arkin, *The Dorp* (1969)
Willa Cather, *My Antonia* (1918)
Sinclair Lewis, *Main Street* (1920)
Ross Lockridge, *Raintree County* (1948)
Don Robertson, *Paradise Falls* (1968)
Ernest Seeman, *American Gold* (1978)
Harold Sinclair, *Everton Trilogy* (1938–41)
Booth Tarkington, *Alice Adams* (1921)
Mark Twain, *The Adventures of Tom Sawyer* (1876)

The First Realistic Look at Small Town Life
E. W. Howe, *The Story of a Country Town* (1883)

■ LET'S PLAY HOUSE

Here is a list of ten houses of words. Do you know who constructed them?

1. *The House of the Seven Gables*
2. *The House at Pooh Corner*
3. *Bleak House*
4. *The House of Mirth*
5. *The House of Bernard Alba*
6. *Heartbreak House*
7. *A House Is Not a Home*
8. *In This House of Brede*
9. *A House for Mr. Biswas*
10. *The House of the Dead*

■ INNOCENTS ABROAD

10 American Novelists' Experiences in Foreign Lands
Nelson Algren, *Who Lost an American* (1963)
Saul Bellow, *To Jerusalem and Back* (1976)
Nathaniel Hawthorne, *Our Old Home* (1863)
Mary McCarthy, *Venice Observed* (1956)
Herman Melville, *Melville's Journal of a Visit to Europe and the Levant* (1954)
James Michener, *Iberia* (1968)
Henry Miller, *The Colossus of Maroussi* (1941)
Paul Theroux, *The Great Railway Bazaar* (1975)
Mark Twain, *The Innocents Abroad* (1869)
Edith Wharton, *Italian Backgrounds* (1925)

10 Americans in Paris
Malcolm Cowley, *Exile's Return* (1934)
Janet Flanner, *Paris Was Yesterday* (1972)
Ernest Hemingway, *A Moveable Feast* (1964)
Matthew Josephson, *Life Among the Surrealists: A Memoir* (1962)
Robert McAlmon, *Being Geniuses Together* (rev. 1968)
Elliot Paul, *Last Time I Saw Paris* (1942)
Samuel Putnam, *Paris Was Our Mistress* (1947)
Ned Rorem, *The Paris Diary* (1966)
Gertrude Stein, *The Autobiography of Alice B. Toklas* (1933)
Alice B. Toklas, *What Is Remembered* (1963)

2 Canadian Writers Remember
Morley Callaghan, *That Summer in Paris* (1963)
John Glassco, *Memoirs of Montparnasse* (1970)

20 Novels of Americans in Europe

In England

J. P. Donleavy, *The Ginger Man* (1958)
Marilyn French, *The Bleeding Heart* (1980)
Henry James, *The Golden Bowl* (1904)
Paul Theroux, *The Family Arsenal* (1976)
Anthony Trollope, *The American Senator* (1877)

In Italy

John Horne Burns, *The Gallery* (1947)
Nathaniel Hawthorne, *The Marble Faun* (1860)
Ernest Hemingway, *A Farewell to Arms* (1929)
John Hersey, *A Bell for Adano* (1944)
William Styron, *Set this House on Fire* (1960)

In France

James Baldwin, *Giovanni's Room* (1956)
Kay Boyle, *Plagued by the Nightingale* (1931)
Elaine Dundy, *The Dud Avocado* (1958)
F. Scott Fitzgerald, *Tender Is the Night* (1934)
Ernest Hemingway, *The Sun Also Rises* (1926)
Henry James, *The Ambassador* (1903)
Henry Miller, *Tropic of Cancer* (1934)
Dawn Powell, *Cage for Lovers* (1957)
James Salter, *A Sport and a Pastime* (1967)
William Wiser, *Disappearances* (1980)

■ INNOCENTS AT HOME

10 Foreign Novelists' Experiences in America
Arnold Bennett, *Your United States* (1912)
Simone de Beauvoir, *America Day by Day* (1952)
Charles Dickens, *American Notes* (1842)
Knut Hamsun, *The Cultural Life of Modern America* (1889)

Henry James, *The American Scene* (1907)
Rudyard Kipling, *American Notes* (1930)
Frederick Maryatt, *My Diary in America* (1839)
Henrik Sinkiewicz, *Portrait of America* (1878)
Anthony Trollope, *North America* (1862)
Mrs. Frances Trollope, *Domestic Manners of the Americans* (1832)

Melting Pot-Boilers: 5 Best Immigrant Narratives
Louis Adamic, *Laughing in the Jungle* (1969)
Mary Antin, *The Promised Land* (1912)
Edward Bok, *The Americanization of Edward Bok* (1920)
Ted Morgan, *On Becoming American* (1978)
Jacob Riis, *Making of an American* (1901)

■ OUR HEMISPHERE

20 Modern Canadian Novelists
Margaret Atwood, *Life Before Man* (1980)
Marie-Clair Blais, *A Season in the Life of Emmanuel* (1966)
Leonard Cohen, *Beautiful Losers* (1966)
Robertson Davies, *Fifth Business* (1970)
Morley Callaghan, *Such Is My Beloved* (1934)
Marian Engel, *The Glassy Sea* (1979)
Mavis Gallant, *From the Fifteenth District* (1979)
Hugh Garner, *Storm Below* (1949)
Hugh Hood, *White Figure, White Ground* (1964)
Margaret Laurence, *A Bird in the House; Stories* (1970)
Andte Langeran, *Dust Over the Town* (1953)
Roger Lemeleu, *The Town Below* (1944)
Jack Ludwig, *Confusions* (1963)
Hugh MacLennan, *Two Solitudes* (1945)
Brian Moore, *The Luck of Ginger Coffey* (1960)
Alice Munro, *Lives of Girls and Women* (1971)
Mordechai Richler, *Joshua Then and Now* (1980)
Gabrielle Roy, *Street of Riches* (1957)
Ethel Wilson, *Swamp Angel* (1954)
Richard B. Wright, *Final Things* (1980)

5 Novels of Mexico
Graham Greene, *The Power and the Glory* (1940)
D. H. Lawrence, *The Plumed Serpent* (1926)
Malcolm Lowry, *Under the Volcano* (1947)
Tom Lea, *The Hands of Cantu* (1964)
B. Traven, *Treasure of the Sierra Madre* (1927)

5 Modern Mexican Masterpieces
Mariano Azuela, *The Underdogs* (1927)
Rosario Castellanos, *The Nine Guardians* (1959)
Carlos Fuentes, *The Death of Artemio Cruz* (1964)
José Ruben Romero, *The Futile Life of Pito Perez* (1967)
Juán Rulfo, *The Burning Plain and Other Stories* (1967)

5 Novels of the West Indies
Graham Greene, *The Comedians* (1966)
Peter Mathiessen, *Far Tortuga* (1976)
Jean Rhys, *Wide Sargasso Sea* (1967)
Simone Schwarz-Bart, *The Bridge of Beyond* (1972)
Phillipe Thoby-Marcelin and Pierre Marcelin, *The Beast of the Haitian Hills* (1946)

5 Modern West Indian Novels
Austin C. Clarke, *The Survivors of the Crossing* (1964)
Roger Mais, *Black Lightning* (1955)
Edgar Mittelhozer, *A Swarthy Boy* (1963)
Shiva Naipaul, *Fireflies* (1970)
V. S. Naipaul, *A House for Mr. Biswas* (1964)

5 Novels of Latin America
Joseph Conrad, *Nostromo* (1904)
Graham Greene, *The Honorary Consul* (1973)
W. H. Hudson, *Green Mansions* (1904)
R. H. Koster, *The Tinieblan Trilogy* (1971–79)
Peter Mathiessen, *At Play in the Fields of the Lord* (1965)

Tales of the Pampas: 5 Gaucho Novels
Eduardo Acevedo Diaz, *Soledad* (1894)
Javier de Viana, *Gaucha* (1899)
Ricardo Guiraldes, *Don Segundo Sombra* (1926)

Eduardo Gutierrez, *Juan Moreira* (1880)
Benito Lynch, *Romance of a Gaucho* (1930)'

The Best Short Story Collection
W. H. Hudson, *Tales of the Pampas* (1946)

---

10 Modern Latin American Classics
Jorge Amado, *Gabriela, Clove and Cinnamon* (1962)
Jorge Luís Borges, *Ficciones* (1962)
Alejandro Carpentier, *Lost Steps* (1956)
Julio Córtazar, *Hopscotch* (1966)
José Donoso, *Sacred Families* (1977)
Guillermo Cabrera Infante, *Three Trapped Tigers* (1967)
José Lezama Lima, *O Paradiso*
Mario Varga Llosa, *Captain Pantoja and the Special Service* (1978)
Gabriel García Márquez, *One Hundred Years of Solitude* (1970)
Manuel Puig, *Betrayed by Rita Hayworth* (1968)

Neglected Classic
Euclides De Cunha, *Rebellion in the Backlands* (1902)
". . . will be recognized, worldwide, as one of the greatest masterpieces of Western prose."

—William Gass

■ BACK IN THE U.S.A.

The Southwest Classics
This list, along with fascinating commentary, is from Lawrence Clark Powell's *Southwest Classics* (Ward Ritchie, 1974). Reprinted by permission of the author.

Josiah Gregg, *Commerce of the Prairies* (1844)
Lewis H. Garrard, *Wah To-Yah and the Taos Trail* (1850)
Susan Shelly Magoffin, *Down the Santa Fe Trail* (1926)
Charles F. Lummis, *The Land of Poco Tiempo* (1893)
Harvey Fergusson, *Wolf Song* (1927)

Mable Dodge Luhan, *Edge of Taos Desert* (1937); *Winter in Taos* (1935)

D. H. Lawrence, *The Plumed Serpent* (1926)

Mary Austin, *The Land of Journeys' Ending* (1924)

Haniel Long, *Interlinear to Cabeza de Vaca* (1936)

Willa Cather, *Death Comes for the Archbishop* (1927)

Erna Fergusson, *Dancing Gods* (1931)

Ross Calvin, *Sky Determines* (1934)

Eugene Manlove Rhodes, *Pasó Por Aqui* (1927)

Ross Santee, *Lost Pony Tracks* (1953)

Stewart Edward White, *Arizona Nights* (1907)

Zane Grey, *Riders of the Purple Sage* (1912)

Oliver LaFarge, *Laughing Boy* (1929)

Will Levington Comfort, *Apache* (1931)

Eusebio King, *Historical Memoir* (1919)

Francisco Garcés, *Diary* (1900)

J. Ross Browne, *Adventures in the Apache Country* (1869)

Martha Summerhayes, *Vanished Arizona* (1908)

John Wesley Powell, *The Exploration of the Colorado River* (1895)

Theodore Roosevelt, *Ranch Life and the Hunting Trail* (1888)

John C. Van Dyke, *The Desert* (1901)

Joseph Wood Krutch, *The Desert Years* (1952)

J. Frank Dobie, *Coronado's Children* (1930)

A classic is a book that doesn't have to be re-written.

—CARL VAN DOREN

The California Classics

Bookman extraordinaire Lawrence Clark Powell prepared this list for his *California Classics* (Ward Ritchie, 1971). Reprinted with permission of the author.

Herbert E. Bolton, *Anza's California Expedition*

Walter Nordhoff, *The Journey of the Flame*

William L. Manly, *Death Valley in '49*

Mary Austin, *The Land of Little Rain*

George Wharton James, *The Wonders of the Colorado Desert*

Louisa Smith Clapp, *The Shirley Letters*
Bret Harte, *The Luck of Roaring Camp*
Mark Twain, *Roughing It*
Gertrude Atherton, *The Splendid Idle Forties*
William H. Brewer, *Up and Down California in 1860–64*
Clarence King, *Mountaineering in the Sierra Nevada*
John Muir, *The Mountains of California*
Richard Henry Dana, Jr., *Two Years Before the Mast*
Robert Louis Stevenson, *The Silverado Squatters*
Frank Norris, *McTeague*
Jack London, *Martin Eden*
J. Smeaton Chase, *California Coast Trails*
Robinson Jeffers, *Give Your Heart to the Hawks*
John Steinbeck, *To a God Unknown*
Charis and Edward Weston, *California and the West*
Idwal Jones, *The Vineyard*
Robert Glass Cleland, *The Cattle on a Thousand Hills*
Helen Hunt Jackson, *Ramona*
Horace Bell, *Reminiscences of a Ranger*
Charles F. Lummis, *Land of Sunshine*
Lincoln Steffens, *Boy on Horseback*
Upton Sinclair, *Oil!*
Harry Leon Wilson, *Merton of the Movies*
Nathanael West, *The Day of the Locust*
Aldous Huxley, *After Many a Summer Dies the Swan*
Raymond Chandler, *Farewell, My Lovely*

The Novel That Gave California Its Name
The Spanish romance *The Adventure of Esplandian* (1510) by
García Ordóñez de Montalvo, which was published a
quarter century before Cortes named what is now the tip of
Baja California, involved a fantastic journey to an island
paradise called "California." The description of that fictive
land proved an inspired and apt designation of the discovered land.

Everything comes to him who waits but a loaned book.
　　　　　　　　　　　　　—FRANK MCKINNEY (KIN) HUBBARD

Hominy Gritty Writing: Some Southern Novelists

5 Old Kentucky Tomes

Harriet Arnow, *Hunter's Horn* (1949)
Wendell Berry, *A Place on Earth* (1966)
Elizabeth Madox Roberts, *The Time of Man* (1926)
Jesse Stuart, *The Land Beyond the River* (1970)
Robert Penn Warren, *Night Rider* (1939)

5 Southern Gothic Classics

Truman Capote, *Other Voices, Other Rooms* (1948)
John Hawkes, *The Cannibal* (1949)
Carson McCullers, *The Heart Is a Lonely Hunter* (1940)
Flannery O'Connor, *The Violent Bear It Away* (1960)
James Purdy, *63: Dream Palace,* (1956)

From Yoknapatawpha to Yazoo: 5 Novels of Mississippi

William Faulkner, *The Sound and the Fury* (1929)
Beverly Lowry, *Come Back, Lolly Ray* (1977)
Elizabeth Spencer, *The Crooked Way* (1952)
Eudora Welty, *The Optimist's Daughter* (1972)
Stark Young, *So Red the Rose* (1934)

Books That Changed the South

From Robert Downs' *Books That Changed the South* (Univ. of North Carolina Press, 1977).

William Bartram, *Travels Through North and South Carolina, Georgia, East and West Florida* (1791)
William Byrd, *History of the Dividing Line Betwixt Virginia and North Carolina* (1841)
George Washington Cable, *Old Creole Days* (1879)
John Caldwell Calhoun, *A Disquisition on Government* (1851)
Wilbur Joseph Cash, *The Mind of the South* (1941)
David Crockett, *A Narrative of the Life of David Crockett of the State of Tennessee, Written by Himself* (1834)
Thomas Dixon, *The Clansman: An Historical Romance of the Ku Klux Klan* (1905)
Frederick Douglass, *Narrative of the Life of Frederick Douglass, An American Slave* (1845)

W. E. B. DuBois, *The Souls of Black Folk* (1903)
Joel Chandler Harris, *Uncle Remus: His Songs and His Sayings* (1880)
Hinton Rowan Helper, *The Impending Crisis of the South: How to Meet It* (1857)
Thomas Jefferson, *Notes on the State of Virginia* (1787)
Frances Anne Kemble, *Journal of a Residence on a Georgia Plantation in 1838–1839* (1863)
Edward King, *The Great South* (1875)
Augustus Baldwin Longstreet, *Georgia Scenes* (1835)
Howard W. Odum, *Southern Regions of the United States* (1936)
Frederick Law Olmstead, *The Cotton Kingdom* (1861)
Thomas Nelson Page, *In Ole Virginia* (1887)
Ulrich Bonnell Phillips, *Life and Labor in the Old South* (1929)
John Smith, *The Generall Historie of Virginia, New-England, and The Summer Isles* (1624)
Mark Twain, *Life on the Mississippi* (1883)
Twelve Southerners, *I'll Take My Stand* (1930)
Booker T. Washington, *Up From Slavery: An Autobiography* (1901)
Mason Locke Weems, *The Life of Washington the Great* (1800)
C. Vann Woodward, *Origins of the New South, 1877–1913* (1951)

I really do think the South tends to produce better writers. There's no mystery about it. We're all Southerners, and we belong to a rural tradition. It's an oral tradition. . . . We like words. We like to tell stories. . . . That's where great literature comes from.

—JAMES DICKEY

■ WRITERS OF THE PURPLE SAGE: BEST BOOKS OF THE WEST

Western Writers' Writers: The Spur Award Winners

The Western Writers of America annually presents the prestigious Spur Award to the author of the best western nonfiction work.

1955: David Lavender, *Bent's Fort*
1956: Paul F. Sharp, *Whoop-Up Country*
1957: Irving Stone, *Men to Match My Mountains*
1958: Robert West Howard, *This Is the West*
1959: Mabel Barbee Lee, *Cripple Creek Days*
1960: Frank Tolbert, *Day of San Jacinto*
1961: No Award
1962: Don Russell, *The Lives and Legends of Buffalo Bill*
1963: Richard A. Bartlett, *Great Surveys of the American West*
1964: William S. Greever, *The Bonanza West*
1965: Ernest Staples Osgood, *The Field Notes of Captain William Clark*
1966: Alvin M. Josephy, Jr., *The Nez Percé Indians and the Opening of the Northwest*
1967: Ray Billington, *America's Frontier Heritage*
1968: John Hawgood, *America's Western Frontier*
1969: Vardis Fisher and Opal Laurel Holmes, *Gold Rushes and Mining Camps of the Early American West*
1970: Nellie Snyder Yost, *Boss Cowman*
1971: Thomas L. Barnes, *William Gilpin: Western Naturalist*
1972: Elliott S. Barker, *Western Life and Adventures 1889–1971*
1973: Tom McHugh, *The Time of the Buffalo*
1974: Richard Dillon, *Burnt-Out Fires*
1975: Paul Horgan, *Lamy of Santa Fe*
1976: Stan Steiner, *The Vanishing Whiteman*
1977: Joyce Gibson Roach, *The Cowgirls*
1978: Janet Lecomte, *Pueblo, Hardscrabble, Greenhorn*

10 Great Westerns
Walter Van Tilburg Clark, *The Ox Bow Incident* (1940)
Harvey Fergusson, *The Blood of the Conquerors* (1921)
Vardis Fisher, *Dark Bridwell* (1931)
Paul Horgan, *The Common Heart* (1942)
Tom Lea, *Wonderful Country* (1952)
Frederick Manfred, *Lord Grizzly* (1954)
Eugene Manlove Rhodes, *The Best Novels* (1949)
Jack Schaefer, *Monte Walsh* (1963)

Frank Waters, *People of the Valley* (1941)
Owen Wister, *Lin McLean* (1898)

5 Tales of the Modern West
Edward Abbey, *The Brave Cowboy* (1958)
William Eastlake, *The Bronc People* (1958)
Larry McMurtry, *Leaving Cheyenne* (1963)
Michael E. Moon, *John Medicine Wolf* (1979)
Max Schott, *Murphy's Romance* (1980)

The First Western
The first novel in English placed in the West was Timothy
Flint's *Francis Berrian, or the Mexican Patriot* (1826).

■ THEY WON THEIR GOLDEN SPURS: AWARDS OF WESTERN WRITERS OF AMERICA

Because it was presented by the writer's peers, a WWA
Spur Award is specially valued by its recipient. In the years
not listed below, no award was given.

Best Western Novels—Traditional
1954: Lee Leighton (Wayne D. Overholser), *Law Man*
1955: Wayne D. Overholser, *The Violent Land*
1956: L. P. Holmes, *Somewhere They Die*
1957: Leslie Ernenwein, *High Gun*
1958: Elmer Kelton, *Buffalo Wagons*
1959: Noel Loomis, *Short Cut to Red River*
1960: Nelson Nye, *Long Run*
1961: Will C. Brown, *The Nameless Breed*
1962: Giles A. Lutz, *The Honyocker*
1963: Fred Grove, *Comanche Captives*
1964: Leigh Brackett, *Follow the Free Wind*
1965: Benjamin Capps, *The Trail to Ogallala*
1966: Benjamin Capps, *Sam Chance*
1967: Herbert R. Purdom, *My Brother John*
1968: Lee Hoffman, *The Valdez Horses*
1969: Louis L'Amour, *Down the Long Hills*

1970: Clifton Adams, *Tragg's Choice*
1971: Ray Hogan, *Jackman's Wolf*
1972: Elmer Kelton, *The Day the Cowboys Quit*
1973: Lewis B. Patten, *A Killing in Kiowa*
1974: Elmer Kelton, *The Time It Never Rained*
1975: Glendon Swarthout, *The Shootist*
1976: Lou Cameron, *Spirit Horses*
Douglas Jones, *The Court Martial of George Armstrong Custer*
1977: Fred Grove, *The Great Horse Race*
1978: Norman Zollinger, *Riders to Cibola*
1979: William Decker, *The Holdout*

Best Western Novels—Historical
1954: Lucia Moore, *The Wheel and the Hearth*
1955: John Prescott, *Journey by the River*
1957: John C. Hunt, *Generations of Men*
1958: Dan Cushman, *Silver Mountain*
1959: Amelia Bean, *The Fancher Train*
1960: John Preggle, *The Buffalo Soldiers*
1961: Will Henry, *From Where the Sin Now Stands*
1962: William Wisre Haines, *The Winter War*
1963: Don Berry, *Moon Trap*
1964: Will Henry, *The Gates of the Mountains*
1965: E. E. Halleran, *Indian Fighter*
1966: Todhunter Ballard, *Gold in California*
1967: Garland Roark and Charles Thomas, *Hellfire Jackson*
1968: Chad Oliver, *The Wolf Is My Brother*
1969: Lewis B. Patten, *The Red Sabbath*
1970: Benjamin Capps, *The White Man's Road*
1973: Will Henry, *Chiricahua*
1976: Matt Braun, *The Kinkaids*
1977: Terence Kilpatrick, *Swimming Man Burning*

The Real West: The Western Heritage Award
    Since 1962 the National Cowboy Hall of Fame and Western Heritage Center of Oklahoma City have presented the Western Heritage Award for the nonfiction book which best preserves "the image of the real American West and the people who were responsible for developing it."

194

1962: *The American Heritage Book of Indians*
1963: John Rouph Burroughs, *Where the Old West Stayed Young*
1964: John Upton Terrell, *Furs by Astor*
1965: C. Gregory Crampton, *Standing Up Country*
1966: *American Heritage History of the Great West*
1967: George W. Groh, *Gold Fever*
1968: John A. Hawgood, *America's Western Frontiers*
1969: Robert Dykstra, *The Cattle Towns*
Laura Gilpin, *The Enduring Navajo*
1970: Merrill J. Mattes, *The Great Platte River Road*
1971: Harry Sinclair Drago, *The Great Range Wars*
1972: Odie B. Faulk and Seymour V. Connor, *North America Divided: The Mexican War*
1973: Tom McHugh, *The Time of the Buffalo*
Grace Dangberg, *Carson Valley*
S. L. A. Marshall, *Crimsoned Prairie*
1974: George F. Ellis, *Bell Ranch As I Knew It*
Richard M. Ketchum, *Will Rogers, His Life and Times*
1975: Benjamin Capps, *The Warren Wagontrain Raid*
Robert O. Beatty, *Idaho: A Pictorial Overview*
Roy P. Stewart, *Born Grown*
C. L. Sonnichsen, *Colonel Green and the Copper Skyrocket*
Margaret Sanborn, *The American: River of El Dorado*
1976: Jeff C. Dykes, *Fifty Great Western Illustrators*
Turbese Lummis Fiske and Keith Lummis, *Charles F. Lummis: The Man and His West*
Don James, *Butte's Memory Book*
1977: No Award
1978: Angie Debo, *Geronimo: The Man, His Time, His Place*
Tim and Ronald McCoy, *Tim McCoy Remembers the West*
1979: Nellie Snyder Yost, *Buffalo Bill: His Family, Failures and Fortunes*
1980: John D. Unruh, Jr., *The Plains Across*

Western Heritage Award Winners: Fiction
The National Cowboy Hall of Fame and Western Heritage

Center presents its award each year for the best western novel. In the years not listed below, no award was given.

1962: James D. Horan, *The Shadow Catcher*
1963: Edward Abbey, *Fire on the Mountain*
1964: Robert A. Roripaugh, *Honor Thy Father*
1965: Thomas Berger, *Little Big Man*
1966: Vardis Fisher, *Mountain Man*
1967: Bill Gulick, *They Came to a Valley*
1968: Robert Flynn, *North to Yesterday*
1969: Fred Grove, *The Buffalo Runners*
1970: Benjamin Capps, *The White Man's Road*
1971: A. B. Guthrie, *Arfive*
1972: Frank Waters, *Pike's Peak: A Family Saga*
1973: Will Henry, *Chiricahua*
1974: Elmer Kelton, *The Time It Never Rained*
1975: James A. Michener, *Centennial*
1978: Dorothy M. Johnson, *Buffalo Woman*
      Bill Brett, *The Stolen Steers: A Tale of the Big Thicket*
1979: Elmer Kelton, *Good Old Boys*
1980: Ruth Beebe Hill, *Hanta Yo*

From Deep in the Heart: 10 Texas Tales
Walter Clemons, *The Poison Tree* (1958)
J. Frank Dobie, *Tales of Texas* (1955)
William Goyen, *The House of Breath* (1950)
John Howard Griffin, *The Devil Rides Outside* (1952)
William Humphrey, *The Ordways* (1964)
Larry McMurtry, *The Last Picture Show* (1966)
George Sessions Piercy, *Hold Autumn in Your Hand* (1941)
Katherine Anne Porter, *Noon Wine* (1937)
David Westheimer, *Summer on the Water* (1948)
Allen Wier, *Blanco* (1978)

A novelist is a person who lives in other people's skins.

—E. L. DOCTOROW

■ PEN AND SWORD: WAR IN FACT AND FICTION

Revolutionary War: 5 Novels
James Boyd, *Drums* (1926)
John Breck, *The Raid* (1951)
Esther Forbes, *Johnny Tremain* (1943)
MacKinlay Kantor, *Valley Forge* (1975)
Kenneth Roberts, *Arundel* (1933)

Civil War: 15 Novels
James Boyd, *Marching On* (1927)
Stephen Crane, *The Red Badge of Courage* (1895)
John William DeForest, *Miss Ravenel's Conversion From Secession to Loyalty* (1867)
John Ehle, *A Time for Drums* (1970)
Shelby Foote, *Shiloh* (1952)
Robert H. Fowler, *Jim Mundy* (1977)
Caroline Gordon, *None Shall Look Back* (1937)
Mary Johnston, *The Long Roll* (1911)
MacKinlay Kantor, *Long Remember* (1934)
Joseph Pennell, *The History of Rome Hanks and Kindred Matters* (1944)
Don Robertson, *By Antietam Creek* (1960)
Evelyn Scott, *The Wave* (1929)
Michael Shaara, *The Killer Angels* (1974)
James Sherburne, *The Way to Fort Pillow* (1972)
Matthew Vaughan, *Major Stepson's War* (1978)

What If?
MacKinlay Kantor, *If the South Had Won the War* (1961)

Best Books on the Civil War.
The Civil War Round Table of New York established the Fletcher Pratt Award in 1957 to honor the best nonfiction book on the Civil War for the past year.

1957: Bruce Catton, *This Hallowed Ground*
1958: Burke Davis, *The Last Cavalier*

1959: Philip Van Doren Stern, *An End to Valor*
1960: Allan Nevins, *The War for the Union: War Becomes Revolution, 1862–1863*
1961: R. Ernest Dupuy and Trevor N. Dupuy, *The Compact History of the Civil War*
1962: Glenn Tucker, *Chickamauga*
1963: Harry Hansen, *The Civil War*
1964: Shelby Foote, *The Civil War: A Narrative*
1965: Clifford Dowdey, *The Seven Days: The Emergence of Lee*
1966: James V. Murtin, *The Gleam of Bayonets*
1967: Charles B. Dew, *Ironmaker to the Confederacy: Joseph R. Anderson and the Tredegar Iron Works*
1968: Glyndon G. Van Deusen, *William Henry Seward*
1969: Edwin B. Coddington, *The Gettysburg Campaign: A Study in Command*
1970: Bruce Catton, *Grant Takes Command*
1971: Frank E. Vandiver, *Their Tattered Flags*
1972: Robert Manson Myers, *The Children of Pride*
1973: John G. Simon, *The Papers of Ulysses S. Grant*
1974: Shelby Foote, *The Civil War: A Narrative*
1975: David H. Donald, *Gone for a Soldier: The Civil War Memoirs of Private Alfred Bellard*
1976: No Award
1977: Richard Wheeler, *Voices of the Civil War*
1978: William C. Davis, *Contribution to Civil War History*
1979: Rowena Reed, *Combined Operations in the Civil War*
1980: Stephen Z. Starr, *The Union Cavalry in the Civil War, Vol. 1, from Fort Sumter to Gettysburg*

World War I

The 10 Best Novels

Henri Barbusse, *Under Fire* (1916)
Thomas Boyd, *Through the Wheat* (1927)
Humphrey Cobb, *Paths of Glory* (1935)
John Dos Passos, *Three Soldiers* (1921)
Timothy Findley, *The Wars* (1978)
Jaroslav Hasek, *The Good Soldier Schweik* (1920–23)
Ernest Hemingway, *A Farewell to Arms* (1929)

Andreas Latzko, *Men In War* (1917)
Frederic Manning, *The Middle Parts of Fortune* (1929)
William March, *Company K* (1933)
John Masters, *Now, God Be Thanked* (1979)
Stratis Myrivillis, *Life in a Tomb* (1930)
Erich Maria Remarque, *All Quiet on the Western Front* (1929)
Ludwig Renn, *War* (1928)
Arnold Zweig, *The Case of Sergeant Grische* (1927)

The Best Memoirs

Edmund Blunden, *Undertones of War* (1928)
Vera Brittain, *Testament of Youth* (1933)
Guy Chapman, *A Passionate Prodigality* (1933)
Robert Graves, *Good-Bye to All That* (1929)
John W. Thomason, *Fix Bayonets* (1926)

The Spanish Civil War: 5 Novels

José María Gironella, *The Cypresses Believe in God* (1953)
Ernest Hemingway, *For Whom the Bell Tolls* (1940)
André Malraux, *Man's Hope* (1938)
Juán Marse, *The Fallen* (1977)
Gustav Regler, *The Great Crusade* (1940)

World War II

10 Best War Novels

Harry Brown, *A Walk in the Sun* (1944)
Tom Chamales, *Never So Few* (1957)
Mitchell Goodman, *The End of It* (1961)
Thomas Goethals, *Chain of Command* (1955)
John Hersey, *The War Lovers* (1959)
James Jones, *The Thin Red Line* (1962)
Edward Loomis, *End of a War* (1958)
Norman Mailer, *The Naked and the Dead* (1948)
Herman Wouk, *Winds of War* (1971)
Irwin Shaw, *The Young Lions* (1948)

The European Perspective

Alexander Baron, *From the City, From the Plough* (1949)
Hans Hellmut Kirst, *The Gunner Asch Trilogy* (1956–59)

Jakov Lind, *Landscape in Concrete* (1966)
Veijo Meri, *The Manila Rope* (1967)
Theodor Plievier, *Stalingrad* (1948)

What If?: Deutschland Über Allies
Len Deighton, *SS-GB* (1979)
Philip K. Dick, *The Man in the High Castle* (1962)
Sarban, *The Sound of His Horn* (1960)

No Atomic Bomb: American Invasion of Japan
David Westheimer, *Lighter than a Feather* (1971)

---

10 Best War Memoirs
Ted W. Lawson, *Thirty Seconds over Tokyo* (1953)
Norman Lewis, *Naples '44* (1979)
George R. Millar, *Waiting in the Night: A Story of the Maquis* (1946)
Farley Mowat, *And No Birds Sing* (1979)
William Manchester, *Goodbye, Darkness* (1980)
Odd Nansen, *From Day to Day* (1949)
Guy Sajer, *The Forgotten Soldier* (1971)
Albert Speer, *Inside the Third Reich* (1970)
Richard Tregaskis, *Guadalcanal Diary* (1943)
William L. White, *They Were Expendable* (1942)

15 Footnotes to the War
Silvano Arieti, *The Parnas* (1979)
Joan Bright Astley, *The Inner Circle: A View of War at the Top* (1971)
Dorothy Baden-Powell, *Pimpernel Gold: How Norway Failed the Nazis* (1978)
Joseph Borkin, *The Crime and Punishment of I. G. Farben* (1978)
Jeanne Wakatusi Houston and James D. Houston, *Farewell to Manzanar* (1973)
Pierre Joffrey, *A Spy for God: The Ordeal of Kurt Gerstein* (1970)
Aubrey Menen, *Four Days of Naples* (1979)

Ewen Montagu, *The Man Who Never Was* (1954)
Frederick I. Ordway III and Mitchell R. Sharpe, *The Rocket Team* (1979)
Oreste Pinto, *Spy Catcher* (1952)
Peter Tomkins, *A Spy in Rome* (1962)
Hugh Trevor-Roper, *Last Days of Hitler* (1947)
F. W. Winterbotham, *The Ultra Secret* (1975)
Miadin Zarubica, *The Year of the Rat* (1964)
Hiltgunt Zassenhaus, *Walls: Resisting the Third Reich* (1974)

Lest We Forget: 25 Novels of the Holocaust
Ilse Aichinger, *The Greater Hope* (1948)
Jurek Becker, *Jacob the Liar* (1979)
Tadeusz Borowski, *This Way for the Gas, Ladies and Gentlemen* (1976)
Michel Del Castillo, *Child of our Time* (1957)
Charlotte Delbo, *None of Us Will Return* (1968)
Richard M. Elman, *The Yagodah Family Trilogy (The 28th of Elul)* (1967)
Leslie Epstein, *King of the Jews* (1979)
Ladislav Fuks, *Mr. Theodore Mundstock* (1968)
Pierre Gascar, *The Fugitive* (1961)
John Hersey, *The Wall* (1950)
Michael Jacot, *The Last Butterfly* (1972)
Stefan Kanfer, *The Eighth Sin* (1978)
Ilona Karmel, *An Estate of Memory* (1969)
Henri Karmel-Wolfe, *The Borders of Jacob Street* (1970)
Jerzy Kosinski, *The Painted Bird* (1965)
W. S. Kuniczak, *The March* (1979)
Anna Langfus, *The Whole Land Brimstone* (1962)
Meyer Levin, *Eva* (1959)
Arnost Lustig, *A Prayer for Katerina Horovitzova* (1964)
Jacob Presser, *Breaking Point* (1958)
Anna Seghers, *The Seventh Cross* (1942)
Jorge Semprun, *The Long Voyage* (1964)
Leon Uris, *Mila 18* (1961)
Elie Wiesel, *Night* (1960)
Fred Wender, *The Seventh Well* (1977)

3 Novels of Hiroshima

Francis Gwaltney, *The Day the Century Ended* (1955)
Masuye Ibusi, *Black Rain* (1969)
Edita Morris, *The Flowers of Hiroshima* (1959)

Korean War: 10 Novels
Thomas Anderson, *Your Own Beloved Sons* (1956)
Clayton Barbeau, *The Ikon* (1961)
William Crawford, *Give Me Tomorrow* (1962)
Pat Frank, *Hold Back the Night* (1952)
Ernest Frankel, *Band of Brothers* (1959)
Michael Lynch, *An American Soldier* (1969)
James Michener, *The Bridges at Toko-Ri* (1953)
Robert Scott, *Look at the Eagle* (1955)
George Sidney, *For the Love of Dying* (1969)
Melvin Voorhees, *Show Me a Hero* (1954)

Vietnam War: 10 Novels
George Davis, *Coming Home* (1972)
Charles Durden, *No Bugles, No Drums* (1976)
Winston Groom, *Better Times Than These* (1978)
David Halberstam, *One Very Hot Day* (1968)
Larry Heinemann, *Close Quarters* (1977)
William Turner Huggett, *Body Count* (1973)
Ward Just, *Stringer* (1974)
Tim O'Brien, *Going After Cacciato* (1978)
Jonathan Rubin, *The Barking Deer* (1974)
Stephen Phillip Smith, *American Boys* (1975)

Vietnam War: 10 Reports from the Front
Charles R. Anderson, *The Grunts* (1977)
Dennis Bloodworth, *An Eye for the Dragon: Southeast Asia Observed, 1954–1970* (1970)
Philip Caputo, *A Rumor of War* (1977)
Frederick Downs, *The Killing Zone: My Life in the Vietnam War* (1978)
Bernard Fall, *Hell in a Very Small Place* (1967)
Ronald J. Glasser, M. D., *365 Days* (1971)
Michael Herr, *Dispatches* (1977)

Ron Kovic, *Born on the Fourth Day of July* (1976)
Tim O'Brien, *If I Die in a Combat Zone* (1973)

World War III?
General Sir John Hackett et al., *The Third World War: August 1985* (1979)

In the Service: 15 Non-Battle Novels

Some Funny
William Brinkley, *Don't Go Near the Water* (1956)
Richard Hooker, *M.A.S.H.* (1968)
Mac Hyman, *No Time for Sergeants* (1954)
Thomas Heggen, *Mr. Roberts* (1946)
Ludwig Bemelmans, *My War with the United States* (1937)

And Some Deadly Serious
Robert Bowen, *The Weight of the Cross* (1951)
James Gould Cozzens, *Guard of Honor* (1948)
James Jones, *From Here to Eternity* (1951)
Carson McCullers, *Reflections in a Golden Eye* (1941)
Richard McKenna, *The Sand Pebbles* (1962)
Anton Myrer, *Once an Eagle* (1968)
William Gardner Smith, *Last of the Conquerors* (1948)
William Styron, *The Long March* (1952)
William Cranford Woods, *The Killing Zone* (1970)
Herman Wouk, *Caine Mutiny* (1951)

The Gray American Novel: Tales of West Point
Norman R. Ford, *The Black, the Gray and the Gold* (1961)
Lucian Truscott IV, *Dress Gray* (1979)

In the Enemy's Camp: POW Memoirs
Philip Deane, *I Was a Captive in Korea* (1953)
Agnes Newton Keith, *Three Came Home* (1947)
George R. Millar, *Horned Pigeon* (1946)
Robinson Risner, *The Passing of the Night: My Seven Years as a Prisoner of the North Vietnamese* (1974)
Giles Romilly and Michael Alexander, *Hostages of Colditz* (1973)

The Bars and Stripes: 10 POW Novels
Pierre Boulle, *The Bridge on the River Kwai* (1952)
Robert Bowen, *The Weight of the Cross* (1951)
James Clavell, *King Rat* (1962)
e. e. cummings, *The Enormous Room* (1922)
Len Giovannitti, *Prisoners of Combine D* (1957)
Sanche de Granmont, *Lives to Give* (1971)
MacKinlay Kantor, *Andersonville* (1955)
Hans Helmut Kirst, *Last Stop Camp 7* (1966)
Francis Pollini, *Night* (1961)
Donald Westheimer, *Song of the Young Sentry* (1968)

Iron Curtains and Bars: Voices from Communist Prisons
Ruo-Wang Ball and Rudolph Chelaminski, *Prisoner of Mao* (1973)
Menachem Begin, *White Nights: The Story of a Prisoner in Russia* (1979)
Joseph Berger, *Nothing but the Truth* (1971)
Vladimir Bukovsky, *To Build a Castle: My Life as a Dissenter* (1978)
Fedor Dostoeveski, *The House of the Dead* (1861–62)
Eugenia Semyonovona Ginzburg, *Journey Into the Whirlwind* (1967)
Anthony Grey, *Hostage in Peking* (1971)
Anatoly Marchenko, *My Testimony* (1969)
Boyd E. Payton, *Scapegoat: Prejudice/Politics/Prison* (1970)
Aleksandr I. Solzhenitsyn, *The Gulag Archipelago* (1974)
Alexander Thomsen, *In the Name of Humanity* (1963)
Richard Wurmbrand, *Christ in the Communist Prisons* (1968)
Pyotr Yakir, *A Childhood in Prison* (1973)

2 Tales from the Gulag
Varlam Shalamov, *Kolyma Tales* (1980)
Aleksandr I. Solzhenitsyn, *One Day in the Life of Ivan Denisovich* (1962)

A book must be an ice-axe to break the frozen seas in our Soul.
—FRANZ KAFKA

> *For a government to have a great writer is like having another government. That's why no regime has ever loved great writers, only minor ones!*
>
> —ALEKSANDR I. SOLZHENITSYN

■ AMERICAN HISTORY: THE PULITZER PRIZE WINNERS

1917: J. J. Jusserand, *With Americans of Past and Present Days*
1918: James Ford Rhodes, *History of the Civil War*
1919: No Award
1920: Justin H. Smith, *The War with Mexico*
1921: William Snowden Sims, *The Victory at Sea*
1922: James Truslow Adams, *The Founding of New England*
1923: Charles Warren, *The Supreme Court in United States History*
1924: Charles Howard McIlwain, *The American Revolution: A Constitutional Interpretation*
1925: Frederick L. Paxton, *A History of the American Frontier*
1926: Edward Channing, *A History of the U.S.*
1927: Samuel Flagg Bemis, *Pinckney's Treaty*
1928: Vernon Louis Parrington, *Main Currents in American Thought*
1929: Fred A. Shannon, *The Organization and Administration of the Union Army, 1861–65*
1930: Claude H. Van Tyne, *The War of Independence*
1931: Bernadotte E. Schmitt, *The Coming of the War, 1914*
1932: Gen. John J. Pershing, *My Experiences in the World War*
1933: Frederick J. Turner, *The Significance of Sections in American History*
1934: Herbert Agar, *The People's Choice*
1935: Charles McLean Andrews, *The Colonial Period of American History*
1936: Andrew C. McLaughlin, *The Constitutional History of the United States*

1937: Van Wyck Brooks, *The Flowering of New England*
1938: Paul Herman Buck, *The Road to Reunion*
1939: Frank Luther Mott, *A History of American Magazines*
1940: Carl Sandberg, *Abraham Lincoln: The War Years*
1941: Marcus Lee Hansen, *The Atlantic Migration, 1607–1840*
1942: Margaret Leech, *Reveille in Washington*
1943: Esther Forbes, *Paul Revere and the World He Lived In*
1944: Merle Curti, *The Growth of American Thought*
1945: Stephen Bonsai, *Unfinished Business*
1946: Arthur M. Schlesinger, Jr., *The Age of Jackson*
1947: James Phinney Baxter III, *Scientists Against Time*
1948: Bernard De Voto, *Across the Wide Missouri*
1949: Roy F. Nichols, *The Disruption of American Democracy*
1950: O. W. Larkin, *Art and Life in America*
1951: R. Carlyle Buley, *The Old Northwest: Pioneer Period 1815–1840*
1952: Oscar Handlin, *The Uprooted*
1953: George Dangerfield, *The Era of Good Feelings*
1954: Bruce Catton, *A Stillness at Appomattox*
1955: Paul Horgan, *Great River: The Rio Grande in North American History*
1956: Richard Hofstadter, *The Age of Reform*
1957: George F. Kennan, *Russia Leaves the War*
1958: Bray Hammond, *Banks and Politics in America: From the Revolution to the Civil War*
1959: Leonard D. White and Jean Schneider, *The Republican Era: 1869–1901*
1960: Margaret Leech, *In the Days of McKinley*
1961: Herbert Feis, *Between War and Peace: The Potsdam Conference*
1962: Lawrence H. Gibson, *The Triumphant Empire: Thunderclouds Gather in the West*
1963: Constance McLaughlin Green, *Washington: Village and Capital, 1800–1878*
1964: Summer Chilton Powell, *Puritan Village: The Formation of a New England Town*
1965: Irwin Unger, *The Greenback Era*
1966: Perry Miller, *The Life of the Mind in America*
1967: William H. Goetzmann, *Exploration and Empire: The*

Explorer and Scientist in the Winning of the American West
1968: Bernard Bailyn, *The Ideological Origins of the American Revolution*
1969: Leonard W. Levy, *Origin of the Fifth Amendment*
1970: Dean Acheson, *Present at the Creation: My Years in the State Department*
1971: James McGregor Burns, *Roosevelt: The Soldier of Freedom*
1972: Carl N. Degler, *Neither Black nor White*
1973: Michael Kammen, *People of Paradox: An Inquiry Concerning the Origins of American Civilization*
1974: Daniel J. Boorstin, *The Americans: The Democratic Experience*
1975: Dumas Malone, *Jefferson and His Time*
1976: Paul Horgan, *Lamy of Santa Fe*
1977: David M. Potter, *The Impending Crisis*
1978: Alfred D. Chandler, Jr., *The Visible Hand: The Managerial Revolution in American Business*
1979: Don E. Fehrenbacher, *The Dred Scot Case: Its Significance in American Law and Politics*
1980: Leon Litwack, *Been in the Storm So Long*

Summary of the Lessons of History in Four Sentences:
1. *Whom the gods would destroy, they first make mad with power.*
2. *The mills of God grind slowly, but they grind exceeding small.*
3. *The bee fertilizes the flower it robs.*
4. *When it is dark enough, you can see the stars.*
　　　　　　　　—CHARLES A. BEARD (FROM *THE PRACTICAL COGITATOR*)

Anyone can make history. Only a great man can write it.
　　　　　　　　—OSCAR WILDE

■ TELLING LIVES: THE BEST BIOGRAPHIES

Classic Collective Biographies
The First: Plutarch, *Parallel Lives of Greeks and Romans* (c. 100)

Suetonius, *The Lives of the Twelve Caesars* (c. 200)
Giorgio Vasari, *Lives of the Artists* (1550)
John Aubrey, *Brief Lives* (1690)
Izaak Walton, *Lives* (1640–78)
Samuel Johnson, *The Lives of the English Poets* (1783)
Alban Butler, *Lives of the Principal Saints* (1756–59)

Royalty
Maria Bellonsi, *The Life and Times of Lucrezia Borgia* (1939)
Vincent Cronin, *Napoleon Bonaparte: An Intimate Biography* (1972)
Antonia Fraser, *Royal Charles* (1979)
Michael Grant, *Julius Caesar* (1969)
Amy Kelly, *Eleanor of Aquitaine and the Four Kings* (1950)
Paul Murray Kendall, *Richard III* (1955)
Harold Lamb, *Genghis Khan, Emperor of All Men* (1927)
Robert K. Massie, *Nicholas and Alexandra* (1967)
Zöe Oldenbourg, *Catherine the Great* (1965)
Lytton Strachey, *Queen Victoria* (1921)

Tudor Lives
J. E. Neale, *Queen Elizabeth* (1934)
Elizabeth Jenkins, *Elizabeth the Great* (1959)
Hester Chapman, *The Challenge of Anne Boleyn* (1974)
J. J. Scaresbrick, *Henvy VIII* (1968)
Lacey Baldwin Smith, *Henry VIII: The Mask of Royalty* (1971)
Mary M. Luke, *A Crown for Elizabeth* (1970)

Scientists
Angus Annilage, *The World of Copernicus* (1947)
Philip Frank, *Einstein: His Life and Times* (1947)
Ernest Jones, *The Life and Work of Sigmund Freud* (1953–57)
Matthew Josephson, *Edison: A Biography* (1959)
Eve Curie, *Madame Curie* (1937)
Ruth E. Moore, *Niels Bohr* (1966)
Muriel Rukeyser, *Willard Gibbs: American Genius* (1942)

Pulitzer Prize: Biography
    Awarded annually for a distinguished biography or auto-

biography by an American author, preferably on an American subject.

1917: Laura E. Richards and Maude Howe Elliott assisted by Florence Howe Hall, *Julia Ward Howe*
1918: William Cabell Bruce, *Benjamin Franklin, Self-Revealed*
1919: Henry Adams, *The Education of Henry Adams*
1920: Albert J. Beveridge, *The Life of John Marshall*
1921: Edward Bok, *The Americanization of Edward Bok*
1922: Hamlin Garland, *A Daughter of the Middle Border*
1923: Burton J. Hendrick, *The Life and Letters of Walter H. Page*
1924: Michael Pupin, *From Immigrant to Inventor*
1925: M. A. DeWolfe Howe, *Barrett Wendell and His Letters*
1926: Harvey Cushing, *Life of Sir William Osler*
1927: Emory Holloway, *Whitman: An Interpretation in Narrative*
1928: Charles Edward Russell, *The American Orchestra and Theodore Thomas*
1929: Burton J. Hendrick, *The Training of an American: The Earlier Life and Letters of Walter H. Page*
1930: Marquis James, *The Raven* (Sam Houston)
1931: Henry James, *Charles W. Eliot*
1932: Henry F. Pringle, *Theodore Roosevelt*
1933: Allan Nevins, *Grover Cleveland*
1934: Tyler Dennett, *John Hay*
1935: Douglas Southall Freeman, *R. E. Lee*
1936: Ralph Barton Perry, *The Thought and Character of William James*
1937: Allan Nevins, *Hamilton Fish: The Inner History of the Grant Administration*
1938: Odell Shepard, *Pedlar's Progress*
Marquis James, *Andrew Jackson*
1939: Carl Van Doren, *Benjamin Franklin*
1940: Ray Stannard Baker, *Woodrow Wilson, Life and Letters*
1941: Ola Elizabeth Winslow, *Jonathan Edwards*
1942: Forrest Wilson, *Crusader in Crinoline*
1943: Samuel Eliot Morison, *Admiral of the Ocean Sea* (Christopher Columbus)

1944: Carleton Mabee, *The American Leonardo: The Life of Samuel F. B. Morse*
1945: Russell Blaine Nye, *George Bancroft: Brahmin Rebel*
1946: Linny Marsh Wolfe, *Son of the Wilderness*
1947: William Allen White, *The Autobiography of William Allen White*
1948: Margaret Clapp, *Forgotten First Citizen: John Bigelow*
1949: Robert E. Sherwood, *Roosevelt and Hopkins*
1950: Samuel Flag Bemis, *John Quincy Adams and the Foundations of American Foreign Policy*
1951: Margaret Louise Colt, *John C. Calhoun: American Portrait*
1952: Merlo J. Pusey, *Charles Evans Hughes*
1953: David J. Mays, *Edmund Pendleton, 1721–1803*
1954: Charles A. Lindbergh, *The Spirit of St. Louis*
1955: William S. White, *The Taft Story*
1956: Talbot F. Hamlin, *Benjamin Henry Latrobe*
1957: John F. Kennedy, *Profiles in Courage*
1958: Douglas Southall Freeman, *George Washington*, Vols. I–VI; John Alexander Carroll and Mary Wells Ashworth, Vol. VII
1959: Arthur Walworth, *Woodrow Wilson: American Prophet*
1960: Samuel Eliot Morison, *John Paul Jones*
1961: David Donald, *Charles Sumner and the Coming of the Civil War*
1962: No Award
1963: Leon Edel, *Henry James: Vol. II, The Conquest of London, 1870–1881; Vol. III, The Middle Years, 1881–1895*
1964: Walter Jackson Bate, *John Keats*
1965: Ernest Samuels, *Henry Adams*
1966: Arthur M. Schlesinger, Jr., *A Thousand Days* (John F. Kennedy)
1967: Justin Kaplan, *Mr. Clemens and Mark Twain*
1968: George F. Kennan, *Memoirs (1925–1950)*
1969: B. L. Reid, *The Man from New York: John Quinn and His Friends*
1970: T. Harry Williams, *Huey Long*
1971: Lawrence Thompson, *Robert Frost: The Years of Triumph, 1915–1938*

1972: Joseph P. Lash, *Eleanor and Franklin*
1973: W. A. Swanberg, *Luce and His Empire*
1974: Louis Sheaffer, *O'Neill, Son and Artist*
1975: Robert A. Caro, *The Power Broker: Robert Moses and the Fall of New York*
1976: R. W. B. Lewis, *Edith Wharton: A Biography*
1977: John E. Mack, *A Prince of Our Disorder: The Life of T. E. Lawrence*
1978: Walter Jackson Bate, *Samuel Johnson*
1979: Leonard Baker, *Days of Sorrow and Pain: Leo Baeck and the Berlin Jews*
1980: Edmund Morris, *The Rise of Theodore Roosevelt*

Best Literary Biographies: National Book Award Winners
Newton Arvin, *Herman Melville* (1950)
W. Jackson Bate, *Samuel Johnson* (1977)
Douglas Day, *Malcolm Lowry* (1973)
Leon Edel, *Henry James, Vols. 2 and 3* (1962)
Richard Ellmann, *James Joyce* (1959)
Justin Kaplan, *Mr. Clemens and Mark Twain* (1967)
Ralph L. Rusk, *Ralph Waldo Emerson* (1949)
Richard B. Sewall, *The Life of Emily Dickinson* (1974)
Roger Shattuck, *Marcel Proust* (1975)
Francis Steegmuller, *Cocteau* (1970)
Aileen Ward, *John Keats: The Making of a Poet* (1963)
Arthur Wilson, *Diderot* (1972)

5 Literary Families
Carolyn G. Heilbrun, *The Garnett Family* (1961)
F. O. Matthiessen, *The James Family* (1947)
John Pearson, *The Sitwells: A Family Biography* (1979)
Lucy and Richard Stebbins, *The Trollopes: The Chronicle of a Writing Family* (1945)
Irene Cooper Willis, *The Brontës* (1957)

A well-written life is about as rare as a well-spent one.
—THOMAS B. MACAULEY

■ FICTIONAL LITERARY LIVES

Writers and Critics: 10 Lit-Crit Hits
George Gissing, *New Grub Street* (1891)
Françoise Mallet-Joris, *The Underground Game* (1975)
W. Somerset Maugham, *Cakes and Ale* (1930)
Anthony Powell, *What's Become of Waring?* (1939)
Philip Roth, *The Ghost Writer* (1979)
Wilfrid Sheed, *Max Jamison* (1970)
Honor Tracy, *Men at Work* (1967)
John Updike, *Bech* (1970)
Geoffrey Wolff, *Inklings* (1978)
May Sarton, *Mrs. Stevens Hears the Mermaids* (1965)

Poetasters' Choice: 10 Fictional Poets
Elliot Baker, *A Fine Madness* (1964)
Anthony Burgess, *Enderby* (1968)
R. V. Cassill, *Clem Anderson* (1961)
Alan Friedman, *Hermaphrodeity: The Autobiography of a Poet* (1972)
Aldous Huxley, *Crome Yellow* (1921)
John Leonard, *Crybaby of the Western World* (1969)
Vladimir Nabokov, *Pale Fire* (1962)
Lore Segal, *Lucinella* (1976)
May Sinclair, *Divine Fire* (1904)
Muriel Spark, *The Girls of Slender Means* (1963)

Glittering Literati: 30 Literary Lives
Gay Wilson Allen, *The Solitary Singer: A Critical Biography of Walt Whitman* (1955)
Sybil Bedford, *Aldous Huxley* (1974)
Quentin Bell, *Virginia Woolf* (1972)
Ann Charters, *Kerouac* (1973)
Marchette Chute, *Shakespeare of London* (1949)
Lester G. Crocker, *Jean-Jacques Rousseau* (1968–73)
Martin Duberman, *James Russell Lowell* (1966)
Paul Ferris, *Dylan Thomas* (1977)
Norma Fruman, *Coleridge* (1971)
John Gardner, *The Life and Times of Chaucer* (1977)

Winifred Gerin, *Charlotte Brontë* (1967)
Amanda Haight, *Anna Akhmatova* (1976)
Michael Holroyd, *Lytton Strachey* (1968)
Edgar Johnson, *Charles Dickens: His Tragedy and Triumph* (1953)
Leslie Marchand, *Byron* (1957)
André Maurois, *Prometheus: The Life of Balzac* (1966)
Nancy Milford, *Zelda* (1970)
Arthur Mizener, *The Far Side of Paradise* (1952)
Harry T. Moore, *The Intelligent Heart: The Story of D. H. Lawrence* (1954)
Peter Quennell, *Alexander Pope* (1968)
Jean-Paul Sartre, *Saint Gene* (1963)
Mark Shorer, *Sinclair Lewis* (1961)
Andrew Sinclair, *Jack: A Biography of Jack London* (1977)
Peter Stansky and William Abrahams, *The Unknown Orwell* (1972)
Elizabeth Stevenson, *Lafcadio Hearn* (1961)
R. W. Stillman, *Stephen Crane* (1968)
A. J. A. Symons, *The Quest for Corvo* (1934)
Lawrence Thompson, *Robert Frost* (1966–76)
Henri Troyat, *Tolstoy* (1968)
Frances Winwar, *The Haunted Palace: A Life of Edgar Allan Poe* (1959)

3 Classic English Lives

James Boswell, *The Life of Samuel Johnson* (1791)
Elizabeth Gaskell, *The Life of Charlotte Brontë* (1857)
John Gibson Lockhart, *The Life of Sir Walter Scott* (1848)

Autobiography: 25 Writers Remember
Edward Dahlberg, *The Confessions of Edward Dahlberg* (1971)
Will and Ariel Durant, *A Dual Autobiography* (1977)
Ford Madox Ford, *Return to Yesterday* (1932)
Hamlin Garland, *Son of the Middle Border* (1917)
Henry Green, *Pack My Bag* (1939)
Frank Harris, *My Life and Loves* (1925)
André Malraux, *Anti-Memoirs* (1968)
Nadezdha Mandelstam, *Hope Against Hope* (1970)

W. Somerset Maugham, *The Summing Up* (1938)
Edwin Muir, *An Autobiography* (1955)
Dom Moraes, *My Son's Father: A Poet's Autobiography* (1968)
George Moore, *Confessions of a Young Man* (1886)
Sean O'Casey, *Mirror in My House: His Autobiographies* (1939–54)
Frank O'Connor, *An Only Child* (1961)
Sean O'Faolain, *Vive Moi!* (1964)
V. S. Pritchett, *Cab at the Door* (1968)
Kathleen Raine, *Farewell Happy Fields* (1973)
John Ruskin, *Praeterita* (1885–89)
Upton Sinclair, *The Autobiography of Upton Sinclair* (1962)
Sir Osbert Sitwell, *Autobiography* (1944–50)
Sacheverell Sitwell, *Journey to the Ends of Time* (1959)
Anthony Trollope, *An Autobiography* (1883)
Edith Wharton, *A Backward Glance* (1934)
William Butler Yeats, edited by Denis Donaghue, *Memoirs* (1973)
Stefan Zweig, *World of Yesterday: An Autobiography* (1943)

Writer-to-Writer: 10 Great Literary Correspondences
The Correspondence of Samuel L. Clemens and William D. Howells, 1869–1910 (1960)
Lawrence Durrell and Henry Miller: A Private Correspondence (1963)
The Van Wyck Brooks-Lewis Mumford Letters (1970)
Arna Bontemps-Langston Hughes Letters 1925–1967 (1980)
Self Portraits: The Gide-Valéry Letters, 1890–1942 (1966)
Dear Scott/Dear Max: The Fitzgerald-Perkins Correspondence (1971)
The Faulkner-Cowley File: Letters and Memoirs 1944–1962 (1966)
W. B. Yeats and T. Sturge Moore: Their Correspondence, 1901–1937 (1953)
Arnold Bennett and H. G. Wells: The Record of Personal and Literary Friendship (1960)
The Nabokov-Wilson Letters: Correspondence Between Vladimir Nabokov and Edmund Wilson, 1940–1971 (1979)

■ WATCHING THE POLS

Best Political Biographies: National Book Award Winners
Catherine Drinker Bowen, *The Lion and the Throne: The Life and Times of Sir Edward Coke* (1957)
James MacGregor Burns, *Roosevelt: The Soldier of Freedom* (1970)
Louis Fischer, *The Life of Lenin* (1964)
James Thomas Flexner, *George Washington: Anguish and Farewell (1793–1799)* (1972)
Christopher J. Herald, *Mistress to an Age: A Life of Madame de Staël* (1958)
Joseph P. Lash, *Eleanor and Franklin* (1971)
W. A. Swanberg, *Norman Thomas: The Last Idealist* (1977)
T. Harry Williams, *Huey Long* (1969)

Presidents
Marquis James, *Andrew Jackson* (1933–37)
Samuel Flagg Bemes, *John Quincy Adams* (1949–56)
Fawn M. Brodie, *Thomas Jefferson: An Intimate History* (1974)
Carl Sandburg, *Abraham Lincoln* (1926–39)
Ralph Ketcham, *James Madison* (1971)
Page Smith, *John Adams* (1962)
Henry Wilson Bragdon, *Woodrow Wilson* (1967)
Dumas Malone, *Jefferson* (1948–74)
Merle Miller, *Plain Speaking: An Oral Biography of Harry S. Truman* (1974)
Theodore C. Sorensen, *Kennedy* (1965)

Morris, Roosevelt, Randall, and Lincoln or Two Couples Who Wrote Independent Biographies of a President and His Wife
Edmund Morris, *The Rise of Theodore Roosevelt* (1979)
Sylvia Jukes Morris, *Edith Kermit Roosevelt: Portrait of a First Lady* (1980)
James G. Randall, *Lincoln the President* (1945–55)
Ruth Randall, *Mary Lincoln: A Biography of a Marriage* (1953)(As a footnote, see Ruth Randall's *I, Ruth:*

215

Autobiography of a Marriage (1968), the self-told story of the woman who married the great Lincoln scholar, James G. Randall, and through her interest in his work became a Lincoln author herself.

Presidential Memoirs
Theodore Roosevelt, *Autobiography* (1913)
Ulysses S. Grant, *Personal Memoirs* (1885)
Calvin Coolidge, *Autobiography* (1928)
Herbert Hoover, *Memoirs* (1951)
Harry S Truman, *Years of Decision* (1955)
Dwight D. Eisenhower, *The White House Years* (1963)
Lyndon B. Johnson, *The Vantage Point* (1971)
Richard M. Nixon, *RN: The Memoirs of Richard Nixon* (1979)
Gerald R. Ford, *A Time to Heal* (1979)

American Political Fiction
Henry Adams, *Democracy* (1880)
Samuel Hopkins Adams, *Revelry* (1926)
Billy Lee Brammer, *The Gay Place* (1961)
Richard Condon, *Death of a Politician* (1978)
Allen Drury, *Advise and Consent* (1959)
Harvey Fergusson, *Capitol Hill* (1923)
Paul Leicester Ford, *The Honorable Peter Stirling* (1894)
John Kenneth Galbraith, *The Triumph* (1968)
Ward Just, *The Congressman Who Loved Flaubert and Other Political Stories* (1972)
Fletcher Knebel and Charles Bailey, *Convention* (1964)
Abigail McCarthy, *Circles* (1977)
Edwin O'Connor, *The Last Hurrah* (1956)
Drew Pearson, *The Senator* (1968)
William Safire, *Full Disclosure* (1977)
Wilfrid Sheed, *People Will Always Be Kind* (1973)
Susan Richards Shreve, *Children of Power* (1979)
Gore Vidal, *Burr* (1973)
Robert Penn Warren, *All the King's Men* (1946)
Tom Wicker, *Facing the Lions* (1973)

Are You Now or Have You Ever Been . . . 10 Novels of McCarthy and the Witch Hunters
James Aldridge, *Goodbye, Un-America* (1979)
Cecelia Bartholomew, *The Risk* (1958)
Elliott Baker, *And We Were Young* (1979)
Ruth Chatterton, *The Betrayers* (1953)
Felix Jackson, *So Help Me God* (1955)
John Lorraine, *Men of Career* (1960)
Olivia Press, *Care of Devils* (1958)
Irwin Shaw, *The Travelled Air* (1951)
William Shirer, *Stranger, Come Home* (1954)
Irwin Stark, *The Subpoena* (1966)

■ HARD WORKS

Striking Prose: 10 Great Labor Novels
William Attaway, *Let Me Breathe Thunder* (1939)
Steve Chapple, *Don't Mind Dying* (1980)
John Dos Passos, *Midcentury* (1961)
Robert Houston, *Bisbee '17* (1979)
Meyer Levin, *Citizens* (1940)
Martin Andersen Nexo, *Pelle the Conqueror* (1906–10)
Wallace Stegner, *Joe Hill* (1950)
John Steinbeck, *In Dubious Battle* (1936)
Harvey Swados, *The Line* (1957)
Émile Zola, *Germinal* (1885)

The First American Labor Novel
Elizabeth Stuart Phelps Ward, *The Silent Partner* (1871)

The Underground Novel: Life in the Coal Mines
Robert Crichton, *The Camerons* (1972)
Albert Edward Idell, *Stephen Hayne* (1951)
Clancy Sigal, *Weekend in Dinlock* (1960)
James Sherburne, *Stand Like Men* (1943)

3 Miner Classics
D. H. Lawrence, *Sons and Lovers* (1913)

Richard Llewelyn, *How Green Was My Valley* (1940)
Émile Zola, *Germinal* (1885)

■ YEARS FOR THE ASKING

Remembering the Sixties
Joan Colebrook, *Innocents of the West: Travels Through the Sixties* (1978)
Sara Davidson, *Loose Change* (1977)
Morris Dickstein, *Gates of Eden: American Culture in the Sixties* (1977)
Joan Didion, *The White Album* (1979)
Thomas Farber, *Tales for the Son of My Unborn Child: Berkeley, 1966–1969* (1971)
Andrew Goldstein, *Becoming: An American Odyssey* (1973)
Warren Hinkle III, *If You Have a Lemon, Make Lemonade* (1975)
Jeremy Larner, *Nobody Knows: Reflections on the McCarthy Campaign of 1968* (1970)
Raymond Mungo, *Famous Long Ago: My Life and Hard Times with the Liberation News Service* (1970)
Howell Raines, *My Soul Is Rested* (1978)
Michael Rossman, *The Wedding Within the War* (1971)
Toby Thompson, *The 60's Report* (1979)
Milton Viorst, *Fire in the Streets: America in the Sixties* (1980)
Tom Wolfe, *The Electric Kool-Aid Acid Test* (1968)

The 10 Least Memorable Memoirs of the Seventies
Maury Allen with Bo Belinsky, *Bo: Pitching and Wooing* (1973)
Rona Barrett, *Miss Rona* (1974)
Anita Bryant, *The Anita Bryant Story* (1977)
Marilyn Chambers, *My Story* (1974)
Monty Hall and Bill Libby, *Emcee Monty Hall* (1974)
Abbie Hoffman, *Steal This Book* (1971)
Liberace, *Liberace* (1974)
Nina Van Pallandt, *Nina* (1973)
Bobby Riggs with George McGann, *Court Hustler* (1973)
Steven Weed, *My Search for Patty Hearst* (1975)

■ AUTOBIOGRAPHY

10 Classics: Old and New
Henry Adams, *The Education of Henry Adams* (1906)
Giovanni Jacopo Casanova, *Memoirs* (1826–38)
Benvenuto Cellini, *The Autobiography of Benvenuto Cellini*
  (1730)
François René de Chateaubriand, *Memoirs* (1848–50)
Thomas De Quincey, *The Confessions of an English Opium
  Eater* (1822)
Benjamin Franklin, *Autobiography* (1791)
Edward Gibbon, *Autobiographies* (1794)
Jean Jacques Rousseau, *Confessions* (1781–88)
Louis de Rouvray Saint-Simon, *Memoirs* (1829)
Malcolm X with Alex Haley, *The Autobiography of Malcolm X*
  (1965)

15 Interesting Lives Well Told
Maurice Baring, *The Puppet Show of Memory* (1929)
Richard Brickner, *My Second Twenty Years* (1976)
Helen Corke, *In Our Infancy: An Autobiography* (1975)
W. H. Davies, *Autobiography of a Super-Tramp* (1908)
Emma Goldman, *Living My Life* (1931)
Ruth Gruber, *Raquela, A Woman of Israel* (1978)
Will James, *Lone Cowboy* (1930)
Michael Kernan, *The Violet Dots* (1978)
Violet Leduc, *Mad in Pursuit* (1971)
Marya Mannes, *Out of My Time* (1971)
Axel Munthe, *Story of San Michele* (1929)
Iris Origo, *Images and Shadows: Part of a Life* (1971)
William G. Owens, *A Season of Weathering* (1973)
Alma Werfel, *And the Bridge Was Love: Memories of a Lifetime*
  (1958)
Ella Winter, *And Not to Yield* (1963)

---

*The main thing to remember in autobiography is not to let any
damn modesty creep in to spoil the story.*

—MARGERY ALLINGHAM

10 Remarkable Minds
Albert Camus, *Notebooks* (1963)
Samuel Taylor Coleridge, *Notebooks* (1957)
Leonardo da Vinci, *Notebooks* (1957)
Albert Einstein, *Out of My Later Years* (1950)
C. G. Jung, *Memories, Dreams, Reflections* (1963)
John Stuart Mill, *Autobiography* (1873)
Bertrand Russell, *The Autobiography of Bertrand Russell* (1967–68)
George Santayana, *Persons and Places* (1944–53)
Albert Schweitzer, *Out of My Life and Thoughts* (1933)
Simone Weil, *Notebooks* (1970)

Holy Writ: 15 Spiritual Autobiographies
St. Augustine, *Confessions* (397–401)
André Frossard, *I Have Met Him: God Exists* (1971)
George Fox,*The Journal* (1694)
Mahatma Gandhi, *Autobiography* (1924)
G. I. Gurdjieff, *Meetings with Remarkable Men* (1963)
Dag Hammarskjold, *Markings* (1964)
Pope John XXIII, *Journal of a Soul* (1963)
Thomas Merton, *The Seven-Storey Mountain* (1948)
John Henry Cardinal Newman, *Apologia Pro Vita Sua* (1864)
Blaise Pascal, *Pensées* (1670)
St. Teresa of Jesus, *Autobiography* (tr. 1870)
St. Thérèse of Lesieux, *Autobiography* (1958)
Simone Weil, *Notebooks* (1970)
John Wesley, *Journal* (1909)
John Woolman, *Journal* (1774)
Paramahansa Yogananda, *Autobiography of a Yogi* (1946)

10 Composite Autobiographies
These "autobiographies" were fashioned from the lifetime's writings of each of the subjects by the editors whose names appear in parentheses after the title.

Sherwood Anderson, *Sherwood Anderson's Memoirs* (Ray Lewis White, 1969)
Lord Byron, *Byron: A Self Portrait* (Peter Quennell, 1950)

Jean Cocteau, *Professional Secrets: The Autobiography of Jean Cocteau* (Robert Phelps, 1970)
Colette, *Earthly Paradise* (Robert Phelps, 1966)
Fedor Dostoevski, *Dostoeveski: A Self-Portrait* (Jessie Coulson, 1963)
D. H. Lawrence, *A Composite Biography* (Edward Nehla, 1958)
Michelangelo, *I, Michelangelo, Sculptor: An Autobiography Through Letters* (Irving and Jean Stone, 1962)
Michel de Montaigne, *The Autobiography of Michel De Montaigne* (Marvin Lowenthal, 1935)
George Bernard Shaw, *Shaw: An Autobiography* (Stanley Weintraub, 1969–70)
Mark Twain, *The Autobiography of Mark Twain* (Charles Neider, 1959)

Diaries, Journals & Notebooks

20 Real Journals

Marie Bashkirtseff, *Journal* (1885)
Charles Baudelaire, *Intimate Journals* (1947)
W. N. P. Barbellion, *The Journal of a Disappointed Man* (1919)
Bernard Berenson, *The Passionate Sightseer* (1960)
James Boswell, *London Journal, 1762–1763* (1950)
Albert Camus, *Notebooks 1935–51* (1962, 1965)
Anne Frank, *The Diary of a Young Girl* (1952)
André Gide, *Journals* (1947)
John Evelyn, *The Diary of John Evelyn (1818)* (1955)
Anne Morrow Lindbergh, *Diaries and Letters, 1922–1944* (1972–1980)
Katherine Mansfield, *Journals* (1932)
Samuel Pepys, *Diary* (1825)
Anaïs Nin, *Diaries* (1966–76)
Ned Rorem, *The Paris Diary* (1966)
Sei Shonagon, *The Pillow Book* (eleventh century A.D.)
Samuel Sewall, *Diary* (1878–82)
Stendhal, *The Private Diaries of Stendhal* (1954)
Kino Tsurayuki, *The Tosa Diary* (tenth century, A.D.)
Edmund Wilson, *Recollections of Northern New York,* (1970)
Virginia Woolf, *Diaries* (1972)

Each of these novels purports to be the diary or notebook of the narrator.

Georges Bernanos, *The Diary of a Country Priest* (1936)
Elizabeth Bowen, *The Death of the Heart* (1938)
Evan S. Connell, Jr., *Diary of a Rapist* (1967)
Richard M. Elman, *Lilo's Diary* (1969)
John Fowles, *The Collector* (1963)
André Gide, *The Pastoral Symphony* (1919)
George and Weeden Grossmith, *The Diary of a Nobody* (1892)
Russell Hoban, *Turtle Diary* (1975)
J. R. Humphrey, *Subway to Samarkand* (1977)
Alex Karmel, *My Revolution* (1970)
Sue Kaufman, *Diary of a Mad Housewife* (1967)
Øren Kierkegaard, *The Diary of a Seducer* (1843)
Doris Lessing, *The Golden Notebook* (1962)
Gavin Lambert, *Inside Daisy Clover* (1963)
Alberto Moravia, *The Lie* (1966)
Rainer Maria Rilke, *The Notebooks of Malte Laurids Brigge* (1910)
May Sarton, *As We Are Now* (1973)
Jean-Paul Sartre, *Nausea* (1938)
Hjolman Soderberg, *Doctor Glas* (1905)
Robert Walser, *Jakob von Gunten* (1909)

Missive Tomes: Letters and Art

Great Letter Writers

John and Abigail Adams, *The Book of Abigail and John: Selected Letters of the Adams Family, 1762–1784* (1976)
James Agee, *Letters of James Agee to Father Flye* (1962)
Lord Byron, *Selected Letters* (1943)
Dora Carrington, *Carrington: Letters and Extracts from Her Diaries* (1971)
Joseph Conrad, *Letters to William Blackwood and David S. Meldrum* (1958)
William Cowper, *Letters* (1904)

Hart Crane, *The Letters of Hart Crane* (1952)
George Eliot, *The George Eliot Letters* (1952–56)
Edward Fitzgerald, *Letters* (1899)
Gustave Flaubert, *Selected Letters* (1954)
Henry James, *Selected Letters* (1960)
William James, *Selected Letters* (1961)
James Joyce, *Selected Letters of James Joyce* (1975)
John Keats, *Selected Letters* (1958)
D. H. Lawrence, *Letters* (1962)
Rose Macaulay, *Letters to a Friend* (1962)
Eric Blom, ed., *The Letters of Mozart and His Family* (1956)
Harold Nicolson, *Diaries and Letters* (1967)
Flannery O'Connor, *The Habit of Being* (1979)
Rainer Maria Rilke, *Letters* (1945–48)
Sidney Smith, *Selected Letters* (1956)
Mary Wollstonecraft Shelley, *My Best Mary* (1951)
Oscar Wilde, *Letters* (1962)
Edmund Wilson, *Letters on Literature and Politics, 1917–1972* (1977)
Virginia Woolf, *The Letters of Virginia Woolf* (1975)

Letter-Perfect Writing: 5 Classics

Lord Chesterfield, *Letters to His Son* (1774)
Lady Mary Wortley Montagu, *Letters* (1763)
Madame de Sevigné, *Letters to Her Daughter and Her Friends* (1648–96)
Vincent Van Gogh, *Letters* (1958)
Horace Walpole, *Correspondence* (1732–47)

10 Epistolary Novels

John Barth, *Letters* (1979)
P. A. F. Chaderlos de Laclos, *Les Liaisons Dangereuses* (1782)
Fedor Dostoevski, *Poor Folk* (1846)
Johann Wolfgang von Goethe, *The Sorrows of Young Werther* (1774)
Günter Grass, *Dog Years* (1965)
Elizabeth Forsythe Hailey, *A Woman of Independent Means* (1978)

Charles de Secondat Montesquieu, *Persian Letters* (1721)
Samuel Richardson, *Clarissa Harlowe* (1747)
Etienne Pevert de Senancour, *Oberman* (1804)
Tobias Smollett, *The Expedition of Humphrey Clinker* (1771)

The letters and records of writers of genius are one of the ways we have of finding out how life was really lived in any given time and place.

—EDMUND WILSON

■ EDUCED AND ABANDONED: THE UNFINISHED NOVELS

Left Unsaid: 20 Novels Left Unfinished by their Authors
Jane Austen, *Sanditon*
James Agee, *A Death in the Family*
Joseph Conrad, *Suspense*
Charles Dickens, *The Mystery of Edwin Drood*
Fedor Dostoevski, *The Brothers Karamazov*
F. Scott Fitzgerald, *The Last Tycoon*
Nikolai Gogol, *Dead Souls*
Nathaniel Hawthorne, *Dr. Grimshawe's Secret*
Gustave Flaubert, *Bouvard and Pecuchet*
Henry James, *The Ivory Tower*
Franz Kafka, *Amerika*
D. H. Lawrence, *Mr. Noon*
Malcolm Lowry, *October Ferry to Gabriola*
Robert Musil, *The Man Without Qualities*
Marcel Proust, *Jean Senteuil*
Sir Walter Scott, *The Siege of Malta*
Stendhal, *Lamiel*
Robert Louis Stevenson, *Weir of Hermiston*
William Thackeray, *Denis Duval*
Thomas Wolfe, *The Hills Beyond*

Left Unread: 15 Novels Often Left Unfinished by Readers
Miguel de Cervantes, *Don Quixote*
Joseph Conrad, *Lord Jim*

Charles Dickens, *Little Dorrit*
Fedor Dostoevski, *The Idiot*
George Eliot, *The Mill on the Floss*
William Gaddis, *JR*
Günter Grass, *The Tin Drum*
Herman Hesse, *Magister Ludi*
Henry James, *The Golden Bowl*
D. H. Lawrence, *The Plumed Serpent*
Thomas Mann, *The Magic Mountain*
Vladimir Nabokov, *Ada*
Thomas Pynchon, *Gravity's Rainbow*
Virginia Woolf, *Orlando*

■ LAST NAMES ONLY PLEASE

Sir Walter Scott's *Waverly* and Mary Shelley's *Frankenstein* are both nineteenth-century examples of novels that take their titles from the surname of the protagonist. Here are ten more to match with their authors.

1. *Sartoris*	A. Vladimir Nabokov
2. *Herzog*	B. Frank Norris
3. *Burr*	C. Sinclair Lewis
4. *McTeague*	D. William Faulkner
5. *Oblomov*	E. John Updike
6. *Pnin*	F. Bruce Jay Friedman
7. *Molloy*	G. Ivan Goncharov
8. *Dodsworth*	H. Gore Vidal
9. *Bech*	I. Samuel Beckett
10. *Stern*	J. Saul Bellow
11. *Pendennis*	K. Rafael Sabatini
12. *Nostromo*	L. James Branch Cabell
13. *Jurgen*	M. William Mackpeace Thackeray
14. *Redburn*	N. Joseph Conrad
15. *Scaramouche*	O. Herman Melville

Answers
1–D, 2–J, 3–H, 4–B, 5–G, 6–A, 7–I, 8–C, 9–E, 10–F, 11–M, 12–N, 13–L, 14–O, 15–K

■ FAMOUS LAST WORDS: A LITERARY QUIZ

Match the novels in the first column with their last words in the second column.

1. *Crime and Punishment*
   Fedor Dostoevski

2. *Don Quixote*
   Miguel de Cervantes

3. *Huckleberry Finn*
   Mark Twain

4. *Lady Chatterley's Lover*
   D. H. Lawrence

5. *Portnoy's Complaint*
   Philip Roth

6. *The Fall*
   Albert Camus

7. *Steppenwolf*
   Herman Hesse

8. *Swann's Way*
   Marcel Proust

A. They endured.

B. Come, children, let us shut up the box and the puppets, for our play is played out.

C. . . . remembrance of a particular form is but regret for a particular moment; and houses, roads, avenues, are as fugitive, alas, as the years.

D. "Now vee may perhaps to begin. Yes?"

E. But I reckon I got to light out for the territory ahead of the rest, because Aunt Sally she's going to adopt me and civilize me, and I can't stand it. I been there before.

F. That would make the subject of a new story; our present story is ended.

G. "Vale."

H. It will always be too late. Fortunately.

9. *The Sound and the Fury*
   William Faulkner

10. *Vanity Fair*
    William Makepeace
    Thackeray

I. One day I would be a better hand at the game. One day I would learn how to laugh. Pablo was waiting for me, and Mozart too.

J. ". . . John Thomas says good night to Lady Jane a little droopingly, but with a hopeful heart."

Answers
1–F, 2–G, 3–E, 4–J, 5–D, 6–H, 7–I, 8–C, 9–A, 10–B

■ THE LAST TEST: BOOKS TO LAST

Each of the statements below refers to a literary work with the word "last" in the title. If you haven't fared too well in the previous tests, this is your last chance.

1. The second of the Leatherstocking Tales; the hero of the title is named Uncas.
2. The final novel of Anthony Trollope's Cathedral Stories.
3. The American title of one of Christopher Isherwood's *Berlin Stories* set during Hitler's rise to power in Germany.
4. Saul Bellow's first play.
5. One of Cornelius Ryan's vivid World War II epics.
6. Walker Percy's second novel.
7. Colorful novel of Boston politics by Edwin O'Connor.
8. Neil Simon's annual hit, this time for 1970.
9. The final volume of a Colette trilogy of the 1920s.
10. This Larry McMurtry novel of a small Texas town was made into a successful motion picture.
11. This novel, left unfinished at his death, may just be F. Scott Fitzgerald's best.
12. An unconventional picture of Jesus by Greek novelist Nikos Kazantzakis.

13. André Schwarz-Bart's semihistorical novel traces the martyr-dom of the Jews through thirty-six generations of one family, culminating in Auschwitz.
14. Early nineteenth-century historical novel by Edward Bulwer-Lytton.
15. A real Black comedy by Ishmael Reed.

Answers
1. *The Last of the Mohicans,* 2. *The Last Chronicle of Barset,* 3. *The Last of Mr. Norris,* 4. *The Last Analysis,* 5. *The Last Battle,* 6. *The Last Gentleman,* 7. *The Last Hurrah,* 8. *The Last of the Red Hot Lovers,* 9. *The Last of Chéri,* 10. *The Last Picture Show,* 11. *The Last Tycoon,* 12. *The Last Temptation of Christ,* 13. *The Last of the Just,* 14. *The Last Days of Pompeii,* 15. *The Last Days of Louisiana Red*

■ THE LAST WORD—LITERALLY

Here is a selection of deathbed utterances of writers. Like us other mortals, most of them found that their life-long knack for turning original phrases deserted them at that critical moment.

Edgar Allen Poe: "Lord help my soul."
George Gordon, Lord Byron: "Now I shall go to sleep."
Thomas Carlyle: "So this is Death—well—."
Johann Wolfgang von Goethe: "More light!"
Washington Irving: "Well, I must arrange my pillows for another weary night; when will this end?"
Robert Burns: "Don't let the awkward squad fire over my grave."
Denis Diderot: "The first step towards philosophy is incredulity."
William Hazlitt: "Well, I've had a good life."
Thomas Babington Macauley: "I shall retire early; I am very tired."
John Keats: "Severn—I—lift me up—I am dying—I shall die easy; don't be frightened. Be firm, and thank God it has come."

Lady Mary Wortley Montagu: "It has all been very interesting."

Blaise Pascal: "My God, forsake me not."

François Rabelais: "Let down the curtain, the fair is over."

Johann Schiller: "Many things are growing plain and clear to my understanding."

Henry David Thoreau: "I leave the world without a regret."

François Marie Voltaire: "Do let me die in peace."

William Wordsworth: "God bless you. Is that you, Dora?"

Of making many books there is no end . . .

—ECCLESIASTES XII, 12
